Toward Heaven On Earth:
Remembering Your Soul

*An Interactive, Life-Transformative
Experience with*

Dr. Mark R. Pitstick

Toward Heaven On Earth: Remembering Your Soul
by Dr. Mark R. Pitstick
$12.00
ISBN 0-9661419-0-3

A portion of the proceeds
from this book will go to
Habitat for Humanity.

Warning/Disclaimer
Every effort has been made to make this collection of materials
as complete and accurate as possible. Nevertheless, information
may change, there may be mistakes, both typographical and in
content. Important data may be omitted. Therefore, this book
should be used as a general guide only and not as a final source of
information.
Further, all statements made by the author, Dr. Mark R.
Pitstick, are based on his own personal research and study; they do
not necessarily reflect the beliefs of all professionals. It should also
be noted that in no way is any information contained herein meant
to take the place of or to provide any kind of professional advice or
treatment, nor does it preclude the need to seek the advice of
professionals on a personal level.

Acknowledgments

To my wife Michelle, daughters Rae Lynn and Faith, and parents Bill and Virginia. To family, friends and my many teachers. To Paul Brown, Lainey Barkley and Otto Collins for proofreading and their valuable Master Mind input. To Tobi Haynes for her editorial expertise and enthusiasm. To Skip Brown for his timely and wise promotional assistance. To all Lightworkers, those Souls consciously assisting a return to peace and joy, love and light. To God and the Heavenly Host for giving us the courage and clarity to realize Heaven on Earth.

"Toward Heaven On Earth" provides a complete overview of how to grow spiritually. It is both thorough and practical. It offers powerful ideas and tools that can transform your life."

Jonathan Robinson, author
The Little Book of Big Questions and The Experience of God

TABLE OF CONTENTS

Laying The Foundation

Preparatory information to launch the life of your dreams;
understanding the goals of *Toward Heaven on Earth*

It Is Time

Namaste! Namaste is a traditional Hindu greeting that means 'I recognize the Divine Light within you. I honor the truth that you and I are one.'

The purpose of *Toward Heaven on Earth* is to help you:

1. absolutely *know* you are an Eternal Soul, an Infinite Spirit who does not die and cannot fail
2. identify and follow your Soul's mission
3. create an *outstanding vitality* of body, mind, and spirit so you can fulfill life's roles *and* your Soul's mission
4. experience a personal utopia now and assist a *global transformation* toward Heaven on Earth in our lifetime

These are the four keys to realizing the potential for an inner and outer Heaven now. Several common interferences and their solutions in parentheses include:

- you're misinformed about spiritual truths because of archaic societal teachings/brainwashing and your personal lack of exploration (study eclectic and updated information about who you are and why you're here)
- you're too ill or chronically fatigued to care or try (reach optimal health via holistic health practices)
- your life is too busy, you don't live in the present moment (take time to care for your body, mind and Spirit; get a life and enjoy it)
- you are controlled by fear and don't trust yourself (see all the above solutions and use life-transformative techniques to reprogram yourself for the better)

I'll address each of these problems and their solutions in further detail throughout *Toward Heaven on Earth*.

Really knowing your Infinite Nature removes fear of death and failure. Then you're free to identify your Soul's purpose and demonstrate your formidable physical, mental, and spiritual potential. You can then enjoy a relative personal utopia that will summate in a literal Heaven on Earth. This may sound impossible given the many problems on Earth but remember: it's always darkest just before the dawn. Now is the time to realize inner *and* world peace!

If this sounds too "New Age" or "Pollyanish," consider the words of the old standard church hymn *We've A Story To Tell To The Nations*: "For the darkness shall turn to dawning, and the dawning to noonday bright; and Christ's great kingdom shall come on earth, the kingdom of love and light." We live in an exciting time when this vision can come to pass!

I was recently driving through the Appalachians mountains at dawn. The sun *seemed* to rise sooner in level areas than in hilly terrain. This was, of course, *an illusion* due to the sun being blocked by the hills. In the same way, Heaven on Earth is a present potentiality, an obtainable reality *now*. Some persons can see that, others cannot because of life's hills and illusions. The sun (the Son, the Christ Light) is present and just waiting to rise in each of us.

Inner peace is available right now—in a heartbeat—the moment you awaken. World peace will manifest when a critical number of Souls awaken. The possibility for both already exist and are realized by removing interferences that block an accurate perception of reality. As Jesus tried to explain, when you have ears that really hear and eyes that really see, you *know* the Father and you are One, that the kingdom of Heaven is at hand and within *now*.

For the first time in history, the accumulated wisdom of every culture is available for sharing and higher learning. Never before has everything been in place for this new era. Critical factors include: availability of information, enhanced communication capabilities, higher literacy rates, more time and societal approval for personal growth, human potential/growth technology, outstanding teachers, past lessons learned the hard way, proof of spiritual dimensions, and humanity's readiness for peace on Earth.

Various ancient prophecies have foretold a coming Golden Age of world peace, cooperation, and respect. The fulfillment of these hopes depends upon each one of us. This new era has been recognized cross-culturally as: the Second Coming of Christ; the Age of Aquarius; the Mayan beginning of Itza—the age of knowledge; the ascension into the 4th and 5th dimensions assisted by wise space beings; the incoming photon belt and Christ Consciousness; or, more secularly, the realization that Earth is a global village and we all are brothers and sisters.

Similar Native American prophecies were recently fulfilled by the birth of a white buffalo that signaled the time for peace among all people. Inca prophecies have long foretold "When the condor of the South meets the Eagle of the North and fly together, then it will be a sign that the Children of Mother Earth are awakening." This prophecy was fulfilled in 1992 when Peruvian priests shared traditions with Native North American elders.

From many diverse viewpoints, then, it is clearly time for humans to realize their True Nature and Essential Oneness with Creator. Yes, my friends, inner and world peace are available *now*. Our task is not so much to set things right as to see things rightly. *Toward Heaven on Earth* teaches how to perceive these truths more clearly.

Reaching Heaven on Earth starts with each one of us. The progression goes something like this: individual-family-neighborhood-community-state-country-world-solar system-galaxy-universe. Like ants in a busy colony, each of us has an important role to discern and fulfill.

I know all too well that most persons are incredibly busy as they juggle many different roles in life. That's why I've searched for "silver bullets", those techniques and understandings that provide inordinately great benefits for a relatively small investment of time, energy, and money. These approaches are time-tested and efficient. There *is* a way to balance all the demands of life and still have time for your self as a person and Soul.

I've included life-transformative technology, as taught by Tony Robbins and others, to *anchor* positive changes quickly and powerfully. If you use these techniques on a regular basis, life will never be the same again! Are you ready for total success and a Heaven on Earth existence? If so, say "yes!"

Thomas Moore, Ph.D., in *Care of the Soul*, states "Soul-making is a journey that takes time, effort, knowledge, skill, intuition, and courage. It is helpful to know that all work with the soul is process—alchemy, pilgrimage, and adventure—so that we don't expect instant success or even any kind of finality." The longest journey starts with the first step. Are you ready to make that step?

A Language For Enlightenment

Deepak Chopra, M.D., says "Although our package of skin and bones looks very convincing, it is a mask, an illusion, disguising our true self, which has no limitations." A predefined terminology assists realizing and communicating this great news, the Truth.

Heaven on Earth is a relative term. Some people currently enjoy a life that is quite heavenly while others are experiencing a veritable hellish existence. Utopia living is our birth right and the predictable outcome when one incorporates the techniques and understandings outlined in this book. God has provided the ever-present potentiality for Heaven; we need only live in alignment with Universal laws to experience peace and harmony.

Similarly, a global transformation toward Heaven on Earth has always been a realistic possibility. Its attainment is an increasingly practical goal as more and more persons experience an individual utopia and serve as they feel called. Our world's status will naturally elevate as more and more people serve in accordance with God's will and their Soul's mission.

Total success means high levels of fulfillment in every part of life: being an outstanding person, spouse, parent, family member, significant other, spiritual server/seeker, worker, community member, athlete, and Divine-Human. Being totally successful means being prosperous, healthy, happy, peaceful, loving, content, committed, service-oriented, and harmonious in life. Outstanding *and* balanced success is the goal.

Terms used synonymously for *remembering your Soul* include: becoming enlightened, knowing the Truth, realizing your True Self, seeing the Light, being saved (from spiritual ignorance), hearing the good news that sets you free, seeing through the illusion, becoming a Divine Human, realizing All is One, and developing a cosmic perspective.

Various terms for *God* include: Supreme Being, Source, Great Spirit, Oneness, Above One, Ground of Being, Creator, Godhead, Prime Creator, Infinite, Great Being, Preexistent One, Divine, Universal Intelligence, Omniscient One, the Most High, and Divine Oneness. The term Mother/Father God recognizes that the Infinite is beyond gender; as such, I refer to the Creator alternatively as He, She, and It.

Heavenly Host or *Heavenly Helpers* is a collective name for God's celestial assistants. (Remember, please, that any model of separateness or duality is allegorical since all life is One.) Heavenly helpers include Ascended Masters, Christed Ones, Arch-Angels, Guardian Angels, and Spirit Guides.

Terms for realms where greater spiritual awareness usually reigns more consistently than on Earth include: Heaven, Home, Nirvana, the Kingdom, the Other Side, the Spirit World, and Paradise. I say "usually" because spiritual enlightenment is more a function of ones state of consciousness than ones location. Some humans experience high degrees of Heaven on Earth while unenlightened Souls may temporarily flounder in darkness even in the Spirit World.

Terms for *entities* who are *living in spiritual darkness*, who are still ignorant of their Spiritual Nature include: "satan, devil, evil spirits, dark ones, dark forces, dark entities, and malevolent forces." These terms are in quotation marks and not capitalized since "evil" and "darkness" have no real substance when exposed to the Light of God and Love. Souls who haven't yet embraced the Light suffer and may cause discord but this is not an irreversible predicament. They need only ask for spiritual help; God and the Heavenly Host will lovingly and immediately welcome them back.

Better terms for the misnomers *death* and *dying* include: "passed over, passed on, left the body, graduated, and dropped the body." I also like "kicking the bucket, buying the farm and, the term popularized by Fred Sanford, 'I'm coming to you, Elizabeth!'" Humorous synonyms for "death" remind us there is nothing to be afraid of; it's OK to laugh at "dying" because it is a joke, a nonexistent illusory phenomenon.

Finally, terms used for the *Soul*, that extension of God in each of us, include: "Real Self, Watcher, Innate Intelligence, Enduring Self, Eternal Self, Divine Self, True Self, Inner Self, Inner Christ, Divine Spark, Observer, God Within, Inner Light, Spirit Within, and Infinite Self." I capitalize these to emphasize our Divine inheritance and vast potential accompanying that status.

Conscious Language

Be honest with yourself for a moment. Are you really happy? Are your relationships loving and positive? Are you enjoying the levels of success in every aspect of life that you thought you would? Do you know why you are on this planet at this time? Do you feel fulfilled and peaceful? If you're like most people—and are brutally honest with yourself—your answers are no, no, no, no and no.

Fortunately, the most important question is: are you ready to change for the better NOW? I don't mean ready to think about it, talk about it, or get around to it someday. If you are ready for transformation of body, mind, and spirit, emphatically say "YES", aloud and in your heart.

By the way, the more you participate in these exercises and life-transformation assignments—like saying "yes" aloud—the more you'll benefit. An *experiential format* increases the program's effectiveness exponentially. If you only read this book passively, you'll miss much of the benefit possible with an interactive mode.

Your bodily state, language, and beliefs dramatically shape your behavior and success. We'll address each of these but changing your bodily state or physiology is the simplest. Four components to reaching *peak state*, an optimal state of preparedness and empowerment are: *changing your physiology*, *empowering feelings*, *power cues* and *inspiring music*. Life-transformative techniques performed while in peak state allow you to break through limiting patterns and install more positive ones. If you are serious about transforming your life and experiencing Heaven on Earth now, please participate fully.

First, to attain peak physiology, *imagine how you would act* if you just won the lottery *and* lasting world peace became a reality *and* your favorite sports team just won the championship *and* you had a great bowel movement after a month of constipation!! Would you sit slumped over, breathe shallowly, and murmur a slow, barely audible "that's good"?

I don't think so! You would stand tall, breathe deeply from the chest, and hold your head high. You would jump up and down, clap, scream, raise your arms above your head, make pumping actions with your fists, and yell "yes!", "great!", "fantastic!", and "thank you God!"

My friend, you are about to win the jackpot of your life: spiritual enlightenment, vibrant health, inner peace, happiness, and success in every aspect of life. You are about to remember your Eternal Nature and achieve your Soul's mission. You are learning strategies to reach your fullest physical, mental, and spiritual potential. You are committing to reach a personal Heaven on Earth existence. You are taking steps to make world peace a reality in our lifetime!

If you feel that's really something to celebrate about, then let your body show it. Just do it—this is crucial! Achieve peak physiology by visualizing the outcomes described in the preceding paragraph. Then stand tall, pump your fists, smile broadly, jump up and down, yell and clap. If you can't at this moment, *imagine* an outrageous celebration then actually do it later as soon as possible.

If you're imagining it, use all of your senses: *see* yourself jumping up and down; *hear* yourself yelling; *feel* yourself clapping. Notice how good it feels as you prepare to eradicate erroneous beliefs and install empowering ones.

Next, *stack* on more positive anchors by connecting with *empowering feelings*. Recall a time when you felt unstoppable, totally alive, and very happy. Maybe you had just received an award or successfully completed a difficult task. Perhaps it was getting married, reaching your personal best, graduating, achieving an important goal, having a baby, or helping some-one.

Recreate those empowering feelings: how did you feel and what did you say? *Intensify* this positive state by turning up the feelings. Feel even more happy, confident, empowered, successful, and unstoppable. Make the picture bigger and brighter so that you can vividly recall these feelings at will.

Now you're ready to identify your *power cues*. These are cues that make you feel peaceful, brave, passionate, determined, and confident. There's no right or wrong answer; don't get too cerebral about it, just let the images appear naturally. Stand in peak physiology, and recall your empowering feelings. Now, with your eyes closed, do the following and make a mental note of what comes to you:

- visualize your power *color*
- see your power symbol, any *geometric shape*
- hear an empowering *sound or word*
- feel a *texture* (e.g., smooth, rough, soft, hard, flowing)
- smell a *fragrance*
- say a *short phrase* that summarizes your *resolve* to change every aspect of your life for the better

Now write down these power cues:

- your color _____
- shape _____
- sound _____
- texture _____
- smell _____
- phrase _____

Finally, choose *inspiring music* that motivates and "jazzes" you. Select music with good associations, that recreates the *passion* you felt earlier. I use: *Life* by Haddaway; *Higher Love* by Stevie Winwood; *I Believe I Can Fly* by R. Kelly; *Peace Train* by Cat Stevens; *Higher Ground* by Stevie Wonder; *The Rain Must Fall* and *After The Sunrise* by Yanni; and *Fly Like An Eagle* by the Steve Miller Band or Seal. After listening to this music repeatedly, you can "play it in your head" and obtain the same results.

Now you have a four part program, all the tools you need to reach *peak state*. You have just assembled an awesome package for massive, rapid, positive change. Now it's time to put it all together!

You can now easily and instantly reach a better state of mind from which to achieve your goals and dreams. This altered state will allow you to shed negative societal trances and self-limiting programs in your mind. With practice, reaching peak state takes only a few seconds. From now on, attain peak state before reading and doing life transformative assignments in *Toward Heaven on Earth*.

Beware of disempowering thoughts like "world peace in our lifetime? Sounds impossible." Or "personal peace and total success? Maybe for a few lucky individuals but not for someone like me." If you detect negative thinking or feel discouraged or fatigued, take a break then resume peak state before reading further.

Relanguaging is a powerful transformational tool. Let a red flag go up when you hear yourself saying words like "I'll try, I should, maybe I can, I can't, if only or that's impossible." Avoid self put-downs, limiting statements, or disempowering words. For example, use "opportunity" instead of "problem" and "challenge" instead of "obstacle." As Albert Einstein said, "In the middle of every difficulty lies an opportunity." The Universe is unfolding as it should; relanguaging will help you remember that truth.

Last year, I walked barefoot on a 12 foot long bed of 1600 degree hot coals. That amazing experience was made possible by using empowering language and being in peak state. Walking on fire was a great paradigm for taking the first step and facing my fears. After walking on those coals, I *knew* I could face any challenge in life.

For another true-life example of how thoughts and words can make or break your life, watch the movie *Shine*. David's father, a survivor of Nazi concentration camps, regularly told him, "You must be tough, life is hard, and no one will ever love you like I do." When those statements were intermittently paired with physical beatings and volatile behavior by his father, David became *very* neurotic.

When David decided to follow his dream of studying piano abroad, his father told him, "If you do, you will be punished for the rest of your life!" When David finally reached success, this self-fulfilling prophecy came true in the form of a massive psychotic break. Only after much time, persistence, and positive messages from loved ones would David's dysfunction subside.

Rapid and massive positive changes can be yours when you read in a peak state and *act* consistently on this information. So, *right now* you are faced with a decision. Are you going to continue on with your life as it's been? Or are you ready to unleash the power within and change for the better? Are you ready to do it, not merely try but do?

Chopra says "Trying is not the way Nature functions. The Earth doesn't try to go around the sun, nor does the seed try to sprout into a sapling. Nature functions with effortless ease, invariably taking the path of least resistance." Remembering your True Nature (who you really are), why you're here (your mission), and how to realize it are really easy, natural processes. Participating in the flow of spiritual unfoldment will create a quality of life you've only dreamed of in the past. So don't try, just do!

Lightworkers

I dedicated this book to all "Lightworkers", those Souls committed to enhancing awareness of God's Love and Light on our planet in this lifetime. Lightworkers (AKA members of the family of light, spiritual servers/seekers, earth-change agents and impeccable warriors) come from all walks of life. They may be of any age, race, gender, sexual preference, religion, culture, or socioeconomic group. Being a Lightworker is about the level of Soul maturity and commitment to assisting peace, love, and understanding among all people.

Family of Light members know they are part of God, gods in amnesia and extensions of God—*and so is everyone else*. (This is the acid-test between the spiritually wise and a psychotic who thinks only he or she is God.) Humans give away much power by believing God is a separate and distant demagogue. We each are part of the phenomena termed God and, as such, can heal and help ourselves and others.

We belittle God's exquisite plan when we believe we are lowly thumb-suckers without personal power and extraordinary abilities. Prime Creator gave each of us roles to play and our Souls agreed to accept the challenges. It's time to remember and fulfill those missions. That's not undermining God's importance, it's showing our appreciation for all our blessings and doing God's work on Earth.

In the area around my office, hotels and office buildings are replacing corn fields. Disrupted animals are trying to develop new ecological niches under my building so I'm livetrapping and taking them to state park land. One young groundhog was pacing frantically inside the cage; as I spoke reassuringly, the animal flattened in a submissive posture and chirped in "groundhogese." I couldn't translate it but instantly the following strong, clear thought *came to me*:

"You seem like a god to this animal because of your size, voice, and ability to trap and transport it. In the same way, primitive humans may have mistaken more powerful beings, like ETs, for God when they were just more advanced technologically." I *felt* the truth of these words and saw a fleeting image of humans in the past who were just as confused and scared as this groundhog.

I realized how limited perspectives from the past have contributed to current spiritual misunderstandings. Lightworkers are Souls who are remembering they are "gods in the making" and co-creators with God. These advanced Souls have congregated on Earth at this time to assist Prime Creator's plan for establishing peace on Earth. They know *it is time* for all to realize their valuable and lofty status.

Now is the time to remember and demonstrate our Divine Humanity and Inner Christ Light. A "wake-up call" is resounding loudly and clearly; earth-change agents are either enthusiastically on the path or they are very agitated right now. An intense *quickening of Spirit* is underway, thus the discontent and searching among so many.

Have you ever tried to remember something—a word "just on the tip of your tongue"—but couldn't? Multiply that frustration many times to capture the angst of impeccable warriors until they remember and answer the call. It's time for spiritual seekers/servers to awaken and follow God's will and their Soul's mission.

As far back as I can remember, I have felt somewhat "out of place" on planet Earth. Recurrent feelings that I was to learn the Truth and teach others kept surfacing. Like Robert Heinlein's *Stranger in a Strange Land*, human ways seemed odd to me. Earthly over-emphases on spectator sports, hunting, and material possessions seemed strange. As a youth, I thought how many wrongs in the world could be corrected with just half the money and energy spent on the Super Bowl.

In my senior year of high school, I was one of three finalists for city government day. I remember thinking what an opportunity it was to plant some seeds and stimulate thought about our future potentials. The other candidates gave a short "rah-rah" speech that was preceded and followed by a crowd of friends cheering and carrying the candidate on their shoulders.

Alone and without banners or fanfare, I spoke about the golden opportunities ahead—how each of us could make a vast difference by considering what our special talents were and using them to better our world. Heavy stuff for high school students; predictably, I came in third. In retrospect, it is the same message I have felt compelled to share throughout my life.

Sharing this message is my *birth-vision*, a calling I cannot ignore. Thus, I have left a comfortable and lucrative professional practice to become "Marky Soul-seed," a 21st century Johnny Appleseed of holistic health and higher consciousness. My mission is to plant seeds of hope, faith, courage, and knowledge to assist the victory of light over darkness, of health over disease, of wisdom over ignorance, of love over hate. This battle is being playing out within each one of us and in our world at large. The Light of God within all life is urging us to remember our True Natures and act as we should.

I recently asked a psychic why I had been so serious and, at times, sad; even childhood pictures show a pensive, thoughtful countenance. He said that in my past three lives I had been a physician or chaplain in war-torn countries; I had seen so much suffering that the sadness had carried over into this in-carnation. I was an old Soul and had been an Essene during the time of Jesus. I was determined in this lifetime to share spiritual understandings with as many others as possible.

Indicators that you may be a Lightworker include:

- you feel different, even alienated, from "average" people and societal norms
- you don't like to be told how to live or what to believe
- you ask "why?" and "how come?" more than usual
- you hear transient electronic buzzing or ringing noises and are bothered by electronic devices
- you question orthodoxy that "just doesn't make sense"
- you are more open minded and less prejudiced than most
- you are interested in information about afterlife, UFOs, consciousness raising and "the paranormal"
- you can see through the scare tactics used to keep others from thinking for themselves
- you're still reading this book

Following ones Soul may, at least initially, result in compli-cations in ones everyday life. Acknowledging your role as a Lightworker may make you seem eccentric or odd compared to "normal" persons. Plato spoke of an "artful madness" that re-sults from avoiding societal constrictions that the Soul finds so bothersome. Following the calling of your Soul may initially lead to conflict and becoming different from the norm. But the exhilaration and freedom of remembering and following ones Spiritual Essence makes any difficulties worthwhile.

Truth Is One

Whatever religion or denomination works for you is fine. Persons of many different *religious* persuasions are on a *spiri-tual* path that recognizes: "Truth is one, paths are many." This is *not* a book about religion. It *is* about *spirituality* and ac-knowledges we are and always will be One with one another and the Creator.

The phrase "Truth is one, paths are many" is a theme of Sri Swami Satchidananda's Integral Hatha Yoga centers. He rec-ognizes that even apparent "evil" and suffering are perfect teachings for those who truly desire to know God. When asked why suffering exists, he uses the analogy of a pregnant female who *asks* to have her labor induced to achieve gains, namely, her baby. Likewise, enlightened Souls ask for, accept, and welcome suffering for the accompanying spiritual gains.

Satchidananda compared life to a movie and said that a movie without a villain or danger would be boring; no one would watch it. Similarly, life without the polarities of positive and negative, good and bad, light and darkness would not be a fertile environment for Soul growth. No one would volunteer for incarnations here. A light bulb needs a positive and negative pole to function properly. Even God, he explained, became bored with constant sameness and therefore explored the unknown, the so-called "dark side."

The Earth experiment, as I understand it, is—in part—to discover how Souls will react when given freedom to choose among different temptations or options. Will the Soul's Light eventually shine through the ignorance and darkness of a relatively unenlightened world? How long will that take? What lessons will be learned in the process by experiencing *the other side* of peace and joy, love and light?

Many spiritual seekers ask: "If all is God, then why go through this illusion with its accompanying pain, darkness, difficulties, and discouragement?" God doesn't create puppets programmed to the ways of Spirit. We have a choice but how can we choose freely until we're aware of all the options? Perhaps this question is best answered by T. S. Eliot: "The end of all our exploring will be to arrive where we started and know the place for the first time."

We need creative tension, struggle, and challenge for optimal learning and fulfillment. Balancing the polarities in life while remembering the Oneness of all creation is a key to inner and world peace. As Deepak Chopra reminds us "At one level, things have to be certain or order couldn't exist. On another level, things have to be uncertain or there would be no newness."

Some would derogatorily label these ideas as "New Age", meaning based on the occult or inspired by the "devil." A study of history and literature reveals there is nothing new about "New Thought" or "New Age" ideas. Karen Armstrong, historian of theology and author of A *History Of God*, explains that the philosophers Plato, Plotinus, Socrates, Pythagoras, and Epictetus inspired metaphysical studies for enlightenment without religion.

Plato's "teachings would help the philosopher to realize his true self, by liberating his soul from the prison of the body and enabling him to ascend to the divine world. It was a noble system, which used cosmology as an image of continuity and harmony... since he was akin to the God who had given life to all things, a philosopher could ascend to the divine world by means of his own efforts in a rational, ordered way."

Third century philosopher Plotinus found Christianity a thoroughly objectionable creed and described the goal of our spiritual quest: "We here, for our part, must put aside all else and be set on This alone... to embrace God with all our being, that there may be no part of us that does not cling to God. There we may see God and ourself as by law revealed: ourself in splendor, filling with the light of Intellect, or rather, light itself, pure, buoyant, aerial, become—in truth, being—a god."

The vision of Plotinus has been echoed in other faiths like the Quakers who preached that everyone has an "Inner Light" that, once discovered and nurtured, leads the way to salvation and peace on earth. The Brethren of the Free Spirit said 'God is all that is, god is in every stone and in each limb of the human body, every created thing is divine. The divine essence is my essence and my essence is the divine essence. Everything that existed yearned to return to its divine Source and would eventually be reabsorbed into God.' This sounds very similar to Unity statements that "there is no spot where God is not" and "there is only one presence and one power — God the good, omnipotent."

I have found the Truth to reside along many paths taken by sincere spiritual seekers. Tolerance for and an appreciation of diverse spiritual paths is a prerequisite for experiencing Heaven on Earth.

Inner Divinity

Meher Baba, a great teacher from India, observed silence for the last 44 years of his life. Speaking was not necessary for "It is love, not questioning, that will bring God to you. There is only one question. And once you know the answer to that question, there are no more to ask. That one question is: *Who am I?...* to attain union with God is so impossibly difficult because it is impossible to become what you already are!" That which we are seeking, we already are!

"Mutants" is an Aboriginal term for those persons who have lost or closed off ancient remembering and wise truths. Being a mutant is a state of heart and mind, not a color or creed. Aborigines echo the importance of realizing ones true nature and inseparability from Divine Oneness. As described by Marlo Morgan in *Mutant Message Down Under*, they hold "if humans know about Divine Oneness and understand that the universe is not a haphazard event but is an unfolding plan, they cannot be fearful. You either have faith or fear, not both."

Many persons have been exposed to the concept that they have a Soul but that truth is not *internalized*. They may have heard, read, or thought about it but don't really *know* it. As such, their life is built on shifting sand rather than solid bedrock that provides an unshakable foundation for a victorious life. R*emembering your Infinite Self*—your inner Divinity—is the key to "the peace that passes all understanding."

Watch the movie *Ghost*, especially the scene in which Demi Moore finally realizes that her "deceased" boyfriend is really alive in Spirit. For her, the "final straw" was seeing the penny float through the air and hearing several pet phrases that only her departed boyfriend knew. Ask Spirit for clear signs so that you'll *absolutely know* your Real Self is eternal.

After that, you'll be born again, saved, enlightened, and transformed forever. After you've "seen the light," you won't ever go back to complete spiritual darkness. That's when life becomes really interesting. No matter what happens in the outer, your calm enlightened center knows it's OK. You're on your way Home or, more accurately, realize *you are Home right now* and never really left. You can then flow down life's path more happily, peacefully, and successfully.

In *Angel Letters*, Sophie Burnham tells about a young couple who had a little girl and a new baby boy. The little girl wanted to be left alone with him but the parents were concerned about the baby's safety. "She begged for days. She was so insistent that the parents finally agreed. There was an intercom in the baby's room... the little girl went in, approached the crib. Alone. She came up to the newborn baby, and over the intercom they heard her whisper, "Tell me about God. I'm forgetting."

That's the problem, isn't it? Many persons have *forgotten* to varying degrees. Like the little girl, there is a still small voice within each of us that cries out to remember. Fortunately, certain techniques and information awaken us from spiritual amnesia. Countless blessings and benefits come from remembering our all loving and forgiving Creator, that there is life after "death", that our True Selves are infinite and there is no eternal "hell."

There are three basic *ways of knowing* that the Spirit World exists and we are eternally part of it. (These will be discussed much more thoroughly in part I.) The first is through *religious faith*. Traditionally, many persons have relied heavily on doctrines of their religion and respective holy books. This is an excellent start but lacks an internalized or experiential component so helpful during life's trials and tribulations.

"Quasi-scientific" *evidence* that suggests a continuity of consciousness is growing in volume and credibility. These include near death experiences, after death contacts, out of body experiences, between incarnation experiences, and paranormal events. Newtonian and Quantum Physics principles also point to the indestructibility of energy, the foundation of our Spiritual Essence.

A third way of knowing is through direct *personal experience*. This is the most subjective but most impressive proof for those fortunate enough to have revelatory or transcendent experiences. This *inner knowing* is ultimately indescribable but radically strengthens ones spiritual faith and knowledge forever.

The level of ones Soul growth prior to this incarnation is no doubt a major factor in the spiritual awakening process. But becoming enlightened in this lifetime is a realistic possibility for everyone who develops strongly internalized spiritual beliefs and habits. The net effect is personally experiencing the kingdom of Heaven.

Why is all this so important? Knowledge of our Infinite Nature consoles and sustains us during suffering. Fear of death and failure, humanity's greatest obstacles, aren't significant factors when we know our True Selves are indestructible. Remembering our Oneness with God sets us free to live full lives with peace, knowledge, and bliss.

It's Time To Awaken

The Soul transcends and exists beyond death. Chopra says "We are not the body. We are not the mind. We are the ones who have mind and body... There is no higher purpose than trying to open your awareness until you can consciously experience the full impact of reality in all its truth, wonder, and sacredness."

Throughout my life, I've been blessed by periodically "hearing" the still small voice of God, the Heavenly Host, or my Enduring Self (all really one and the same.) These revelations had a supernatural quality about them; time seemed to stand still and each experience left a yearning for more contact with this wise Source. Traditionally, Native American youth had a *vision quest* to contact the Great Spirit and understand their mission in life. My experiences certainly felt something like that.

After these experiences, I felt closer to God and less fearful of "death." I knew the Supreme was a benevolent Force that loved us and, despite Its vastness, wanted personal contact with each of us. God then seemed more like a friend than a vengeful, fearsome despot.

Musician and spiritual teacher Iasos says the Earthly dimension was designed as a "platform for evolution for three distinct kingdoms; the Human Kingdom, the Angelic Kingdom, and the Elemental Kingdom. These three kingdoms were designed to have complementary inter-locking roles or functions, within a synergistic whole. None of them are any 'higher' or 'more evolved' than any other, since in each kingdom there is unlimited room for further expansions into Light and Consciousness."

He continues, "The beings in the Human Kingdom were created as step-down transformers for divine thought-forms, to remanifest the heavens of the higher spiritual planes onto the denser planes of form and matter. Humans are all embryonic sun-gods and sun-goddesses in training, and the earth is our incubator." We each are magnificent spiritual beings, much grander than most of us can imagine.

Ruth Montgomery, in *A World Beyond*, reports these words of wisdom by Arthur Ford from the Other Side: "each person is a continuing entity through all eternity. No beginning and no ending... There has never been a time when we were not, and we always will be, even though in constantly changing forms and stages, for we are as much god as God is a part of us... Each of us is incomplete without the totality of humanity."

"It is the totality that makes us the whole of the Universal Spirit which we are wont to call God. The clergy may not like this concept, but if you think about it awhile you realize that it is much nearer to fulfilling Christ's commandment 'Love One Another,' and His teaching that 'The Kingdom of god is within' than all the stuffy preaching about a God who sits on high to judge the quick and the dead. We are all a part of that godhead."

A patient who heals with polarity and herbs recently came to my office for a chiropractic adjustment. As soon as I touched her back, I received vivid images of a female healer many centuries ago. She, too, used natural healing approaches but in those dark ages, she was burned to death as a witch. I briefly felt the sadness, anger, and fear of those spiritually ignorant times. I then clearly felt it was time for her to forgive and forget the past, to boldly share her healing gifts, and to transform fear into power.

When I shared these messages, her eyes filled with tears. "Thank you," she said "I've been wrestling with fears and doubts about increasing my outreaches in natural healing. That's ex-

actly what I needed to hear at this time." Similarly, it is time
for each of us to awaken to our true spiritual nature, to courageously share our unique gifts and speak our highest truth.
The world is waiting patiently for that supreme moment when
a sufficiently critical number of us do so and usher in Heaven
on Earth!

Jean Houston, Ph.D., author of *The Possible Human*, says
the key is to see through societal-induced trances and see all
people as God-in-hiding. "The moment is always there; the totality is always there. Know at every moment that this is it! It
isn't a future event; it is the radical now. Have that excitement, then join with other groups of people... I believe we are
at the most critical place and time in human history. Indeed,
these are the times and we are the people who must act. If not
now, then when? If not you, who? What we do makes a profound difference."

It's time to awaken, remember, and act upon these truths.
More and more persons are hearing the voice of Spirit and are
bravely sharing their inner truths. A spiritual revolution is
underway and we're each being called to participate fully.

Age Of Love And Light

In his 1994 inaugural speech, South African President
Nelson Mandela said "Our deepest fear is *not* that we are in-
adequate. Our deepest fear is that we are powerful beyond
measure. It is our light, not our darkness, that frightens us.
We ask ourselves, who am I to be brilliant, gorgeous, talented
and fabulous? Actually, who are you not to be? You are a child
of God. Your playing small doesn't serve the world. There's nothing enlightened about shrinking so that other people won't feel
insecure around you. We were born to manifest the glory of
God within us. It's not just in some of us; it's in everyone. And
as we let our own light shine, we unconsciously give other people
permission to do the same. As we are liberated from our own
fear, our presence automatically liberates others."

We're not alone in this process of realization; we have *limitless assistance* from within and all around. In years past,
humans have suffered under misconceptions they were lowly

creations, born in sin and prone to evil. Many were entrapped by this erroneous, limiting teaching. The age of darkness and confusion has passed; now is the time to realize our lofty calling and limitless possibilities. We are entering a golden age of peace and joy, love and light.

This New Age offers wonderful new possibilities for our world. Yes, there are still significant problems requiring creative "soul-utions." Darkness seems to be stronger than Light at times, in part, because issues that have been hidden for a long time are coming out in the open. Blatant discrimination against females, children, non-whites, gays, elderly and lower socio-economic groups has long occurred and needs to be properly addressed by society.

That's one reason why so much crap is hitting the fan. Also, in the past, many persons have given their power away to individuals in control. It's time for each person to regain his or her own power and recognize the sacredness of all life.

Sociologist Paul Ray calls this new social order "transmodernism" and says 44 million U.S. adults, the "cultural creatives," are standard bearers of a new integral culture. Strongly held values include: environmentalism, ecological sustainability, globalism with love of travel to foreign places, planetary stewardship, altruism, feminism and involvement in women's issues, self-actualization, alternative health care, spirituality, personal growth psychology, a greater social conscience and social optimism.

Ray says we should take heart. We are traveling in the midst of an enormous company of allies, a large population of creative people who are the carriers of more positive ideas and values than any previous renaissance period has ever seen. And they can probably be mobilized to act altruistically on behalf of our future.

Some persons believe that, in addition to help from Earthly workers and God, we are also aided by a wide array of higher spiritual Beings—some from formed, some from formless dimensions.

Whatever your model, it's clear that powerful energies of transformation abound. Each of us plays an important part in the unfolding of these new possibilities—the movement toward Heaven on Earth. As our hearts open and we remember our true identities as Eternal Souls, we will step forward to contribute our special talents. We each have a special calling to assist the unfoldment of this new era.

As this evolution of consciousness accelerates, Spirit speaks to all via an intensification of spiritual energies. Some people are not prepared for these changes and are experiencing drastic upheavals in various aspects of their lives. Those who can handle the energy flow will be teachers for those who have not yet learned how.

This intensification of energies is like fire that improves the quality of life if channeled properly or burns if not. Intense spiritual energies—kundalini energies in the Eastern model—are rising. Some persons are in the flow with these changes while others resist and get burnt. Both paths teach valuable lessons but the former is much more pleasant. Those who ignore this call will learn the hard way until they realign aspects of their lives that are not in harmony and balance.

These consciousness shifts will eventually summate into a virtual utopia. Realizing Heaven on Earth is a result of both grace *and* works; God helps those who help themselves. With ever-present help from God and the Heavenly Host, we surely can reach greater heights. When enough persons share this vision, it will become a reality. The plans and mechanisms for it are already in place. In fact, the kingdom of Heaven is—could we only see clearly—an established reality *here and now*.

We live in a totally lawful and orderly Universe that is exquisitely designed for our *spiritual* unfoldment and growth. From a purely secular perspective, life seems capricious and cruel; God seems to be uncaring, impotent, or nonexistent. Look at life from the standpoint of *soul-growth*; the mysteries and seeming injustices on earth will eventually make perfect sense.

Cooperation, rather than competition, characterizes this New Age of enlightened humanity. The contribution of persons from all walks of life is important. And remember, little changes make a huge difference over time. Our church recently changed the words of *Amazing Grace* from "saved a wretch like me" to "saved a Soul like me." This is one small example of a paradigm shift that creates infinite positive outcomes.

Anchor and Celebrate

Let's review the highlights so far:
- total success in every aspect of life is achievable now
- conscious language and technology for change enables rapid, lasting, and positive changes
- members of the Family of Light are awakening to Spirit
- a number of different and valid paths exist to the Truth
- the real you is an Eternal Soul, not just a mind and body
- it's time to awaken to and demonstrate that True Nature
- humanity is ready for a New Age of peace, joy and love

To really internalize the importance of these points, use the Life-Transformative Techniques to reach peak state: attain peak physiology, remember empowering feelings, use your power cues, and listen to or recall inspiring music. Reread the highlights above, then celebrate by moving your body and cheering. Feel the great news we've just discussed and *give thanks* for powerful information and techniques that will transform your life. Doing so signals you are ready to change past patterns and *break through* to new levels of happiness, success, and service.

PLEASE don't continue reading until you've integrated this new information into your body, mind, and spirit with a celebration. If you can't physically celebrate now because you're in public and worry you'll be institutionalized, internally rehearse it until you can outwardly celebrate.

The various *methods* used to reach enlightenment are secondary in importance to an *earnest desire* to know and follow God's will and your Soul's mission. Yet, there are techniques and understandings that have consistently helped others *awaken.* You're now ready for part I information to help trigger a *profound remembrance* of your True Self.

Part I:

REMEMBERING YOUR SOUL

Evidence suggesting a greater spiritual reality and
continuation of consciousness; ways of *knowing*
the real you is Eternal Soul and Spirit

Acknowledge The Divine In All Life

"Oh, then, soul most beautiful among all the creatures, so anxious to know the dwelling place of your Beloved that you may go in quest of Him and be united with Him, now we are telling you that you yourself are his dwelling... his secret chamber and hiding place."

—St. John of the Cross

In theology school, God was defined as the highest power that we can conceive of. I do not view God as a huge superman in the sky who rules, judges, and punishes. God is Ultimate Energy, Force, Power, Peace, Knowledge, Bliss, Consciousness, Love, and Intelligence. God imbues every aspect of life—including you and me. As Islamic poet Rumi wrote, "God is like a vast ocean of love, and the Milky Way galaxy is but a speck of foam floating in that ocean."

Edgar Mitchell, former astronaut and founder of the Institute of Noetic Sciences, says "If you search for God, you will find it. It is right there within yourself... The reason it's hard for some to find God is that most of our ideas about God were imprinted at a very early age. Later information we receive about ourselves and the universe is often rejected because it doesn't match up with what we were taught as young children. We tend to interpret new information in accordance with our early ideas. So to find God, we first have to become aware of our programmed concepts of God and change them if they don't match up with our present day experience."

I asked God and Christ into my life privately at a young age, publicly at age 18, and have continued to do so nearly every day since. For 25 years, I have prayed that God use me as a channel, a vehicle for Her plan. I have asked to know God's will for me, to remember and perform my Soul's mission.

Everything is, in reality, a manifestation of God so it's a stretch to speak of inviting something in that already is everywhere. From the perspective of duality, Divine Oneness does not intrude on our free will but waits to be invited into our consciousness. Whether you're a dualist, monist, pantheist, agnostic or atheist, take a moment right now and open your heart to your Higher Power. Humbly ask for guidance from God and the Heavenly Host. Then give thanks and know your request has been heard and the ball is rolling.

Depending on your level of spiritual maturity or understanding, you may need or want an intermediary between you and God. Some persons can't relate to or comprehend Prime Creator and are more comfortable with a Divine go-between like Jesus, a saint, or a guru. All sincere paths lead to God so choose the ones that seem best for you. Remain flexible and open as your relationship with the Divine strengthens and changes.

Eventually, you'll reach a point where you realize that *God is in and is all*. You'll come to understand that you have the same Inner Christ Spirit that imbued Jesus and others around whom religions have formed. Deepak Chopra, M.D., states "deep inside you there is a god in embryo, and it has only one desire. It wants to be born."

We each have a "birth vision", our Souls' plan for this earthly incarnation. Few persons have remembered or followed this vision because of life's challenges, religious misconceptions, societal teachings, and fear. Acknowledge the Divine within and all around; ask for assistance in remembering and achieving your birth vision. Pray that you will contribute to the "world vision" of utopia, Heaven on Earth, in our lifetime.

Personal Experience

"Wilt thou love God, as he Thee? Then digest, My Soul, this wholesome meditation: How God, the Spirit, by Angels waited on in heaven, doth make his Temple in thy brest."
—John Donne *Divine Poems XV*

There's no substitute for firsthand experience to really see through life's illusions. Those who have glimpsed the Divine need no further proof. A personal relationship with the Creator and realizing ones Soul has been described as "seeing the light", "being saved" and "getting happy feet" (the latter being a term by comedian Steve Martin that never quite caught on in theological circles).

Personal experience of the Divine *convinces* us of a spiritual reality that eludes the five senses yet is more real than anything our senses reveal. Life is but a dream. As Richard Bach explained in *Illusions*, "This is a dream. It's a different space-time and any different space-time is a dream for a good sane earthling, which you are going to be for a while yet. But you will remember, and that will change your thinking and your life."

I retained a glimpse from the Other Side; at age 5, I told my parents that a beautiful sunset "looked like God." I had two auditory and cognitive revelatory experiences at age 11 as described in *Balanced Living*. Since then, I have periodically felt or heard Divine counsel.

Another, more subtle, sign took 35 years for me to understand. I was about 7 years old when I first heard the term *master* as in "master's degree"; time slowed for a moment and my mind whirred quickly, as if trying to recall a distant memory. Although I didn't know what it was, I made a mental note to become a "master" someday. I forgot those childhood thoughts even when I earned my master's in psychology although part of me felt disappointed—like "Well, you've got that master's degree, now what?"

Two years ago, in a moment of reverie, I recalled my thoughts at age 7 and reflected how the master's degree didn't seem like that was it. I wondered if my childhood fascination with the term "master" was because I dimly remembered studying under spiritual masters. Or maybe I recalled my birth-vision to remind myself and many others of our lofty birthright.

I've been blessed with several peak experiences of glimpsing the Divine through meditation. In 1974, I was meditating while lying on the grass on a warm spring day. After a 20 minute TM meditation, I felt as if my body were becoming part of the Earth. At that moment, my fear of death and separation decreased dramatically. I *knew* through firsthand experience that there was a Divine plan and love that surpassed human understanding. I had glimpsed Oneness!

Near the end of a recent ninety minute yoga and meditation session, I was silently working with the mantra "OM" when, spontaneously, a louder and deeper chorus of "OM" resounded within. I smelled an unknown but wonderful fragrance although the windows and doors were shut. Then I felt what seemed to be Divine love and peace. This peek of the Beloved was so over-whelming and beautiful that tears welled up in my eyes.

It seemed that information and energy for future use was being transmitted to me. The power and splendor was so great that, after just a minute, I felt I couldn't handle the current. I murmured aloud, "Oh my God!" and the glimpse was over. But that sweet memory will carry me through life's challenges and remind me I'm always Home, no matter what the external cir-cumstances.

One teaching from that event is that I was not prepared to directly experience the Divine for very long. The Beloved's Power blew my mind's circuit breakers; my nervous system wasn't strong enough to handle the current. This experience motivates me to live as Godly a life as possible so I can increas-ingly sustain that energy level.

That's the main reason for practicing centering techniques: not to work oneself toward God—the Divine is always present. Such methods help upgrade our body/mind/spirit *receivers* so we can perceive reality more accurately. God, Life, Energy, Love, Peace, Joy, and Harmony are the totality of life. All else is an illusion; certain techniques and understandings help us remem-ber and experience that truth.

My most recent experience proving the existence of the Spirit World occurred at a spiritual retreat. I was walking to-ward the ocean and clearly saw two people swimming and standing in the water. As I waded in, I saw a tall male with dark hair and a shorter female bobbing and diving under the water. As I approached even closer, the female waved at me and I recognized her as my good friend "Elaine."

I wondered who the man was since her husband is shorter and has white hair. I couldn't see him and figured he was hold-ing his breath under water. When I reached Elaine, I looked all around and asked "Where's that guy?" She looked at me like I was crazy and said "What guy? I've been out here by myself for 20 minutes." I described the fellow I had seen as clearly as I had seen her. "Maybe you saw my Spirit Guide." Maybe!

Some persons are born into this life with a significant remembrance of the Truth. Jesus was one such person and thus could teach elders and scholars at age 12. In *Autobiography of a Yogi*, Paramahansa Yogananda wrote "I find my earliest memories covering the anachronistic features of a previous incarnation. Clear recollections came to me of a distant life in which I had been a yogi amid the Himalayan snows."

Years ago, my wife and I had just finished reading our 4 year old daughter a bedtime story. As she drifted off to sleep, she murmured "I remember before I came to be with you. The sun always shined, it never rained, and I always wore pretty dresses. And, oh yes, Greg was there too!" (Greg was a 4 year old friend she had met at preschool with whom she had an unusually immediate and strong mutual attraction.) And then she stopped. We waited, then quietly prompted her by asking "Tell us more, what happened then?" Our questions awakened her and she said "I must have been dreaming." Actually, much of what we perceive as waking reality is really a dream.

Firsthand experience or remembrance of the Divine is the most important proof of a greater spiritual reality. Then the whole ballgame changes radically and forever for the better. All the other evidence and techniques assist reaching this level of knowing.

S.S. Satchidananda, in *To Know Your Self*, says "Why did God create this material world and put us into this game? The only One who can fully answer this question is the One who made everything. But when you see Him you probably will say 'I've been meaning to ask You this and that, but now that I see You, I don't have anything to ask.'"

Enlightened Spiritual Paths

There are thousands of different religions or denominations and there are just as many spiritual viewpoints as there are people. Just as each snowflake is different, each of us has a unique perspective on life's ultimate matters. An in-depth, open-minded look at some religious approaches suggests they owe more to the hands of humans than they do to the hand of God.

The more fundamentalist denominations describe an eternal Soul-life in Heaven as an outcome only for a relatively few true believers in their way. Fortunately, most religions also have *esoteric* denominations that recognize the Divinity within each individual and teach techniques to discovering that potential. These include Sufism in Islam, Cabalistic and Liberal sects of Judaism, and more enlightened denominations such as Unity, Science of Mind, Religious Science, Unitarian-Universalist, United Church of Christ and Christian Science. Most Eastern religions and Native spiritual approaches include Higher Thought as an integral part of their teachings.

For example, Unitarian-Universalism has long led the way in advocating women's rights, enlightened mental health treatment, gay rights, tolerance of other faiths, and recognizing universal salvation. Early members included Henry David Thoreau, Clara Barton, Ralph Waldo Emerson, Emily Dickinson, Nathaniel Hawthorne, Walt Whitman, Dorthea Dix, Horace Greeley, Susan B. Anthony, and Thomas Jefferson.

Universalist member, physician and signer of the Declaration of Independence, Dr. Benjamin Rush, stated "a belief in God's universal love to all His creatures... God will finally restore all of them who are miserable to happiness." This was a remarkable statement in an age when belief in eternal hellfire and damnation was very common; the belief that the whole human race will be "saved" was condemned as heresy by "church" councils in 544 AD.

In the 18th century, Thomas Starr King said "The one (Universalists), think God is too good to damn them forever and the other (Unitarian) thinks they are too good to be damned forever." They were, of course, both right and the two groups eventually merged. I'm thankful for enlightened churches that share a message of tolerance, love, and the sanctity of each person and other religions.

Jack Miles, author of *God: A Biography*, states "Much that the Bible says about him (God) is rarely preached from the pulpit because, examined too closely, it becomes a scandal." He cites examples of God destroying most humans in the flood described in Genesis 8, a race He had created and described as "very good" just a few pages earlier. Like Miles, I and many others also have trouble believing other Biblical stories, for example, that God would demand Abraham to sacrifice his son, even as a test. The concept of original sin, that—because "Adam" sinned—we all are born into sin, seemed idiotic when I was young and strikes me as even more ridiculous now.

Many religious/mythical explanations of the world are crude and absurd. Yet some persons think that believing in unintelligible dogma is a test of true faith. More and more, though, sophisticated spiritual seekers don't view God as a separate super-person who rules the world from above but as the Ultimate Ground of Being manifest in all life. .

Take religious teachings seriously, not literally. In *A History of God*, Armstrong states: "Once the Bible begins to be interpreted literally instead of symbolically, the idea of its God becomes impossible. To imagine a deity who is literally responsible for everything that happens on earth involves impossible contradictions. The 'God' of the Bible ceases to be a symbol of a transcendent reality and becomes a cruel and despotic tyrant."

She notes the rise in "fundamentalism" in Christianity, Islam, and Judaism: "A highly political spirituality, it is literal and intolerant in its vision. In the United States, which has always been prone to extremist and apocalyptic enthusiasm, Christian fundamentalism has attached itself to the New Right. Fundamentalists campaign for the abolition of legal abortion and for a hard line on moral and social decency... (they) seem to have little regard for the loving compassion of Christ. They are swift to condemn the people they see as the 'enemies of God.' Most would consider Jews and Muslims destined for hellfire, and Urguhart has argued that all oriental religions are inspired by the devil."

Such a stance misses the compassion, acceptance and love that the founders of these religions encouraged. It is time to remember that we each are children of the One God and treat each other accordingly. A number of elders who regularly attend more orthodox churches have thanked me for tackling thorny theological issues that never made sense to their hearts and minds.

Enlightened spiritual paths don't scare people with erroneous notions of "hell" and "devils." Some persons have become afraid to think for themselves and trust their own feelings. Preachers thumping pulpits and yelling about eternal damnation have not been helpful. They spread fear and misinformation while turning many thoughtful persons away from God.

Thomas Jefferson wrote, "The religion builders have so distorted and deformed the doctrine of Jesus, so muffled them in mysticisms, fancies, and falsehoods, have caricatured them into forms so inconceivable, as to shock reasonable thinkers."

For example, the following ad ran periodically in our newspaper's classified column: "Free: Eternal Life. To receive this gift from God, ask Jesus to come into your heart as your Lord and Savior. To keep this gift you live with all your heart by the New Testament of the Christian Bible. Choose Heaven; Hell is hot. For Jesus said 'But those mine enemies which would not that I should reign over them, bring hither and slay them before me.' (Luke 19:27) 'And whosoever was not found written in the Book of Life was cast into the Lake of Fire.' (Rev. 20:15)"

More succinctly and sickeningly, I recently saw a sign supposedly designed to save souls: "Jesus or burn!" I hate to give these ludicrous interpretations and fearful messages further press but they explain perfectly why so many persons want nothing to do with religion. Fortunately, God and Christ don't need "hell", fear, coercion, and threats to fulfill their plans for redemption of all. Remember, religious teachings that would offend a child's sensibilities about God cannot be true.

The truth is, there is no eternal fiery hell for anyone. Dr. R. Errico, Aramaic scholar, states that the word "hell" originally denoted *a condition of mind* when we're separated from God and the truth of our Eternal Nature. Hell did not refer to a place! Yes, humans can choose to create a temporary, self-imposed hell. But heavenly states of consciousness are always available as soon as we remember our Inner Divinity and Oneness with God.

Errico says the original meaning for "demon possession" or being influenced by the "devil" was *having a wrong concept* or 'trapped energy that is wild and chaotic.' Again, these words have been misunderstood and misused over time to convey something very different from the original meaning. The result is much confusion and fear among the laity.

The root word for heaven means "expanding." We enjoy a heavenly quality of life when we *expand our centers*, our hearts and minds, sufficiently to realize we are Divine Humans at one with God. Open-minded, love-centered denominations in every religion recognize the Inner Divinity in all individuals. Worship with enlightened spiritual groups to help remembering your Soul.

Be Here Now

Everything that has happened is in the past; anything that is yet to come will happen when it's time. We just need to focus on the present moment. Living with *present time consciousness* is a major key to remembering we are Souls. The "eternal now" moment is all there ever is. The past is over and tomorrow never comes. When we really internalize this, we experience a peace that escapes those reliving the past or worrying about the future.

Alan Watts, in *The Book: On The Taboo Against Knowing Who You Are*, says that after understanding "that, beneath everything, 'I' and 'universe' are one, you ask 'So what? What is the next step, the practical application?'—I will answer that the absolutely vital thing is to consolidate your understanding, to become capable of enjoyment, of living in the present, and of the discipline which this involves. Without this you have nothing to give... Without this, all social concern will be muddlesome meddling and all work for the future will be planned disaster."

Heaven can be experienced right now on Earth and other dimensions. Heaven is a state of consciousness, a level of being, a vibrational rate of energy. Some persons have written off this Earthly lifetime as a horrible experience in a place controlled by the "devil." They live with the hope of heaven at a future time and different location.

Yes, there are more consistently spiritually harmonious realms than Earth but don't discount the potential for Heaven on Earth here and now. We each have experienced times when life was heavenly, when we felt happy, joyous, peaceful, and loving. We can pray, will, intend, and affirm to be fully here now, to remember our Infinite Selves, to enjoy Heaven each moment, and assist others to do the same.

Being here now occurs optimally when we love, accept, and forgive ourselves and others. *Love* because we are by birthright inherently lovable, *we are love*—a unique part of Creation—and so is everyone else. *Acceptance* because we can't change the past and we always do the best we can given what we have to work with. The best way to grow and improve is to accept where we are now and go forward.

Forgiveness because we can always choose to forgive others and ourselves, just as God has forgiven us. In fact, as *A Course In Miracles* points out, "God does not forgive because He never has condemned." Breathe in deeply and, as you exhale, give thanks for this mini-healing that allows you to live fully in the golden present moment.

I comforted my daughter after a nightmare: "It's just a bad dream, nothing can hurt you" I reassured her. She could sense the truth of my words and felt better. The dominant Earthly perception of reality is a type of dream; we can't really be hurt here either. I know all too well that people suffer and die but this pain is very transitory in comparison to Eternity. The biggest step in knowing this good news is letting go of fear.

Brian Weiss, M.D., author of *Many Lives, Many Masters*, *Through Time Into Healing* and *Real Love*, states "if people knew that 'life is endless; so we never die; we were never really born,' then this fear would dissolve. If they knew that they had lived countless times before and would live countless times again, how reassured they would feel. If they knew that spirits were around to help them while they were in physical state and that after death, in spiritual state, they would join these spirits, including their deceased loved ones, how comforted they would be."

"If they knew that acts of violence and injustices against people did not go unnoted, but had to be repaid in kind in other lifetimes, how much less anger and desire for vengeance they would harbor... But how to reach people with this knowledge? ...if faith is not enough, perhaps science will help. Perhaps experiences such as Catherine's (one of his patients) and mine need to be studied, analyzed, and reported in a detached, scientific manner by people trained in the behavioral and physical sciences."

In *Teaching Your Children About God*, Rabbi David Wolpe recounts an old Jewish parable about twin fetuses in the womb that is wonderfully instructive of this physical life and the afterlife. One believes there is life beyond the womb while the other thinks there is no other life except in his uterine home. When the "believer" is forced through the birth canal, the remaining fetus is saddened, convinced his companion has died forever. "Outside the womb, however, the parents are rejoicing. For what the remaining brother, left behind, has just witnessed is not death but birth." This classic tale reminds us that, despite appearances to the contrary, life does not end but continues 'after death' in a wondrous way that most humans can't imagine. Being here now, trusting, studying and growing will eventually teach all persons that there is nothing to fear.

The rest of section I consists of current information, much of it from respected doctors and scholars, that points to a greater spiritual reality.

Reincarnation

Understanding that a "cyclical life" process is operative in the Cosmos is another important step in remembering your Soul. Reincarnation is the philosophy that we live not just one but many lives. We will return to physical planes like the Earth for further lessons until we have perfected ourselves. We will merge with the Divine when our energy vibrations are powerful and harmonious enough to handle the frequency of the God Force.

I recently saw a little girl whose glance mesmerized me for a moment; she at once looked both childish and wise beyond her years. As our eyes met, a powerful message flashed: "Consider how many beautiful children like her have been molested, tortured, and killed by others. Don't you think God has a plan—like continued existence of an Eternal Soul—in which hope and justice ultimately prevail despite human cruelties?"

What about the widely different environments that two children might grow up with? One has a happy, loving, healthy, intelligent, prosperous family and all the accompanying blessings. Another is born into poverty, abuse, ignorance, neglect, and turmoil. Where is the equality? Where is the justice unless there is some great equalizing factor?

The Bhagavad-Gita stated "As a man, casting off worn-out garments, taketh new ones, so the dweller in the body, casting off worn-out bodies, entereth into others that are new. For sure is the death of him that is born, and sure the birth of him that is dead; therefore over the inevitable thou shouldst not grieve."

Throughout history, a majority of the world's religions and populations have believed in reincarnation. Famous persons who believed in reincarnation include: Plato, Socrates, Pythagoras, Plotinus, Origen, St. Augustine, Cicero, Marcus Aurelius, Hume, Kant, Hegel, Schopenhauer, Nietzsche, William James, Henri Bergson, Goethe, Hugo, Sand, Blake, Wordsworth, Whitman, Shelley, Kipling, Voltaire, Tennyson, Browning, Alcott, Emerson, Thoreau, Poe, Whitman, Wagner, da Vinci, Benjamin Franklin, Luther Burbank, Edison, Henry Ford, Edgar Cayce, General Patton, and Harry Houdini.

Unity minister James Dillet Freeman, in *The Case For Reincarnation*, says it is one of the earliest, oldest, and most universal ideas human beings have had. He has written and lectured about reincarnation in the hope that others will "find meaning in what often appears to be a meaningless world... I look at reincarnation as not only completely compatible with the important teachings of Christianity, but I think it makes Christianity more Christian."

In *Tying Rocks To Clouds* by William Elliott, Rabbi Zalman Schacter-Shalomi stated "In mystical Judaism, we believe in reincarnation. It's call *gilgul*. We believe each time we incarnate, we move a step forward. Coming down one time prepares

me for the task I have to do the next time. Whatever I conclude
in this lifetime, if I come back again, I can take up from where
I left off—not with the same memory, mind you, but with the
same traces and vibrations and merit and clarity and God-con-
nection that I had. Then I can go farther in the next incarnation to provide more input. If I learned a lot this time around,
I get to teach the next time around! If I did wrong this time, I
may get a chance to fix some of the wrong I did."

Reincarnation was a widely held belief in the time of Jesus
and early Christians until patriarchal councils in the 5th century A.D. decided what future generations would be taught.
However, there are a number of references in the Bible that
escaped deletion by men who deemed themselves to be God-
ordained censors.

Even as a youth, I was puzzled by John 9:2 as the disciples
asked Jesus "Rabbi, who sinned, this man or his parents, that
he was born blind?" A person born blind to learn from past
transgressions could only have sinned in a previous life. Duh!

In Matthew 17:12-13, Jesus said "'Elijah has already come,
and they did not know him, but did to him whatever they
pleased. So also the son of man will suffer at their hands.' Then
the disciples understood that he was speaking to them of John
the Baptist." In Matthew 11:11-15, Jesus said "Truly, I say to
you, among those born of women there has risen no one greater
than John the Baptist... and if you are willing to accept it, he
is Elijah who is to come. He who has ears to hear, let him hear".

An understanding of reincarnation helps explain another
otherwise abstruse passage in Rev. 3:12 "Him that overcometh
will I make a pillar in the temple of my God, and he shall go no
more out." These passages highlight how much the law of karma
and reincarnation were part of standard thinking during the
time of Jesus.

Reincarnation was still a common belief among early Christians despite having been rejected as heresy by church councils, most notably the Second Council of Constantinople in 553
AD. After these councils, only the church and its officials could
forgive sins, receive Divine revelation, properly interpret Scripture, and decide what kind of afterlife a person would have.

That was a powerful combination no doubt designed, in part, to keep the church and its ministers well-heeled and in absolute power.

Surprisingly, there was no popular outcry after the councils ruled belief in reincarnation as heresy. This was most likely because living conditions were so miserable that few wanted a series of such deplorable lives. Still, most persons continued to consider reincarnation as part of their basic religious philosophy, especially those with better education and socioeconomic status.

The largest such group in Europe was called the Cathari; in France, they were called the Albigenses. These peaceful and gentle people believed that material power had corrupted the church. The word 'catharsis' stems from their philosophy of purging themselves from the temptations of the material world until, after a series of lifetimes, they became pure spiritual beings at one with God.

Their beliefs spread and the church suffered a decline. Citing their threat to Catholicism, Papal authorities started a crusade and slaughtered hundreds of thousands of innocent men, women, and children. Despite this widespread carnage, belief in reincarnation persisted and actually increased in the following years. Then the church founded the Inquisition that was primarily designed to extinguish such beliefs; those who dared differ from church doctrines were tortured or killed.

The Inquisitions continued for 300 years, frightening and killing people and ensuring power of the medieval church. Enlightened Christian beliefs like reincarnation were driven underground. Centuries of persecution created deeply rooted fears about avoiding dissension with established powers. Some spiritual seekers living today were possibly tortured and killed in past lives during the Dark Ages. Fortunately, all this is in the past. Now it's time to forgive and realize a Golden Age.

There are a number of classic "proofs" that suggest the reality of reincarnation. Some of the most impressive evidence comes from children who spontaneously report information. Melvin Morse, M.D., pediatric researcher of near death experiences in children, reports children who "met souls in heaven waiting to be reborn. This bothered them because it seemed contrary to their religious training, yet they did meet these souls." Why would children, who had no prior exposure to the idea of reincarnation, witness such a process unless it is true?

A number of children have reported past life details that have been verified. In Western cultures, there is little understanding of the principles of reincarnation; as such, claims of previous lives would be met with amusement or ridicule. However, in cultures where reincarnation is a widely accepted phenomena, claims by children are more thoroughly investigated and considered as possibly factual. The story of Shanti Devi is a famous one in the field of paranormal occurrences.

Born in 1926 in Delhi, India, Shanti chattered at a young age about her husband and children. At age nine, she told her parents about her previous life in a town 100 miles away and that she had died during childbirth. Her parents contacted her previous family and, without any help, Shanti correctly picked family members from another lifetime out of a crowd.

Again, without any assistance, she led the way to her former home and pointed out where a well used to be and where she had buried an exact sum of money. She discussed private matters with her ex-husband that only a former wife would know. There are many such cases that have been investigated and confirmed by professors from universities in India.

Child prodigies are another phenomena that suggest the existence of previous lifetimes. A number of children have demonstrated virtuoso musical abilities despite little or no practice at that instrument. Other children have spoken several languages fluently without any exposure to them in the present lifetime, a phenomena termed *'xenoglossy'*. Dr. Frederick Wood, in *After Thirty Centuries*, describes such a young girl, Rosemary, who spoke fluent Egyptian and was knowledgeable about their ancient ways.

Familiarity with places and persons is another set of puzzling events unless reincarnation is true. Some persons, upon arriving at a country or city for the first time, know directions and locations of landmarks. More common is the occurrence of meeting someone for the first time and having a strong sense of having known each other before. This may partially account for the instant fondness or dislike we feel toward new acquaintances.

Nature's cycles further suggest a series of changing but never ending life stages. Consider nature's seasons, ocean tides, sunrise and sunset, lunar stages, plant stages, and animal metamorphoses. Surely humans have as many chances to get it right as nature does. The idea of cyclical life stages for Souls until we graduate from caterpillars to butterflies makes perfect sense to me.

The First Law of Thermodynamics, the Law of the Conservation of Energy, recognizes that energy cannot be destroyed but merely changes form. Things change from one form to another. It's logical, then, that this is also true of our spiritual energy. Our Souls merely change their outward form and location but do not perish.

Quantum physics describes reality as an interplay between "solid" matter and formless energy. Human Beings are manifestations of Spirit/Energy taking on incarnations to learn, grow, teach, and serve. Science only substantiates what ancient religions have been teaching for thousands of years. Krishna, speaking in the Bhagavad Gita, says "If the slayer thinks he slays, or if the slain thinks he is slain, neither of these knows the truth about himself. For the Self is never born and never dies."

Another "proof" of reincarnation is that it's *logical*. Astronomers report hundreds of billions of stars in each galaxy and billions of galaxies in this universe. Given the magnitude of Creation, isn't it conceivable there are more options than just one Earthly life, then Heaven or "hell" for eternity? It's rather closed minded to rule out such possibilities; as Eleanor Roosevelt pointed out, the idea of being born *again* doesn't seem any more fantastic than being born this time.

Past life regressions, under hypnosis, allow recall of past lives and are another "proof" of reincarnation. Several trusted friends had told me of past life regressions that were very meaningful to them, but I viewed regressions with skepticism until I experienced them firsthand. Read Dr. Weiss' books for fascinating accounts of past life memories made available through hypnosis.

Weiss describes events that cannot be easily explained unless past life regression is a valid phenomena. For example, a mother and daughter with a horrible relationship went, unbeknownst to each other, to two different hypno-therapists. After learning they had been enemies in a past life, their relationship healed even before they compared notes and discovered their identical regression experiences. Says Dr. Weiss "With this startling and illuminating new perception, their relationship finally transcended the fixed script of endless competition and hostility."

The greatest potential for this work, in addition to convincing us of spiritual realities, is the rapid emotional and spiritual healing that may not be possible with more traditional therapies. After his new work with regression therapy, Dr. Weiss noticed "I felt more hope, more joy, more purpose, and more satisfaction in my life. It dawned on me that I was losing the fear of death. I wasn't afraid of my own death or of nonexistence. I was less afraid of losing others, even though I would certainly miss them."

He continues "How powerful the fear of death is. People go to such great lengths to avoid the fear: mid-life crises, affairs with younger people, cosmetic surgeries, exercise obsessions, accumulating material possessions, procreating to carry on a name, striving to be more and more youthful, and so on. We are frightfully concerned with our deaths, sometimes so much so that we forget the real purpose of our lives."

In *The Secret Of Healing*, Hans Holzer, Ph.D. describes bioenergetic healer Ze'ev Kolman's abilities to know and use past-life information. Says Holzer, "Increasing numbers of doctors take quite seriously symptoms caused by situations in previous lives that are unknown to the sufferer, because there are positive results to back them up. When the patient understands the origin of the affliction, it appears that the matter is solved..."

A series of past life hypnotic regressions was one of the most fascinating experiences in my life. My analytical brain thought: "My imagination could be making all this up" but several aspects of the experience were significant. First, I was so "clocked out" that I drooled, having forgotten to swallow—usually an unconscious reflex. In over 20 years of meditating and relaxing with different techniques, I have never slobbered, especially in front of a new acquaintance and health care colleague.

During the regression, tears of sadness and joy streamed down my face although I had not cried for over 20 years. It was as if a deeper self—not "Mark the Earthling"—was having a catharsis. I felt a strange detachment as I "saw" myself living and dying in former incarnations. It was like impassively watching a movie of myself through a heightened identification with the "Observer" role. The sessions left a sense of closure with old, unsettled emotions. I felt more peaceful, calm, and confident of my Eternal Nature.

(Parenthetically, the analogy between life and a movie is closer than most of us realize; this may be one reason why movies are so entertaining. Even though I was watching possible earlier versions of myself dying and suffering, there was not much more emotion involved than when I watch a movie on TV. This puts life's tragedies into true perspective; a movie may be sad but we know the actors and actresses don't really die or suffer. In the same way, the "tragic" events of our lives are relatively very transient and illusory. In the movie of life, no one really dies and suffers either; it just seems like it for awhile. Seeing through this illusion breaks the bondage to fear, despair, and confusion.)

Some ask 'If reincarnation is true, why don't we remember details of past lives?' If we remembered all that we knew before, we wouldn't learn our lessons here. If a schoolteacher gave all the answers to the students, who would study? As Souls, we chose to experience a particular set of challenges that would impart lessons most needed for spiritual growth. Remembering past lives would prevent us from gaining the full impact of life's lessons.

Why should we be able to remember the details of past lives? I can't even remember details of last year! Think how confusing life would be if we did remember details from thousands of past lives. Our computer-brain would be so clogged with minutia that we couldn't react quickly or make small decisions without reconfiguring tons of data. I'm confident the current setup is a fine one.

We do retain the most important *insights* from the past. Past life experiences contribute to who and how we are *now*. We retain accumulated wisdom from the past and an inner knowledge we are Eternal Souls. That helps us keep going with hope, faith, and courage.

An understanding of reincarnation helps explain many of life's quandaries. Altruistic acts that endanger ones life have long puzzled social scientists. The instinct for survival is usually the strongest yet many persons have risked or lost their lives trying to save complete strangers. Perhaps in a moment of passion and human need, the Higher Self instantly shines through and overcomes basic survival instincts. Maybe unconscious memories of the Soul's imperishability overcome the rescuer's regard for self-preservation. Could it also be that the person in need wasn't a "complete stranger" but was connected through past lives?

Consider the attraction between couples of widely varying age, appearance, or interests. Perhaps they unconsciously recognize a familiar Soul in each other, thereby rendering physical criteria unimportant. Other couples who stay together despite endless unhappiness may need problems from past lives healed to break quarrelsome patterns.

What about criminals and societal offenders who seem to get off scot-free? What about those who don't seem to get a fair shake—children who die young, the retarded, addicts, and those who suffer greatly? If this lifetime is all there is, justice does not always prevail and many persons have a valid grievance. Reincarnation and karma are the great equalizers that explain countless seeming human injustices.

Recently, a propane gas tank exploded and destroyed a home in our area. Of the four children in the family, one was away on a trip, one was thrown clear unharmed, one was 90% burned, and another died. Can that incredible array of outcomes be just randomness—good or bad luck? How can we make sense

of such tragedy? Must we be satisfied with the perplexing plati-
tude that it's God will?

There's only one answer that sufficiently explains life's
seeming inequalities and injustices. Life is eternal but is always changing. Our Souls have lived before and will continue
to live after this lifetime. There is a perfect and lawful design
in the Universe. The Real Self, *in tandem with* the wisdom of
God and the Heavenly Helpers, chooses probable life events
for spiritual growth to proceed optimally.

Perhaps one child's Soul was ready to graduate so she
passed on. Or maybe she volunteered to die prematurely to
improve Soul growth for herself and others. The badly burned
boy may have hurt others in another life and chose karmic
retribution to learn his lessons the hard way. Or, more likely,
he may have volunteered to awaken others through his suffering. The community has certainly pulled together in a heart-
warming outpour of donations and love.

Maybe the two who were unharmed weren't in need of or
ready to teach and learn such drastic lessons. No one knows
for sure but a cyclical model of changing lives throughout eternity offers a greater option of sensible answers to life's difficult
questions.

The movie *Defending Your Life* portrays recently deceased
adults who face a life review and are judged whether they can
move on to higher planes or must repeat the Earthly classroom experience. One adult asked 'what about children who
die?' His counselor told him "children don't have to defend themselves; when a child is taken, they automatically move on."
That's comforting and makes sense. Maybe children who die
prematurely don't have as much spiritual work to accomplish
and can leave the Earth plane sooner than "slow learner" adults.

As noted, many outstanding persons in every culture
throughout history have believed in reincarnation. But we in
the West have been strongly influenced by institutions that
limited information about reincarnation. Persons who know
their inherent Eternal Nature are harder to control and collect
money from. Why would enlightened persons pay for fancy

churches and furnishings when we ourselves and every aspect of creation are God's temple?

Why would wise, enlightened humans fight wars to make a few powerful persons rich? No wonder the powers-that-be haven't busted their chops to teach the masses about their True Nature. Established powers of church, big business and government all lose when people know about their Inner Divinity. Some authors even contend that *malevolent extraterrestrials* have historically benefited by keeping humanity in spiritual ignorance. More about that later.

That's why reincarnation and related topics may sound foreign or crazy at first. We have been denied the truth about ourselves. We each are much more wise, infinite, special, powerful, and beloved by God than we can imagine. Knowledge of reincarnation, that our Souls do not die but continue to change form and grow toward God, is a key to becoming free. Those who know their Divine Nature no longer fear death, failure, and social censure that keep so many relatively impotent.

In *The Case For Reincarnation*, James D. Freeman says "If there is a God, He has to be Intelligence. He has to be Justice and Order. I think He even has to be Love. There's no way Intelligence and Justice and Order and Love could make us to live this one life and then judge us for eternity on how we managed to live it. Such a world is too unfair a world! If there is a god, two things have to be true: One—I am an immortal being. Two—I draw my own life to me."

Of life's seeming injustices and tragedies, Freeman writes "The only reasonable way I can explain this, unless I believe the whole thing has no meaning and is an accident, is to believe in reincarnation. I am what I am because I grew to be this in former existences; and I will go on after death into further existences... because I believe in God and believe that He's love and intelligence, I also believe I'm growing to be the spiritual being He made me to be. I have lived before and I will live again. My life is what it is now because of what I was in former lives, and my future life will be what it will be because of what I am now... To me it's the only way you can make this life make sense."

Reincarnation provides us with a vastly improved model for viewing reality. Remember, though, that it is still a *relatively limited* way of viewing reality. The most accurate description of reality is a dance of energy, the Divine at play, manifesting and changing extensions of Itself through eternity. In truth, there is no duality, no separateness, no barriers in all Creation. All is One, with unfolding *perpetual change* within the constancy of Life.

In *Running from Safety*, Richard Bach's character is asked if he believes in reincarnation: "No. Reincarnation is a series of lifetimes, isn't it, one after the other, in order, on this planet? That feels a little limiting, it fits a little tight across the shoulders." "What fits you better?" "An infinite number of beliefs of life experiences, please, some in bodies, some not, some on planets, some not; all of them simultaneous because there is no such thing as time, none of them real because there's only one Life."

Well put, as always, Richard. Unfortunately, the idea of no separateness, time, or space is difficult for most persons to comprehend. The model of reincarnation is an *improvement* over old ways of viewing reality. It helps us understand that our Real Selves are eternal, that our Essence did not begin at birth and does not end with death. Reincarnation captures the open-ended nature of God's plan, a design for the salvation of all without limits of time and space. Some erroneously describe God's plan of redemption as a very limited window of opportunity: one life time lasting a few seconds to many years and that's it before judgment day

Those few years—with all the confusion, temptation, fear, and ignorance on earth—determine whether we frolic in Heaven or roast in "hell" for eternity? That's a pretty poor plan for even a deranged human, let alone an all loving, omniscient, omnipresent and omnipotent Creator. The God I know can do much better than that.

I'd like to end this section with quotes about reincarnation by some great minds:

• *"I am certain that I have been here as I am now a thousand times before, and I hope to return a thousand times."*

—Goethe

• *"I know I am deathless. No doubt I have died myself ten thousand times before. I laugh at what you call dissolution, and I know the amplitude of time."*

—Walt Whitman

• *"As far back as I can remember I have unconsciously referred to the experiences of a previous state of existence."*

—Thoreau

• *"Believing as I do in the theory of rebirth, I live in the hope that if not in this birth, in some other birth I shall be able to hug all humanity in friendly embrace."*

— Mohandas D. Gandhi

• *"My doctrine is: Live so that thou mayest desire to live again—that is thy duty—for in any case thou wilt again!"*

—Nietzsche

• *"It is the secret of the world that all things subsist and do not die, but only retire a little from sight and afterwards return again."*

—Ralph Waldo Emerson

• *"It is not more surprising to be born twice than once; everything in nature is resurrection."*

—Voltaire

Near Death Experiences

The massive amount of research on Near Death Experiences (NDEs) constitutes the most scientific proof that consciousness survives bodily death. A Gallup survey estimates that more than 8 million Americans have had NDEs. Taken together with other evidence, NDEs are the "final straw" that help many realize our Real Selves do not die.

Tens of thousands of NDE cases, documented by doctors and scientists, demonstrate a continuation of awareness beyond "death." Most persons are familiar with the stages: being out of the body, hearing a buzzing or ringing sound, going through a tunnel, seeing radiant light, meeting departed loved ones and Spiritual Beings, seeing beautiful scenes and colors, hearing angelic music, feeling peaceful and at Home, learning lessons, being told it's not ones time to stay on the Other Side, and a rapid journey back into the successfully resuscitated body.

Many persons who have a NDE describe meeting familiar appearing loved ones who have passed over before them. These long departed Souls appear in a comforting way, often as the nearly dead person last saw them: Grandma looks 70 and cousin Joey looks 5 years old as they did when they passed over. Souls on the Other Side take on physical appearances that *reassure* the recently "deceased" entity.

Souls in nonphysical dimensions have the ability to focus their energy and create a varying outward appearance as needed. After the NDE, Grandma and Joey can go about their spiritual business with another formed or formless countenance. "Young Souls" need the reassurance of loved ones appearing in familiar forms. "Old Souls" with advanced spiritual growth who have experienced rebirth many times don't need a welcoming committee from the Other Side. They zip right into the Spirit World without any fanfare; after many rebirths and "deaths", the experience becomes routine.

One of my favorite NDE cases is about a woman who nearly died and, while going away from Earth through the tunnel of light, met her close friend coming back through the tunnel. 'Don't worry,' her friend assured her, 'It wasn't my time to die and it's not your time either. I'll talk to you soon.' The first woman shared this experience with her family after she had been resuscitated. 'That's impossible,' her family said, 'we just talked with her last week and she was completely healthy.' The woman insisted they call and, as reported, her friend had also just nearly died.

Stanislav Grof, M.D., researcher and author of *Books of the Dead* and *Holotropic Mind*, stated "The most extraordinary and fascinating aspect of NDEs is the occurrence of 'veridical' (verifying) out-of-body-experiences (OOBEs), a term used for experiences of disembodied consciousness with accurate extrasensory perception. Thanatological studies have repeatedly confirmed that people who are unconscious or even clinically dead can have OOBEs during which they observe their bodies and the rescue procedures from above, or perceive events in remote locations. Current thanatological research now focuses on confirmation of some preliminary observations of these experiences occurring with congenitally blind people."

Out of body experiences can occur without nearly dying. A patient of the Sikh religion told me that, after earnestly praying, he felt his consciousness levitate to the ceiling and saw his inert body lying on the couch. While in this OOBE state, he saw Jesus, Krishna, and Guru Nanak (founder of the Sikh religion). He felt instantly relieved about his worries; the blessed nature of those moments still moves him to tears when he recounts the experience.

Willis Harmon, Ph.D., author of *Higher Creativity* and *Global Mind Change* states "there is a tremendous amount of empirical, anecdotal, clinical, and traditional evidence suggesting that in some sense the essence of the person survives physical death, and that the realm of the after-death is not so discontinuous with earthly life as we might have been led to assume... death appears less as an extinction than as an awakening to 'where one was all along'. At death, the center of awareness shifts from the physical to higher planes (with perhaps a period of confusion and/or sleepy resting in between). We don't go somewhere at death; we are already there. As this new view becomes real in our lives, fear of death disappears. We couldn't nonexist if we wanted to."

NDEs were reported thousands of years ago, as described in the Tibetan and Egyptian Books of the Dead but this information was lost or little known for centuries. Similar or identical revelatory experiences have been reported by persons taking consciousness altering substances, for example, LSD in the Harvard "Good Friday" research conducted by Drs. Timothy Leary and Richard Alpert (AKA Ram Dass.)

Years ago when "Dolora" told me of the recent death of her beloved husband and dog, I started to console and remind her that she would see them again. She excitedly interrupted, "Oh I know that! I had a near death experience 20 years ago and I *know* death isn't the end."

At age 82, she was recently told she had terminal liver cancer. She consoled her doctors, saying "Don't worry about me. I'll be waiting to greet you when you pass over!" The hospice was called in and she was given 2 months to live. One year later, she looks great, takes no drugs, and is going strong. Her lack of fear about death and surety of an afterlife is probably a major reason she's still alive.

Such faith and assurance are indicators of a true NDE, paranormal event, angel encounter, or other revelatory experience. These dramatic lessons impart a lasting hope, faith, and assurance of things not seen but nevertheless vitally real. Says Nancy Bush, president of the International Association for Near-Death Studies, "Most near-death survivors say they don't think there is a God. They know."

The March 31, 1997 *U.S. News & World Report* stated "No matter what the nature of the (near-death) experience, it alters some lives. Alcoholics find themselves unable to imbibe. Hardened criminals opt for a life of helping others. Atheists embrace the existence of a deity, while dogmatic members of a particular religion report feeling welcome in any church or temple or mosque."

Raymond Moody, M.D., Ph.D., found that those who had undergone NDEs became more altruistic, less materialistic, and more loving. Psychiatrists Bruce Greyson and Ian Stevenson "are intrigued by reports of the chronically ill regaining their vigor, and even 'miraculous' cures from cancer or HIV infection" after NDEs. They also observe that, having stared eternity in the face, those returning from NDEs often lose their taste for ego-boosting achievement.

After Death Contacts

After Death Contacts (ADCs) are another "proof" that our Spirits survive bodily death. The term ADC describes contact with a deceased person that involves sensing (seeing, hearing or feeling) them while awake or dreaming. A recent National

Opinion Research Center poll reported 42% of adult Americans and 67% of all widows have had an ADC.

Read *We Don't Die* and *We Are Not Forgotten* by Joel Martin and Patricia Romanowski for a fascinating description of psychic George Anderson's conversations with and messages of love and hope from the Other Side. The book *Hello From Heaven* by Bill and Judy Guggenheim describes hundreds of such encounters. Their confirmation and validation ADCs are most impressive and convincing.

"Confirmation ADCs" are experienced by more than one person at a time and thus lend increased credibility to the experience. For example, Lauren saw the form of her "deceased" brother Donald outside the church window during his funeral service. He was strolling happily and peacefully, without the limp and pain he had suffered with for years. After the service, Lauren's sister-in-law, Joyce, approached her excitedly and said "Did you see Donald? I saw him too!"

"Validation ADCs" involve information that couldn't be known unless, in fact, a genuine ADC had occurred. One such example reported by the Guggenheims was shared by Denise whose husband Louis had died 9 months earlier. In her dream, Denise was talking with her departed husband who was happy and laughing. Louis said "Guess who is up here? He hasn't changed a bit" and told Denise their priest, Father Antonio, had just joined him on the Other Side. The next morning, Denise recalled the dream as the phone rang. Another priest called to tell her that Father Antonio had died just last night but, of course, she already knew that.

A church member, "Evelyn," passed on several years ago and her sister told me the following story. Evelyn's daughter, "Lisa", was beside herself with grief after her mom's passing. She couldn't quit crying and the family was concerned that she might need sedation. Lisa was alone in her room, sobbing uncontrollably, when she heard Evelyn's voice. Lisa looked up and saw a gauzy version of her mother. "You must stop this carrying on", Evelyn told her, "I'm at peace and I'll see you again. It's time for you to remember that and calm down."

Lisa immediately stopped crying and rejoined the other family members. They couldn't believe the *sudden, total and lasting transformation* in her appearance and behavior. She continued to enjoy a peaceful state of acceptance and knew her loving relationship with her mother would never end, despite outward changes.

Such experiences used to be considered paranormal, defined as "beyond the range of scientifically known or recognizable phenomena; rare; unusual; supernatural." As the spiritual revolution intensifies, such reports are becoming increasingly common. Fewer persons are afraid of seeming weird or different and are reporting paranormal occurrences.

The night her mother died, my wife who lived 20 miles from the hospital awakened at the time of "death" and knew she had just passed over. Her brother-in-law who lived some distance away had the very same experience.

Another brother-in-law, "Tim", shared some amazing ADCs that occurred after his dad, "Harold", passed over. Harold had an old rose bush that hardly ever bloomed despite all his efforts. Harold and "Kent" (his son-in-law) had made a deal: whoever "died" first would try to make the rose bush bloom as a sign to the other from the Spirit World. They had told no one else about this pact.

The morning after Harold's funeral, "Wanda" (Kent's wife and Harold's daughter) told her family "I had the strangest dream last night! You know that old sickly rose bush? I dreamt it had bloomed full of healthy roses."

Harold also had an old thorn tree that he wanted to cut down but his wife disagreed. He had often said, "I'm going to cut down that tree if it's the last thing I do!" The night of his passing, a "freak" windstorm blew down the tree.

Another friend knew when the phone rang that it was news of her father's passing. As she hung up the phone, she felt a hand on her shoulder and a voice gently say, "I love you. I'm at peace. Don't worry about me. We'll meet again." Another friend feels her "departed" brother communicating his presence whenever a clock he gave her starts vibrating and moving for no apparent reason.

"Dr. Smith" gave an inspiring seminar to several hundred persons and was surrounded during a break. I felt moved to ask if he had ever experienced a revelation that fueled his mission for excellence. When I did, the blood drained from his face as if I had looked into his Soul. He excused himself from the crowd and led me to a deserted area of the convention center. "Only my immediate family knows about this but since you asked, I'll tell you" he said.

Several years previously, Dr. Smith had purchased a couple businesses and wasn't giving 110% to his practice, research, and teaching. Then his sister, who lived across the country, told him of her young daughter's rare illness. He tried to help but she was in the advanced stages. Before "Jenny's" funeral, Dr. Smith sat alone by the casket and cried tears of remorse. He had become so busy that he hadn't really known his niece or provided preventive holistic health care for her. He felt totally discouraged and depressed.

Suddenly, he saw a series of colorful 3-D images projected on the wall behind the casket. The first was Jesus dressed in white robes, standing at the foot of Jenny's coffin, and reaching out to her. The second was Jenny sitting up and reaching out to Him. The third was Jesus walking and Jenny skipping into a spiritual realm of billowy clouds and iridescent light.

When he told his sister of his visions, she cried tears of joy. "You weren't around Jenny much so you couldn't know," she said "but before she became ill, Jenny always skipped and never walked." This experience transformed his life and he committed himself fully to teaching advanced chiropractic care, literally until the moment he died.

When I worked in hospitals, several older but completely coherent patients told me about their visions of departed loved ones. The Spirits, usually a parent or spouse, stood by the patient's bed, smiled, and said they would be reunited soon. These patients told me in hushed but excited voices, "I haven't told anyone else but there's something about you" and shared their story. Each patient passed on in the next several days.

Ask your friends and family if they or anyone they know have ever had any ADC experiences. You'll be surprised at the frequency of such incidents that comprise yet another body of evidence about Spiritual realities.

Angel Encounters

"He shall give his angels charge over thee, to keep thee in all thy ways. They shall bear thee up in their hands, lest thou dash thy foot against a stone."

—Psalms 91

Angel encounters are another indication there is more to life than meets the eye. Numerous authors, poets, painters, and visionaries have described Angelic encounters.

Many books and documentaries by persons from all walks of life describe Angel experiences. We might discount an occasional paranormal event but, as with NDEs, the greatest proof is the sheer bulk of material especially those confirmatory in nature.

I believe I experienced the grace and beauty of an Angel's visit as I was completing my first book. While writing early one morning, I suddenly felt ecstatic for no apparent reason. I heard a slight rustling and, from my peripheral vision, saw a white, gauzy form like the fine lace-work of a wedding dress. I turned to see it more clearly and it was gone. I felt I had been blessed and given a sign that my work was in flow with Divine Will and my Soul's mission.

Angels and Divine-helpers from other dimensions can't assist unless they are asked. You have to invoke them; you have to request their assistance. Angels often appear in the form that humans expect them to look like although others are seen as apparitions of light or as appearing like humans. Like greeters in a NDE, Angel forms are optional.

Eileen Freeman, theologian and author, says "Angels transcend every religion, every philosophy, every creed." Ancient Native American religions, Judaism, Islam, Hinduism, Buddhism, and Christianity all recognize Angelic intermediaries who operate between the Divine and Earthly.

Angels have, no doubt, taken the rap for heinous acts committed by powerful but unenlightened beings. The Old Testament describes an "angel" who slew 185,000 Assyrian enemies of Jerusalem and another who engineered the "heaven-sent" pestilence that destroyed 70,000 people during the reign of King

David. Angels?! A more likely explanation would be the work of powerful but malevolent extraterrestrials.

Heaven-sent Angels save, love, help, and inspire. In years past, humans may have mistakenly called any being that appeared in the sky an "Angel" but Angels and the Heavenly Host have no need for mass destruction. Forces of darkness and ignorance cover those bases very well, thank you, without help from God's Crew.

Tennyson wrote "For nothing worthe proving can be proven, nor yet disproven: wherefore thou be wise, cleave ever to the sunnier side of Doubt." I maintain a healthy skepticism until I've investigated a topic. All the evidence I've seen convinces me of the reality of the Angelic realm and their *loving* assistance on Earth.

At a holistic health conference, one doctor told of a childhood experience that convinced him of the authenticity of Guardian Angels. He was in the bathtub when the bathroom light shorted out; his little sister brought in a goosenecked lamp so he could finish his bath. Just as the lamp was accidentally knocked into the water, he saw two strong, hairy arms yank him out of the water and throw him to safety. But there was no one else around.

Sophie Burnham says many dying children see Angels. "Don't cry," one boy comforted his mother. "Do you see my angel out the window? She's telling me I am going fishing."

We're never alone and are especially administered to by Angels during tragedies. The obvious question inevitably arises, 'If Angels assist some persons, why don't they help everyone in distress?' My understanding regarding this excellent question includes:

- Angels and the Heavenly Host do not impose their will on others. If a person has made a decision to hurt or destroy themselves, that's their free will.
- We first need to ask for assistance, then realize it may not always arrive how, when, and where we expect it.
- We will never know how often we are helped. Assistance may be subtle, undetectable, and preventive.

- Souls may have chosen suffering to assist spiritual growth and Angels wouldn't interfere with this plan.
- Earth is designed to be a place of learning. If the Heavenly Host intervened and prevented all suffering, much of the earthly curriculum would be omitted.

Iasos says "beings of the Angelic Kingdom have the function of administering to the spiritual needs and emotional needs of both the Human Kingdom and Elemental Kingdom. They 'take care' of us... Their role is to radiate the aura of God to humans and elementals, to help them and comfort them on their path, and to remind them of their celestial source and heritage."

He says that every human has at least one personal or guardian Angel. "Many light workers have a number of them. If you want your personal angels to work even more closely with you, you can first of all acknowledge them and thank them from your heart for their undying (and usually unappreciated) service to you. Then you can do your best to make your personal aura as sweet, harmonious, and loving as you can. Remember—the sweeter your energies, the closer your angels will want to 'hangout' in your aura."

Between Incarnation Experiences

I coined the term "between incarnation experiences" (BIEs) to describe events *in between lifetimes*. Webster defines *incarnation* as "a taking on or being manifested in a fleshly body." BIEs, then, describe Soul events that occur in-between formed incarnations on Earth or other physical dimensions. BIEs are experienced during hypnosis, dreaming, or spontaneous remembrance.

NDEs have paved the way for understanding BIEs. Just two decades ago, NDEs were widely considered delusional; now most persons know someone who has experienced a NDE and believe in their validity. The stages typically experienced by the person who nearly dies are common knowledge. BIEs simply take up where NDEs leave off. That is, what does the Soul experience when the person's body *isn't successfully resuscitated*?

This information is largely based on *Journey of Souls* by Michael Newton, Ph.D., and writings by Edgar Cayce and Ruth Montgomery. BIE data explains that different Souls need different environments after bodily "death." Some are weary and need rest; others *feel* broken and need mended. Some have been ensconced in evil and need deep sleep followed by extensive counseling. Still others are so spiritually elevated that they hit the ground running on the Other Side.

Given, then, that each Soul has unique needs and lessons in between incarnations, here are some common stages in the Spirit World. After "death", Souls are surprised at being alive and elated about freedom from pain and restriction. Some stay around Earth for a few days—a few minutes in Soul time—to comfort grieving loved ones or recover from the shock of "accidental" death.

Souls meet with their Spirit Guides next to review the past life, to learn from mistakes and receive praise for victories. Counseling sessions and "healing energy showers" start the recovery process from physical and emotional wounds. A sense of euphoria grows as Souls more fully realize all the Earthly burdens they have left behind. Souls begin to remember the Spirit World as their Real Home and feel quite harmonious as they enjoy their new orderly, Heavenly abode.

After this initial reentry and rehab process, Souls are ready to greet beloved Soulmates whose hugging would appear, Newton says, as "two masses of bright light whirling around each other." Souls have access to any other Souls or beatific physical surroundings merely by willing or intending it. Eventually, Souls spend more and more time with close Souls, those of their 'pod, cluster, or hive.'

These Souls have enjoyed interactions and mutual assistance for eons. Dr. Newton describes clusters of about 20 Souls who help each other toward the One over many life times. As you might imagine, these Souls know each other very well and can't rationalize, intellectualize, or otherwise BS their way out of mistakes. Some Soulmates agree to visit Earth or reincarnate together while others stay in the Spirit World to act as Guides.

The Soul cluster may enjoy physical landmarks such as schools, temples, homes, or other familiar places. In addition to Soul growth and learning, Souls play, sing, dance, enjoy recreation and play pranks. Additional sessions with Spirit Guides and spiritual teachers are held. Some Souls have "parallel lives", i.e., spend part of their energy in the cluster and part in another formed or formless incarnation simultaneously.

Says Newton "(Q) Do all parts of our soul energy go out of the spirit world when we incarnate? (A) Part of us never leaves, since we do not totally separate from the maker. (Q) What does the part that remains in the spirit world do while we are on Earth in one or more bodies? (A) It is more dormant, waiting to be rejoined to the rest of our energy... if our souls are all part of one great oversoul energy force which divides, or extends itself to create our souls, then why shouldn't the offspring of this intelligent soul energy have the same capacity to detach and then recombine?"

After a few or many Earth-years, the Soul becomes ready for another physical incarnation. Spiritual training sessions, a collaborative effort with Soulmates and Guides, analyze karmic factors, spiritual growth goals, and missions in alignment with God's will. In "life progressions", Souls glimpse possible future scenarios that may result from certain choices. The future is not predetermined but likely outcomes or probabilities can be explored.

Exit interviews with Spirit Counselors are held to assess the Soul's readiness to leave the Spirit World. Once a Soul decides to incarnate again, it's time to choose who to be, who to be with, and where to live. The *place of life selection* is accessed to program in optimal choices for the next life.

Just before Souls reenter a physical incarnation, *recognition classes* are held to plan *memory triggers*. "Signs", "flags", or "markers" involve one of the five senses and help Souls recall prearranged plans or reunions with Soulmates. When I read about these, I immediately thought of my refracted sunlight in the kitchen experience at age 11. Perhaps that was a visual signal pre-designed to remind me of my birth-vision and mission on Earth.

As one of Newton's clients explained, "the road signs kick us into a new direction in life at certain times when something important is supposed to happen... The signs are supposed to click in our memory right away and tell us, 'Oh, good, you are here now.' Inside us... we can say to ourselves, 'It is time to work on the next phase.' They may seem like little insignificant things, but the flags are turning points in our lives."

When it's time to return to another incarnation, Souls prepare themselves as if for battle. They experience mixed feelings of excitement, apprehension, concern, and sadness about leaving the Spirit World for a time. Final interviews with ones Guides are held and cluster-mates say "see you later." Souls enjoy full recognition of their Oneness with all Creation before spiritual amnesia temporarily sets in.

The sensations of *entering the womb* are usually briefer but more physically shocking than "dying." As the Soul consciousness and fetal energy merge, the Soul is free to come and go, especially until birth and even until age 5 or 6. After that, most children "shut down" and completely forget their essential Spiritual Nature due to societal hypnosis that they are only a physical being. The Soul is not trapped in the body, however, and can explore and play while the human sleeps, meditates, or is under anesthesia.

Read Newton's book and *feel* your response to the information above. Does it seem vaguely familiar and does it make sense to you? Your remembrance of or excitement about this data constitutes another "proof" of our Eternal Heritage.

Miraculous Evidence

> *"Any man who does not believe in miracles is not a realist."*
> —David Ben-Gurion

Miracles are another way of remembering that Spirit is our Eternal Nature and Home. Many persons have experienced mini-miracles but doubt their senses and dismiss them as figments of their imagination. Some skepticism is healthy but excessive doubt blocks our appreciation of the miracles all around us. In truth, all life is a miracle: a mighty oak from an acorn, a fully formed baby nine months after two cells join, nature's spring renewal.

In *Balanced Living*, I shared the "D.C." miracle that happened to me several years ago. Miracles may be God's way of staying anonymous but the *God-within* has operated under anonymity long enough. Humans have suffered under delusions and illusions long enough; it's time to see clearly. The truth is, miracles abound; this is evident when we really open our eyes, ears, hearts, and minds. Every aspect of life is unbelievably miraculous but that's not enough for some doubting Thomas's. So, periodically, really unique and impressive miracles happen.

Edgar Mitchell stated "There are no unnatural or supernatural phenomena, only very large gaps in our knowledge of what is natural... We should strive to fill those gaps of ignorance." What once seemed miraculous is experienced and achieved by persons with vision.

Barbara Mark and Trudy Griswold, authors of *Angelspeake*, say we'd see the daily miracles our angels create for us if we paid closer attention. Can what we classify as coincidence, serendipity or synchronicity often be attributed to angels? "We probably don't have quite as much free will as we think when we are living a life of service. If we have turned over much to God and have entrusted Him to arrange what it is we can do to accomplish His work, He is going to make sure we're not wasting time. Our angels tell us that we can't possibly conceive of the complexity sometimes involved. They work on arrangements weeks and years in advance. When you experience what appears to be synchronicity and you think back to all the pieces of the puzzle that had to fit at the right time, you become overwhelmed by the power and possibilities."

Read *Teachings Of The Far East Masters* by Baird T. Spaulding for descriptions of miracles that have been reported in the Far East for centuries. Spaulding and a team of scientists observed and later learned how to walk on water, walk through walls, and be in more than one place at a time. Marlo Morgan describes Aboriginal telepathic communication, advanced healing, and other "miracles."

Deepak Chopra tells of research conducted while a medical student in India. A swami or wise man with "miraculous" abilities was buried six foot under for six days. When the experimenters dug him up, he had no measurable heart beat or respiration and appeared to be dead. After a few minutes, however, his vital signs began to return. The swami opened his eyes and said "Could I have a glass of milk, please?"

The many triumphs of individuals in the face of seemingly insurmountable odds are also miracles. Consider the challenge of being blind and deaf from birth that Helen Keller overcame. She stated "I have never believed that my limitations were in any sense punishments or accidents. If I had held such a view, I could never have expected the strength to overcome them."

Don't underestimate the miracles in your life and all around you. And don't limit those that can happen in the future! Ask for clarity to detect life's miracles and feast on yet another "proof" of spiritual realities.

"Paranormal" Input

Researcher H. J. Eysenck stated "Unless there is a gigantic conspiracy involving ... highly respected scientists in various fields, many of them originally hostile to the claims of the psychic researchers, the only conclusion the unbiased observer can come to must be that there are people who obtain knowledge existing in other people's minds, or in the outer world, by means yet unknown to science."

Two excellent books by psychics who help Souls from the Other Side speak to earthbound loved ones are *The Eagle and The Rose* by Rosemary Altea and *Life After Death* by Mary T. Browne. Both have assisted many clients in understanding the reality of life after death. The veil between the physical and spiritual worlds is revealing itself to be very thin. Strong thoughts between realms can be transmitted and received by a growing number of persons.

With their special gifts, genuine psychics learn intimate details from departed ones that provide proof to loved ones on Earth. One skeptical male client was convinced when Altea described the type of candy his dad often gave him when he was a boy. As with all valid spiritual contacts, psychic-assisted communications create lasting and positive change. Such paranormal input reminds us that "death" is merely rebirth into Spirit.

Rosemary was consulted by a woman seeking reassurance that her husband was OK after death. The psychic described in detail a man carrying a white goose under both arms. The woman was overjoyed at this description of her husband and their beloved pet geese that had also "died." No psychic could have known how important this detail was to her unless it had indeed been conveyed by a departed loved one.

Joan Borysenko, Ph.D., author of *Minding the Body, Mending the Mind* and *The Power of the Mind to Heal*, shared a beautiful lesson she learned during her mother's death. Her mother had long been cynical about and critical of Joan's spiritual work. Joan and her son Justin were present as her mom passed on; at that moment, the room was filled with light and both realized what Justin verbalized:

"You must be so grateful to your mother. You know, she was a very great soul. And she embodied to take a role that was much smaller than the wisdom in her soul and she did it as a gift for you so that you'd have something to resist against." This wonderful story gives us another glimpse of the intelligence and Divine Design always operative in the universe, even when we can't fathom it. Maybe the person who is driving you crazy has purposely taken on what I call a "contrast incarnation" to assist your spiritual growth.

A friend whose dad committed suicide asked me to conduct the funeral service. I met with the family two days before the funeral to gather input for creating a meaningful ritual. We discussed that his severe, chronic depression had been more than he could bear and God understood when someone escaped the pain through suicide. We talked about the Soul's continuity after death and that "Bob" was no doubt sending messages of love to remind his family they would meet again. I mentioned that Bob's Soul was probably present in the room at this moment.

Just then, the grandmother, who seemed to have been dozing up to this point, bolted upright in her chair and exclaimed "That reminds me! I heard Bob and my (late) husband talking this morning in the room as I awakened. I heard them so clearly that I was surprised when I didn't see their bodies. They were talking about going on a trip somewhere together." That broke the gloom and everyone laughed and cried together.

After that, everyone felt more sure that Bob was alive and well in Spirit and was sending reassurance to the family. The sudden and marked change in everyone was proof enough that we were blessed with a message from Spirit. The family was so energized that they spent the next several, usually very difficult, days consoling others. I felt honored to participate in a transformation of a tragedy into a teaching that "death" is not an end and our Creator understands, loves, and forgives more than we can imagine.

An interesting "paranormal" follow-up story occurred with "Ted", whose lung cancer due to smoking was described in *Balanced Living*. His widow, "Elizabeth", shared this story that occurred after she had prayed for a sign from above that Ted was at peace. In the first spring after Ted's burial, the family planted flowers by his grave and videotaped the scenery. As soon as they arrived at the grave site, a sparrow flew to Ted's monument and perched there, cocking its head and looking intently at the family.

Elizabeth remarked that it seemed as if the sparrow was trying to tell them something or that perhaps Ted's Spirit was communicating through the bird. Throughout their visit, the same sparrow continued to chirp and hop on the grave stone. The family excitedly videotaped the bird with the idea of showing it to other family members. But when they played the tape at home, there was the grave site, grass, trees, family members, and flowers—but no sparrow! This event corroborates reports that Spirit Beings are difficult to capture on film.

These examples of how the Divine works in the midst of tragedy demonstrate that, although evil may have its day, good and God are ultimately all that exists. Paranormal experiences, whether assisted by psychics or occurring spontaneously, further point to the existence and continuity of the Soul.

Limited Perception

"Everyone who is seriously involved in the pursuit of science becomes convinced that a Spirit is manifest in the Laws of the Universe."
—Albert Einstein

We are Beings of Energy who appear to be solid matter, an illusion that confuses us at every turn. Science has long proven that "solid matter" is largely space and energy but most persons haven't realized the implications of this research. For example, if a hydrogen atom's nucleus were the size of a marble, its single electron would be a quarter mile away! This model helps us fathom our true nature: not solid matter but space, energy, light, Spirit.

In *Quantum Theory*, physicist David Bohm wrote "the world cannot be analyzed correctly into distinct parts; instead it must be regarded as an indivisible unit in which separate parts appear as valid approximations only in the classical (i.e., Newtonian) limit. Thus, at the quantum level of accuracy, an object does not have any 'intrinsic' properties (for example, wave or particle) belonging to itself alone; instead, it shares all its properties mutually and indivisibly with the systems with which it interacts."

Here's another scientific fact that highlights the brain's limited perceptual ability that contributes to humanity's collective delusion. Even though we appear to be standing still, the Earth travels at 66,000 miles per hour and completes a trip of 595,000,000 miles around the sun every year. At the same time, the Earth rotates around its own axis. How can we fathom our true reality as Spirit when we can't even sense we aren't standing still?!

States Dr. Chopra, "Sight, hearing, touch, taste, and smell serve to reinforce the same message: Things are what they seem. According to this reality, the Earth is flat, the ground beneath your feet is stationary, the sun rises in the east and sets in the west, all because it seems that way to the senses... (The truth is) I am not my atoms, they come and go. I am not my thoughts, they come and go. I am not my ego, my self-image changes. I am above and beyond these: I am the witness, the interpreter, the Self beyond the self-image. This Self is ageless and timeless."

Heisenberg's Principle of Indeterminacy recognizes that, in any subatomic scientific experiment, the very act of observation changes what is happening. To look, light is needed; light waves strike molecules and change their behavior. The point is that science is not as objective as once thought; all life is interwoven and interdependent. Techniques in Part II such as prayer, yoga and meditation improve the clarity of our perception of reality.

Satchidananda says "atomic vibration is in everything, whether it appears to be moving or unmoving. Science says all is made from the atom. God says all comes from Adam. In Sanskrit, they call it *Atman* which is the true Self. See how close we always are? Everything has consciousness because the vital energy of that hum or first manifestation is causing movement or current everywhere. That movement is omnipresent in every atom... Like electric power, God steps Himself down to us from the Absolute through sound and then form until we can benefit from Him."

He continues "We are all like gadgets plugging into His power, which he has limited so that we can make use of Him. There is just this constant flow of the cosmic energy, or Universal consciousness, that we call God. It flows multivariously and in so doing forms different waves or bubbles. Some of those forms or bubbles are we... We are all different shapes of the same matter. Through Yoga, you can experience this yourself."

Friedbert Karger, German physicist at Munich's Max Planck Institute, has extensively studied afterlife phenomena. Says Karger "The consciousness—or soul—of a man lives beyond the body. The body is a tool that consciousness uses. When the body dies, the soul remains." He calls the paranormal "a challenge for physics," a next step after quantum physics. Many famous physicists have expressed an interest in the spiritual world; Max Planck, founder of quantum physics, said "Spirit is the original basis of all matter, reality, true existence... I am not afraid to call the mysterious creator by the same name as civilizations of Earth for past centuries: God."

He further states "Death is not an end but a transition from one state to another... souls have 'gravity': the heavy souls of people oriented toward the material struggle slowly and painfully to separate themselves from the body. The lighter souls of people geared toward the spiritual separate more quickly and easily. It is not necessary to know physics to understand the laws of the spirit."

It's a scientific fact that our five senses are limited in perceiving reality. Humans can't hear a dog whistle. Hummingbirds can differentiate between eight shades of white that appear identical to humans. What appears to our eyes as white light reveals its true nature as a rainbow of colors when cast through a prism or crystal. The electromagnetic spectrum contains many wavelengths, x-rays for example, that humans can not detect.

In *Doors of Perception*, Aldous Huxley postulated that "mind-expanding" chemicals like LSD relax inhibitory centers in the brain. He noted that about 90% of the brain's function is inhibitory, that is, adaptively dampens or filters incoming information. Light and sound waves are transmitted through time and space indefinitely; we couldn't function without sensory selectivity. The brain filters sensory input so we can discern only that information necessary for survival and optimal functioning.

Understanding this provides another piece of the puzzle for spiritual seekers. Buckminster Fuller stated that 99% of reality is invisible. Important phenomena like air, electricity, gravity, love, and God are real yet escape detection by human senses. The point? There's more to life than meets the five senses. If we believe only what we can see, hear, touch, taste, and smell, we are missing out on much of reality.

Scientific validation of the brain's limited perceptual abilities gives me more faith in spiritual realities. In 1995, I was awakened from sleep by a gentle wise voice thought that said "To increase in wisdom, view all aspects of the creation as molecular manifestations of spiritual energy, as a collection of atoms imbued with the Spirit of God."

Remember, there is a visible physical and an invisible spiritual world; the latter contains all the potential just as an acorn contains an oak tree. What is real never changes and cannot be destroyed. Our task is to remember and demonstrate the power of Spirit.

We Are "gods"

"I have said, ye are gods; and all of you are children of the most High."

—Psalms 82:6

Of the Inner Divinity in all life, Alan Watts states "How is it possible that a being with such sensitive jewels as the eyes, such enchanted musical instruments as the ears, and such a fabulous arabesque of nerves as the brain can experience itself as anything less than a god? (Especially) when you consider that this incalculably subtle organism is inseparable from the still more marvelous patterns of its environment—from the minutest electrical designs to the whole company of the galaxies..."

All life is a *manifestation* of God; everything and everyone is an extension of the Divine. God has been described as a Cosmic Dreamer, Painter, or Sculptor that dreams, paints, or sculpts Itself into many different formed and formless aspects. This critical point is essential for an accurate comprehension of ones Soul.

In Sufism, it is said "I looked into myself and saw that I am He." The Upanishads proclaim "I am everywhere, shining forth from all beings." "All life is One, God is All, The Father and I are One, All is Allah, Isness Is, God is One, I Am That I Am": these are various ways of stating there is no separation or duality in life. As Joel Goldsmith wrote in *The Infinite Way*, "That which I am seeking, I am." Any other understanding is an *illusion* that has created untold suffering and confusion.

God is in everything and each one of us. If this sounds too pantheistic for you, consider the words of the old standard church hymn *This Is My Father's World*: "He shines in all that's fair; in the rustling grass, I hear Him pass, He speaks to me everywhere." Our task is to remember we are Spiritual Beings, one with God, who have temporarily taken on physical bodies for a specific reason.

We each are part and parcel of any accurate definition of the Divine. Consider the words of Paul in his letter to the Ephesians (4:6) stating "One God and Father of all, who is above all, and through all, and in you all." Besides proving Paul was a Southerner, these quotes support the Truth that God is in each of us, we each are gods in process, co-creators and One with the Great Spirit.

Abraham Maslow, Ph.D., stated "We find another kind of resistance, a denying of our best side, of our talents, of our finest impulse, of our highest potentialities, of our creativeness... It is precisely the god-like in ourselves that we are ambivalent about, fascinated by and fearful of, motivated to and defensive against."

Dr. Wayne Dyer says that there are two basic theories about the nature of God and life:

1. God is outside us, the boss, a very large man, is separate from and superior to us, and had only one son.

2. God is in all things, Her name is not important, all life is connected, the ego mistakenly believes there is separation, God is in each of us *and* potentially in every part of our life, we each are sons and daughters of God but are afraid to realize our lofty calling as part of God.

Trine says that humans are capable of becoming *God-man and woman* and differ from God only in quantity or degree of God essence — not quality. "In the degree that man opens himself to this divine inflow does he approach God... the only limitations man has are the limitations he sets to himself, by virtue of not knowing himself."

The concept that humans are in the process of becoming gods and One with Father/Mother God has persisted through time in various cultures. That's the good news that sets us free and further points to our true Soul Nature. That's the message of Jesus that I hear woven throughout the New Testament, an enlightened message that has survived 2000 years of translations, interpretations, and outright purposeful changes.

Reinforce Part I

You have just been exposed to a lot of information that assists remembering your Soul. Reading it once will help some but really *anchoring* this information with life-transformative technology will change your life forever! Let's review the topics in Part I that indicate our Eternal Nature:

- acknowledge God's presence in your life
- personal revelatory experiences or those of friends
- teachings of enlightened religions and spiritual paths
- reincarnation evidence, some substantiated by scientists
- near death experiences with scientific confirmation
- after death contacts, especially validation types
- angel encounters and their messages that humans and all creations of God are One in Spirit
- between incarnation experiences via hypnotic regression
- miracles that point to an unseen spiritual reality
- our brains are limited perceivers of reality
- quantum physics' description of reality as energy
- "paranormal" input, spontaneously or via psychics
- theological recognition of our oneness with the Creator

That's a lot of outstanding news! Let's review the four steps to reaching *peak state*:

1. assume peak physiology by standing tall, breathing deeply and alternatively clenching and relaxing your fists

2. recall exhilarating, empowering memories from the past when you felt totally committed and unstoppable

3. recall your sensory power cues (color, shape, sound heard, texture, fragrance, and phrase spoken)

4. listen to or cognitively recreate inspiring music

Get in peak state, then reread the above list of proofs aloud and with enthusiasm and animated gestures. Just as a great professional speaker would, jab the air with a finger, make fists, wave and open your arms, raise your eyebrows, and smile. The more you incorporate your entire body, the more you will *own* this good news. Using life-transformative technology allows you to *break through* old, erroneous limiting beliefs and reprogram yourself with newer, more accurate data.

Now celebrate by jumping, clapping, cheering, and giving thanks! Compliment and reward yourself for having the discipline to do this life-changing work. Take 5 minutes a day for the next two weeks to deeply reinforce a *total knowing* that the Real You is immortal and unstoppable!

These methods reprogram your entire being—body, mind, and spirit—and are much more powerful than just a sterile, intellectual understanding. PLEASE don't proceed to part II until you've celebrated and really absorbed this life transforming information.

Now list three experiences discussed in part I (e.g., a NDE, ADC, or Angel encounter) that you or someone you know has had:

1. _____

2. _____

3. _____

Write a few sentences about how this information *makes you feel*. What old limitations are minimized or removed by knowing all this evidence that points to a continuation of consciousness through eternity?

_____

_____

_____

_____

Next, share this information as soon as possible with three of your closest "Soulmates"—family and friends with whom you can safely discuss your deepest hopes and dreams. These three will become part of your *Master Mind Group*, trusted and loving individuals who will help you reach your fullest potential physically, mentally, and spiritually.

Now you're ready for the next step: identifying and following your Soul's mission!

Part II:

IDENTIFYING AND FOLLOWING YOUR SOUL'S PURPOSE

Remember your Soul's mission (God's will for you),
then start fulfilling that calling

First Things First

Before proceeding, remember the basics. *Acknowledge* the reality of God and Christ Consciousness in your life. Remember you are an Infinite Spirit, one with the Ultimate. *Ask* the Great Spirit within and all around you for direction and guidance. *Pray* to communicate with the Infinite. M*editate* to receive input from God, the Heavenly Host and your Self. Reach peak state before each session of reading, especially before life-transformative assignments. These *daily* practices set the stage for knowing and achieving your Soul's mission.

Follow Your Bliss

"If you follow your bliss, you put yourself on a kind of track that has been there the whole while, waiting for you, and the life you ought to be living is the one you are living."
—Joseph Campbell

Follow your heart, do what you feel called to do. You have a wise inner voice that guides you toward your mission in life. The pieces of life's puzzle will fall in place as more and more persons—starting with you—pursue their bliss. Our Souls came to Earth to learn and teach lessons, love and serve one another, and enjoy life. Spiritual realization decreases fear and increases faith and courage to follow our inner callings.

Thoreau wrote, "Go confidently in the *direction* of your dreams, live the life you have imagined." Goethe said, Whatever you can do, or dream you can do, *begin* it. Boldness has genius, power and magic in it." Both authors emphasized the importance of getting started, of taking the first step. Universal Intelligence assists those who are committed to working toward their dreams. That's when windows of opportunity open and "serendipity" occurs.

Our Souls, in alignment with God's plan, chose a mission before they came to Earth. That mission is our heart and Soul's dream. Everyone has a life-vision, a special talent they were meant to share. Universe totally supports those who assist God's plan to bring peace, joy, love and light on Earth.

Follow your heart and Soul's longing—you can't go wrong. In *The Teachings of Don Juan*, Carlos Castenada was told to ask "does this path have a heart? If it does, the path is good; if it doesn't it is of no use... One makes for a joyful journey; as long as you follow it, you are one with it. The other will make you curse your life. One makes you strong; the other weakens you."

This is not just lofty impractical spiritual advice; it's useful information that increases the quality and quantity of this Earthly lifespan. For example, the most common time for heart attacks is early Monday morning. Day after day, year after year of following 'a path with no heart' literally destroys ones anatomical heart.

I've counseled a number of persons who hated their work but were afraid to follow their bliss. "After I retire, then I'll start that little business I've always dreamed of" they say. When I ask about their life's dream, they invariably pause for a moment. Then their eyes light up as they describe what they would do "*if* only..." The truth is, each person *can* follow their calling; doing so, at least part time, is a key to experiencing Heaven on Earth.

In *Bridges to Heaven* by Jonathan Robinson, Levar Burton stated "Right now I am totally energized around my work— what I consider my destiny path. As I write and direct these days, I feel so much in alignment with my life's purpose. When I came into this body, I made an agreement to do specific work along the lines of waking up humanity to the truth of our spiritual journey. When I am engaged in that process, I strongly feel the presence of God in me and working through me."

Can you feel the passion and commitment in his words? I got goose-bumps when I first read them. What a powerful statement of how you can feel when you follow your bliss. Resolve to do *whatever it takes* to feel that juiced about your life's work. Decide right now to identify and reach your birth-vision as soon as possible. How about now?!

Attending to the Soul's mission is usually a multidimensional process. We each have numerous roles in life—family member, significant other, friend, worker, church member, community participant, individual, etc. Following your bliss doesn't mean forsaking all other roles and just focusing on the spiritual aspect. On the contrary, for most of us, being totally successful and achieving our Soul's mission means meeting all our roles impeccably.

Fulfilling our various roles, doing meaningful work, and making space for Spirit is a challenge but is possible. Make a commitment right now to identify and pursue your dreams. Some persons will have the circumstances and courage to make abrupt changes, to follow their bliss full time. Others may choose to make a more gradual transition over time. Whichever path you choose, start *now*!

Let your heart and Soul dream for a moment using your fullest imagination and passion: if you knew you could not fail, what would you do? Let the images flow and feel the excitement as—perhaps for the first time—you become aware of your Soul's calling. You came here to fulfill a mission; until you start working toward it, you'll never experience the joy and peace that is your birthright.

In *I Had It All the Time*, Alan Cohen states "It is not selfish to be happy. *It is your highest purpose.* Your joy is the greatest contribution you can make to life on the planet. A heart at peace with its owner blesses everyone it touches.... by what means would God speak to you except through the deepest inclinations of your heart?"

Your initial reaction to this message of following your bliss may be, Alan notes, "'But if everyone follows their spirit without hesitation, the world will be swallowed up in chaos! Self-centered egomaniacs would go around raping and pillaging. There would be no integrity, no commitment, nothing would get done, and the world would fall apart.' The scenario just described is exactly the world engendered when we do *not* follow our spirit without hesitation. The message is to follow your spirit, not your fear... As spiritual beings, our nature is loving, and so to follow your spirit is to live in the constant expression of love. Love does not go around raping, pillaging, or hurting others. Love seeks to serve and create peace and harmony."

To begin identifying your Soul's calling, close your eyes, let yourself become relaxed, and ask for assistance from God and the Heavenly Host. Give thanks for guidance and clarity in realizing your Soul's mission. Then listen quietly for that still small voice within. Now answer the following questions by noting your very first response that spontaneously arises. Note any clues that arise spontaneously such as words, pictures, feelings, colors or other persons and places.

1. What are you naturally good at?

    _____

    _____

2. What would you do if money were no object?

    _____

    _____

3. What would you do if you had only one year to live?

    _____

    _____

4. What would you do if you knew you couldn't fail?

    _____

    _____

5. What would you do without pay because you enjoy it?

    _____

    _____

6. What do you read and talk about in your spare time?

    _____

    _____

7. What chokes you up, gives you goose bumps, cold chills, tears in your eyes, or pressure over your chest?

    _____

    _____

8. How do you feel called to assist Heaven on Earth?

    _____

    _____

Most persons have glimpsed their calling periodically over the years but thought they were "just" dreaming or daydreaming. Depending on your predominant sensory orientation (auditory, kinesthetic, or visual), you may have briefly heard, felt, or seen yourself reaching these goals. These visions usually recur and leave one with an inner excitement and longing.

Your *higher purpose* involves sharing your Inner Light, speaking your higher truth, helping, healing, teaching, and comforting others in some way. The opportunities and vehicles for such work are endless; every role creates an opening for serving others. Don't be discouraged because you can't be influential on a large scale. Brighten the corner where you are, follow your calling, and trust that Universal Law will manifest that energy as needed.

Your calling doesn't have to be something earth-shaking or exotic. The dream of "Tom", an accounting controller, was to own a small business, live more simply, and escape corporate pressures. His wife, "Debbie", had long dreamed of raising several children although her health only permitted giving birth to one child.

They bought a cemetery monument business and rescued two grandchildren by raising them. At their shop, they provide excellent service at fair prices and really care for their recently bereaved customers. At home, they are raising their grandchildren like their own. They will never be in *People* magazine or receive Nobel Prizes but they are among the growing ranks of those following their dreams *and* making the world a better place.

It is time for *everyone* to recognize the spark of the Divine within and share that Light. There is a totally perfect order and purpose, the beauty and magnitude of which we can only glimpse. Your mission is to discern your part and trust your feelings. Diane Roger said "Your hopes, dreams and aspirations are legitimate. They are trying to take you airborne, above the storms, above the clouds-if you will only let them."

Heed the parting words from the Palaedians in *Bringers of the Dawn* channeled by Barbara Marciniak: "we speak into the soul and heart of everyone of you. We ask you to hear the call, to recognize it, and to step forward as members of the Family of Light. Have the courage in all the days you walk this planet to live that light and share it with all you encounter. This does not mean to preach or sell that light. It means to live the light you know you are, to discover in the simplicity of your being the purpose of your existence, to blossom with it, and to reseed this place that is Planet Earth in its deepest time of transition."

Creative Discontent

"We are on a market trip on earth; whether we fill our baskets or not, once the time is up, we go home."

—Ibo, Nigeria

Many awakening persons are experiencing an inner turmoil and existential angst. Creative or Divine discontent signals it is time for adjustments in ones life. Discontent has a purpose and is nothing to be afraid of; it signals we are *unfinished* and have inner work to do.

At a Native American ceremony, Kristy talked about following ones heart, even if others consider it "kooky" or "on the fringe". Fabric, she explained, consists of stable weaves in the middle and looser fringe around the borders. Being on the fringe is where the action and excitement is. It's good to be on the fringe, at least in some aspects of your life. Otherwise, life becomes predictable, boring, stuffy and lacks Spirit.

God never gives us a dream without the means to fulfill it. When you were a kid playing outside, your parents wouldn't call you inside and then—just before you reached the door— lock you out. In the same way, God doesn't call us to enter a door that's locked—although we may have to jiggle the handle, push, pry, and work at it a bit. To achieve dreams, we must also be willing to risk pain and potential setbacks.

The 'unfolding' process is fierce at times; awakening to ones calling has been termed a "magnificent obsession" or "terrible blessing". Divine discontent motivates us to reach meaningful life goals and break old cycles. Creative discontent signals that messages from the Soul are waiting to be expressed. The totality of our being, our Divine-Humanity, cries out to be recognized and demonstrated.

Following ones bliss is not always a popular move. Friends and family may criticize or tell you to "be sensible!" But every

aspect of your life will be ruined if you don't follow your calling. Nature prods gently at first and later, if necessary, uses a
two-by-four to get your attention. Your health, happiness, relationships, and job success will all be adversely affected if
you're not listening to Spirit's call.

Make it a priority to identify and contribute your Soul's
special talent. Listen to your inner urges and wrestle with your
creative discontent. Focus on serving others and avoid the pitfalls of *excessive* power, fortune, fame and sex. When you do
follow your Soul's path, the ego may "raise cane" for awhile
because it's afraid of the unknown. It's exciting but a little scary
to become free and secure enough to take the road less traveled.

Treat the ego like a fearful child. Reassure it but resolve
that no amount of crying or whining will halt your Soul's mission. You have listened to ego's voice of fear and "reasonable-
ness" for too long; now it's time to listen to your heart and Soul
and follow God's will for you. That is the message of creative
discontent.

Suppose for a moment that your inner discontent is trying
to tell you something about your Soul's mission. Write out the
first feelings and thoughts that come to mind for the following
questions:

1. What do you love most in life?
   _____
   _____

2. What do you want in life and what are you committed
   to?
   _____
   _____

3. What life changes would ease your creative discontent?
   _____
   _____

4. If you were not afraid, you would:
   _____
   _____

Remember, focus on what you want—not on what you don't want! Answering these questions and doing the life-transformative exercises will open doors and increase your motivation. Rediscover the hunger for what you want most in your life. Having sufficient drive will overcome your fears and resistance.

Cut off all possibilities except achieving your goal. Anything you can dream, you can do. It's time to live the life you were born to live; you were born at this time in this place for a great reason. You are an extension of God's love; fulfill His plan for you on Earth. As Helen Keller said "Life is either a daring adventure or it is nothing." Make it a daring adventure.

You are here for greater reasons than you know. Never take your eyes off your purpose. Periodically ask yourself "Is what I'm doing taking me closer to my dream?" Take this simple test. Examine every aspect of your life. Keep and move toward what nourishes your spirit; discard and move away from what is loathsome to your spirit. Use creative discontent to fuel your mission and an attitude of gratitude to receive the riches that surround you.

Service To Others

Serving others is a key to identifying and following your Soul's mission. When I asked my Dad what his idea of Heaven was, he replied it would be working with and helping others in different ways. That's what my parents do now for family, church, Lion's club, Good Samaritan, Children Services and Community Action. They're enjoying Heaven here on Earth.

One of my recommendations for depressed persons (in addition to aerobic exercise, chiropractic care, optimal nutrition, stress management and mind reprogramming) is to get out and serve others. Being isolated, self-absorbed, and unfulfilled contributes to depression. We always get back more than we give when serving from the heart. Focus on others and the Enduring Self becomes freer and happier.

A wonderful true story illustrates the power of serving others. A woman with terminal cancer decided to spend the last year of her life helping other cancer victims. She advertised her willingness to feed, visit, and care for others and was overwhelmed with responses. Her doctor tried to discourage her as she didn't have time for proper rest, diet, or exercise. After her one year re-exam, her doctor—choked up and unable to speak—wrote her a note: "there is no trace of cancer in your body."

Some people hesitate to act because they're not sure which way to serve. How can you best discern the voice of Spirit? How do you know if your idea is a brainstorm or a brain-spasm? Here are some suggestions:

- listen for messages that come clearly and spontaneously to you *versus* you actively thinking of it
- look for signs that come in threes; e.g., if you hear about a seminar three times within a couple weeks, maybe you should attend
- you feel strongly *drawn* to something, as if a magnetic attraction were involved
- your surroundings seem more vibrant and vividly colorful just before or during Spirit-filled decisions
- you *feel good*—excited, tingling, energetic—when you follow the right path
- things usually flow smoothly and, when they don't, you don't feel like giving up
- signs of chakra activation occur
- unexpected verifications, "coincidences", or Heavenly hints that you're on track, occur
- there is a deep *inner knowing*, a surety that you can't describe but you know is right

We each have a special gift to share with others. Our biggest mistake is doing nothing because we think we can't do a lot. *What* we do isn't so important as the Spirit behind the action. Don't be discouraged because you're not famous and a recognized VIP. Persons at those levels often have a tough job even remembering there is a spiritual path, let alone staying on it.

Elisabeth Kubler-Ross, M.D., says one of her most important teachers was a janitor in her building. Remember, appearances can be deceiving. In the *Star Wars* trilogy, Luke Skywalker couldn't imagine that a little, odd looking creature like Yoda was a wise master. That's why it's so crucial to remember our Inner Divinity; without an emphasis on the Spirit within, we become misled by outer illusions.

While staying at a Signature Inn, I read a tract entitled "To Our Guests." At first, I figured it was just another piece of promotional literature but the words had a definite spirit to them. It read "In ancient times, there was a prayer for 'The Stranger within our gates.' Because this motel is a human institution to serve people, and not solely a money-making organization, we hope that God will grant you peace and rest while you are under our roof... We are all travelers. From 'birth till death' we travel between the eternities. May these days be pleasant for you, profitable for society, helpful for those you meet, and a joy to those who know and love you best."

I was impressed, especially when I saw the staff putting this philosophy into action: a friendly front desk person at 1 AM and a kindly waitress taking time to visit with an elderly man dining alone. It helped me remember how all the ways of serving God and others are important. It's also a benchmark of this New Age; everyone benefits from a soulful, service orientation.

Focus on serving others and follow your bliss. Grass roots movements have always been the most lasting and effective. We *can* change the world *one person at a time*. Do your best and know that is sufficient.

Resolve To Fulfill Your Mission

An Aboriginal Real Person asked Marlo Morgan "if it was true some people live their entire lives and never know what their God-given talents are?... Yes, I had to admit, many Mutants did not think they were given any talent, and they did not think about the purpose of life until they were dying. Big tears came into his eyes as he shook his head, showing how difficult it was to believe such a thing could happen: 'Why can't Mutants see, if my song makes one person happy, it is a good job? You help one person, good job!'"

Take a moment *right now* to take stock of your life. Are you happy and fulfilled with your life work? Are you following your inner dream, at least part time? If not, when will you take steps toward reaching your purpose? I'll give you a hint: the answer is never "tomorrow." Tomorrow never comes so start today!

In 1965, at age 12, I was sitting alone in our kitchen, eating a bowl of cereal and reading the front page obituary of a prominent local man. Sunlight refracted through our beveled window panes and multicolored light shone into my peripheral vision. As I looked up into that light, a calm, clear voice or thought said "This man just ended his time on Earth. Someday you will likewise die. What will you do with your time until then? Will you help others and leave the Earth a better place? Or will you merely take up space?" This was the first time I had experienced this input that seemed both internally and externally oriented.

I periodically recalled that inspiration and planned to become a physician, psychologist, or minister so I could help people. I worked in hospitals for six years, attended theology school, earned a masters in clinical psychology, and started work in mental health centers. In 1980, I started writing a book but got off track while earning my doctorate, getting married, having children, moving repeatedly, starting practice, ETC.

In 1991, I told the doctor I practiced with that I wanted to treat patients only 3 days per week so I could teach and write more. That was unacceptable so I started my own practice in 1992. I told my practice consultants that my ultimate goal was to teach and write while practicing only part-time. "No problem", they said, "Build a big clinic, hire associate doctors, manage them, and you'll have plenty of time to teach and write."

In 1993, I was so busy with my practice, associate doctors, and new building plans that I didn't even have time to promote *Balanced Living* when it was published. In the winter of 1994, we moved into our new office as associate doctors Larry, Moe, and Curly self-destructed one by one.

In the spring of 1994, I became *painfully* aware it was time to radically shift the emphasis of my life work. I suddenly felt an *intense* discontent and unhappiness as I was riding our lawn tractor. I was blessed with a beautiful family, good friends, spiritual growth, great health, and ample material goods but something was missing. After much prayer, meditation, and talking with loved ones, I realized my Soul needed more time and space to really live. And it was finally time to write, teach, and learn more!

Later that autumn, I visited friends in Florida; my friend Joe had earlier given me a CD of beautiful music by "Greg." As we walked along the ocean, Joe told me that Greg had written, performed, and produced this music and was ready to follow his bliss. He had quit his full time job and was ready to journey across the country promoting his music. As Joe told me this story, I felt a wave of excitement and surety that I too would achieve my mission. I went into the water and held up my arms to celebrate. I expressed gratitude to Creator for assistance in discerning and achieving my Soul's mission.

At that moment, Greg "just happened" to be jogging by; he stopped and told about his imminent plans to go for it. I had never seen anyone so excited, determined and alive. Even though he and his wife would be living week to week financially, they were following their calling and taking a leap of faith. That magic moment with Joe, Greg, my family, the ocean sunset, and God is etched into my memory forever and motivates me to just do it!

It was definitely time for me to learn and teach more about spiritual matters. It was time to write *Toward Heaven on Earth* and remind others—and, most of all, myself—about our True Nature. But what about the practice and building? Plan A was to sell everything and immediately write and teach full time. Despite being on the market for 2 years, my office building didn't sell and several potential buyers of the entire practice didn't pan out. It apparently wasn't time or I had the wrong plan.

Plan B was to find a partner to buy half the business, reduce my practice hours by half, and sell the building as soon as possible. But, while waiting for all this to happen, I became *proactive*. There weren't enough hours in the day to do everything so I carved out 16 hours per week for writing and teaching by *temporarily* reducing my leisure, exercise, yoga, and sleep time. Almost immediately, I felt happier and more peaceful; no matter how long it took, I was going *in the direction* of my dreams.

I took concrete action steps and got the ball rolling enough to temper my creative discontent. Then doors started opening that allowed me to pursue my dream full time. I found another doctor to purchase my practice; he and I had both been praying for an optimal work relationship and were connected by a mutual friend who is on the spiritual path. The many steps in that transition *flowed* smoothly and easily; it apparently was the right time, person, and plan.

The last several years were a difficult and seemingly chaotic process; in retrospect, there was a rhyme and reason to the timing and events. I never gave up on my dream no matter how many times I seemed to get sidetracked and I'm sure those "obstacles" contained important lessons. I now trust much more in the Divine flow in all things.

You can do the same; *brainstorm* how you can start moving in the direction of your dreams. Just because you can't do it all today is no reason not to get started. *Resolve* to know and fulfill your Soul's mission.

Reinforce Part II

To make optimal use of this information, attain peak state via peak physiology, empowering feelings, inspiring music, and power cues. Then answer the following:

A. Why do you feel your Soul is on Earth at this particular time? That is, what is God's will for you?

_____

_____

_____

_____

B. What are five of your special talents and strengths?

1. _____

_____

2. _____

_____

3. _____

4. _____

5. _____

C. What are five negative, limiting beliefs that—in your
heart of hearts—you *know* you need to change?

1. _____

2. _____

3. _____

4. _____

5. _____

D. What are the negative and unacceptable consequences
for each limiting belief listed in C? That is, how will your health
and happiness, your family and friends be adversely affected
unless you *break through* old erroneous beliefs?

1. _____

2. _____

3. _____

4. _____

5. _____

Read what you have just written and realize your formidable potential (A. and B.) *Resolve* to reprogram your limiting
beliefs (C.) so you, your loved ones, and the world doesn't suffer negative repercussions (D.) Are you ready to let go of old
baggage and emerge as a totally successful Divine-Human?

Such a lofty goal is a lifelong process, a journey that never ends but a *quantum leap* forward is achievable *now* with these understandings and methods!

Are you ready? If so, say YES! *Yes* to God and the Heavenly Host. *Yes* to your Soul's Light that has been waiting so patiently to shine through. *Yes* to a life of happiness and total success. *Yes* to the love and peace that invariably comes when we are willing to take action steps for the betterment of Self and others.

The following exercises take about 30 minutes. You'll need pen, paper, and a place where you can yell, celebrate, and possibly cry. Nature is a perfect setting and transformational energies are proportional to the square of the number of dedicated persons doing the exercises together.

In *A Christmas Carol* by Charles Dickens, Ebenezer Scrooge changed instantly after visits by the ghosts of Christmas Past (how his life had been), Present (how his life currently was), and Future (how his life would be). You also can change quickly and dramatically by vividly visualizing your negative limiting beliefs and their predictable consequences. This painful exercise gives you sufficient *leverage* and motivation to change for the better.

You've already written these out in C and D. Now *picture, feel, and hear* how your life will be unless you exchange negative limiting beliefs for more empowering, positive ones. The next exercise is, I promise, the *only* time I'll ask you to focus on negativity. Assume a *down* (versus peak) *state* with your shoulders slumped forward, head down, shallow breathing, and a lifeless physiology. Close your eyes and imagine what your life will be like in *five years* if you don't reprogram negative patterns and follow your Soul's mission.

Consider how every aspect of your life will be hampered or ruined: relationships, physical health, happiness, job success, mental well being, relationships, income, spiritual growth, and so on. See yourself in the mirror *5 years* from now; how will you look and feel if you haven't broken through the barriers that are choking off your potential? What are you saying to yourself about the quality of your life? (Hint: if it contains the phrase "this sucks!" that's not a good sign.)

Now go out *10 years* from now. How will every facet of your life be worse if you haven't made the changes *you know* in your heart are needed? Have you lost valued relationships because of continued negativity? Has your health status declined, perhaps irreversibly so? How do you feel about your job, income, and opportunities for advancement? Are you at all happy? Do you recognize or like your reflection in the mirror? What bad news do you hear yourself and others saying about your life?

Finally, visualize yourself *20 years* from now if you don't follow your heart and Soul's calling. Will you even be alive? What important relationships have ended or are merely existing? What are your children or grandchildren like after emulating your bad points? Do you hear yourself and others saying "What a wasted life, I don't know what happened. So much promise years ago!" Have you given up on your dream or forgotten you ever had one? Do you feel discouraged, hopeless, and helpless about reaching your dreams? Does "reaching total success" sound like an impossible dream or a motivational sales pitch?

If you've participated fully in this exercise, you're feeling discomfort, sadness, and anxiety. Trust me, the pain is well worth it IF you make necessary changes. Humans are motivated by gaining pleasure *and* avoiding pain. This program emphasizes *both* to trigger massive positive change now. We may never pass this way again; please use this opportunity to erase those negative tapes!

Continue in *down state* and, in a weak whiny voice, state your first limiting belief (under C): "I *used* to think..." Then immediately refute that disempowering misconception by rapidly assuming *peak physiology* (upright posture, loud confident voice, clenched fists, slapping your chest) and state with absolute surety "But that's bullshit! The truth is...!" That is, dynamically replace your old limiting belief with a more accurate and positive one.

For example, one of my negative limiting misconceptions was "I used to think I don't have enough time and energy to do everything I need to do." The refuting statement is "But that's hippopotamus shit! I have all the time and energy I need to meet my priorities. I *make* the time and I create the energy that's needed!"

Another was "I used to think I have too many stresses, demands, and responsibilities in my life." My new reply to that past limiting statement? "But that's elephant shit! I have many opportunities, options, and blessings. The stress was only a signal that changes were needed. I'm moving toward a balanced life of happiness and total success *now!*"

Repeat this process *five times* for each of your five old limiting beliefs. Do so with as much animation, intensity, volume, passion, and energy as possible. Like every thing else, the more you put into it, the more you get out of it. Make a commitment to repeat this process (saying your old limiting beliefs in down state and your empowering new beliefs in peak state) every day for the next 14 days. This eight minute process anchors positive changes so deeply that you'll never be crippled by old limiting beliefs again. If you ever start to whine from a disempowered state, your mind will recognize it *automatically* for the absolute bullshit that it is.

Now you're ready for the *coup de grace* to those old erroneous notions. First, attain a totally empowered peak state. Rewrite the five limiting beliefs (from C.) then *cross them out* with great gusto. Now write your new beliefs that you just anchored ("the truth is...")

Next, visualize, feel, and hear yourself in *five years* having changed radically for the better after implementing these *major positive changes*. Consider how every aspect of your life will improve as you continue to live according to these new marvelous beliefs. Imagine every aspect of your life changing for the better: relationships, job, income, health, happiness, and inner peace. See yourself in the mirror and notice how much happier and more vital you look.

Visualize yourself in *ten years* as these new wonderful cycles reinforce more grand outcomes. Hear yourself and others raving about your improvements. See how much happier and healthier you look. Feel how good it is to experience total success. Finally, picture, feel, and hear how outstanding your life has become in every way after *twenty years* of consistent, unlimited belief living.

This awesome reconfiguration for total success and happiness calls for a celebration! Achieve peak state with physiology, feelings, music and power cues. As you play the music, yell, clap, dance, jump, and act like a total lunatic. It's only fitting since you just lost your mind—at least the negative, limiting portion of it!

Quickly review your statements under #1-4 on page 79 and A and B on pages 85-86. Then close your eyes and vividly see/ hear/feel yourself identifying and following your Soul's mission. Hear the praise from within and from others as you achieve your dreams. Feel the gratitude and courage as you transform toward your best.

You have just completed a *massive reprogramming* by erasing limiting bunk and inserting more accurate input. Use this technique for any other limiting beliefs you uncover in the future. Remember, this works best when you vividly recite them daily for two weeks. Then *maintain* your gains by repeating the process once a week until you have thoroughly internalized it. *Commit* to identifying and achieving your Soul's mission. You *can* transform your life for the better and experience Heaven on Earth.

It takes energy to make your life extraordinary. The upcoming techniques and information in Part III will increase your total well being so you can consistently be a strong spiritual server/seeker.

Part III:

REACHING TOTAL WELLNESS
OF BODY, MIND, AND SPIRIT

Techniques and information for *outstanding vitality*;
so you can fulfill all your roles impeccably *and*
achieve your Soul's mission

Before a Native American vision quest, spiritual seekers are advised to prepare by:
- eating more purely to cleanse the body and nervous system
- exercising to strengthen the physiology
- praying, chanting, and singing spiritual songs

In the same way, we can purify and strengthen ourselves for this life journey by following wise life-style counsel.

We each are at different points along life's path and, as such, our needs vary. For example, an overly disciplined and hard driving person may need to let go, kick back, and remember "easy does it." A person with too little drive may want to turn up the fires a notch and add more discipline to their regimen. Listen quietly for the Tao, the middle road, your chosen path toward optimal living.

Jonathan Robinson wrote "I like to think everyone has a combination-type lock on his or her heart and soul. Our mission, should we decide to accept it, is to figure out the combination to that lock... The more approaches we try, the more likely it is that we'll find the magic combination that opens the door to a much deeper experience of God. In addition, the more paths we know to the 'kingdom of heaven within,' the more opportunities we have for diving into the divine."

My 25 years in medical, theological, psychological, and chiropractic fields have given me an uncommon depth and variety of experiences and insights. I also have been blessed with an unending thirst for the Truth and am grateful to have learned some great distinctions and answers to life's ultimate questions.

See my first book, *Balanced Living*, for important background information and additional techniques, especially regarding exercise, nutrition, chiropractic, chakras, vegetarianism, rest and sleep, stress management, and maintaining a healthy internal and outer environment.

Please note an important distinction: techniques and methods are *not* necessary to work your way to God or into Heaven. Rather, they assist *opening* to the realization that God and Heaven are inside and all around each of us now. Having realized this, we will *want*, not need, to fine-tune our body/mind/

spirit to thank Creator and be optimal spiritual servers/seekers.

As you learn and apply these advanced approaches for becoming all you can be in body, mind, and spirit, remember the focus: to be worthy servants of God and all people, how shall we prepare?

Prayer

"Prayer does not change God, but it changes him who prays."
— Soren Kierkegaard

Prayer is communicating with God, the Heavenly Host *and* our Inner Selves. Fervent prayers from the heart are answered *if* the prayer is in accordance with Universal Law. A Divine Perfection exists that humans can usually only glimpse occasionally. What *we* think should happen isn't always in our best interest or that of others. That's one reason some prayers aren't answered as we would like.

So if a particular prayer isn't answered, it's probably best. Prayers aren't always answered when, how, and where we expect. Maybe the right combination of people, places, and events hasn't occurred yet. That's why the best prayer is to know and follow God's will which is the same as your Soul's mission.

Australian Aborigines recognize that the best way to communicate with God is not talking but listening. They clear thoughts out of their minds and wait to receive, recognizing "You cannot hear the voice of Oneness when you are busy talking." They preface their prayers with the affirmation that their lives "help the most people everywhere."

Alan Cohen reminds us "Appreciation accelerates manifestation. The difference between a prayer of 'I want' and 'Thank you' is like that between a propeller-driven airplane and a jet. More exactly, it is the difference between getting somewhere and already being there. There is no bridge to cross; you are already home."

For example, "If you want to demonstrate greater prosperity, you must think prosperity thoughts, speak prosperity words, and take prosperity action; if you want more rewarding relationships, you need to become engrossed with what is working in your relationships, rather than what is not. If you want to live a life of constant celebration, start by appreciating the gifts already given instead of complaining about the lack of those you await."

I give thanks each day for a new opportunity to love, serve, grow, enjoy and create. I thank God for all my blessings: loving relationships with friends and family, great health, prosperity, and assistance with my Soul's mission. I especially give thanks for the growing awareness that we each are, in truth, Eternal Souls.

I thank Mother/Father God for Divine love, guidance, assistance and inspiration. I give thanks for the increasing realization that my True Nature is love, hope, peace, faith, mercy, goodness, compassion, patience, harmony, balance, joy and abundance.

Finally, I express thankfulness for my daily walk with God and Christ as I grow in understanding of and follow God's will for me. I thank God for helping me realize, open to, and demonstrate my Inner Divinity and Christ Light. I daily renew my willingness to serve as a conduit and vehicle for God's work on earth. Then I meditate.

Meditation

Paramahansa Yogananda said "Why should you think He is not (everywhere)? The air is filled with music that is caught by the radio—music that otherwise you would not know about. And so it is with God. He is with you every minute of your existence, yet the only way to realize this is to meditate."

Father Thomas Keating said "Silence is the language God speaks, and everything else is a bad translation." God appears with the disappearance or quieting of the mind. The best way to reach that inner silence is meditation. Sitting quietly enables getting to the space between thoughts, to the unified field of all possibilities. So few are able to enjoy pure silence; those who do are greatly rewarded.

You don't have to *do* anything to realize your True Self, you just have to *stop doing anything* for a short while each day.

Western cultures have, unfortunately, historically lacked training in centeredness and meditation. Perhaps people will pray and meditate more regularly as additional research at leading universities demonstrates many mind/body/spirit benefits.

In J.D. Salinger's short story, *Teddy*, he said "You know that apple Adam ate in the Garden of Eden... You know what was in that apple? Logic. Logic and intellectual stuff... what you have to do is vomit it up if you want to see things as they really are." When asked how he would change educational systems, Teddy replied "I think I'd first just assemble all the children together and show them how to meditate. I'd try to show them how to find out who they *are*, not just what their names are and things like that... I'd want them to *begin* with all the real ways of looking at things, not just the way all the other apple-eaters look at things."

If you unhook your TV from the antenna or cable hookup, you'll get poor reception. No connection, no clear picture. In the same way, humans are beings of energy who function best with strong connections to their Source. Meditation allows *getting clear*, being connected to the Ground of All Being, cultivating higher powers that assist us in knowing and doing God's will.

We choose whether life is like Heaven or "hell" by our thoughts, words, and deeds. Light and "darkness" can't occupy the same space. Divine intelligence, clarity and faith aren't on compatible energy levels with ignorance, confusion and fear so they can't coexist. Regular meditation allows a firsthand experience of God and inner peace. It's the best single way to remember and demonstrate our kinship with the Great Spirit.

Resolve to *make the time* to meditate daily. Optimal times of day are dawn and dusk, 20 minutes each. That's a bit of time but how serious are you about remembering your Soul? Some Souls spend lifetime after lifetime "wanting" to become enlightened but don't make the necessary sacrifices to reach those sublime states of being. How much do you want to experience Heaven on Earth?

In *The Tenth Insight*, James Redfield says everyone is born with positive intentions to remember their *birth vision* and fulfill their *world vision*. Yet, many persons "go unconscious" and live in a trance, get socialized into cultural norms, and forget their True Nature. "After that, all we can remember are these gut feelings, these intuitions, to do certain things. But we constantly have to fight the Fear. Often the Fear is so great we fail to follow through with what we intended, or we distort it somehow."

An older couple began receiving treatment from me recently and were endlessly rehashing their aches and pains. I tried to break their pattern and asked how long they had been married. "Forty seven years!", one said. "That's a rarity these days with all the divorces." Then they took turns reciting a long list of negatives: "and all the drug addicts, and all the teenage pregnancies, and all the alcoholics, and all the murderers, and all the welfare bums." It was a perfectly choreographed negative incantation.

God knows how long they would have continued if I had not interrupted: "Actually, the great majority of people are good and loving." They both got a blank look and didn't say anything; the new input apparently did not compute. I realized that a direct cause of their physical condition was "the evening news mantra." They had exposed themselves to negative media so long and so often that they were deluded and brainwashed.

In truth, of the 5 billion people on our planet, over 99% are wonderful as many world travelers will attest. That leaves only a small fraction of bad eggs that newscasts selectively and heavily focus on. That's why so many people mistakenly believe the world is going to hell in a hand-basket.

Regular prayer and meditation provide a spiritual foundation and allow us to see through the fearful illusions of physicality. Practiced regularly, they are keys to absolutely *knowing* there is an exquisitely perfect Divine design despite appearances to the contrary. A Yogaville teacher, Swami Gurucharananda, shared this beautiful lesson at the end of a meditation session: "Be still and know I am God. Be still and know I am. Be still and know. Be still. Be." Meditation helps us *embody* this wisdom.

Time Isn't Really Real

"The secret of life is enjoying the passage of time... the thing about time is that time isn't really real, it's just your point of view, how does it feel for you, Einstein said he could never understand it all."

—James Taylor

Time's illusory nature is a difficult concept to grasp, especially when indicators of "human time" are on walls, wrists, in cars, and incessantly announced on TV and radio. The effort is well worthwhile, though, since comprehending the *relative reality* of time greatly assists experiencing Heaven on Earth.

All eternity is comprised of a series of "eternal now" moments. Or, more accurately—but harder to conceptualize—there is no such thing as time. All life is one endless dance of energy, God manifesting itself in varying ways throughout Eternity. Infinity.

Earth's indigenous cultures view time as a circular or cyclical, rather than linear, phenomenon. The symbol for infinity is a horizontal figure eight that has no beginning and no end. Many persons have become prisoners to the almighty clock that constantly reminds us the meter is running. We have forgotten that time is a human invention, an aid for our convenience. In God's Grand Design, there are no limits of space or time.

Time measurements are useful for organization and productivity. Time deadlines also motivate us to get on with our dreams. Just remember to view time as a servant not a master. Past and future are illusory; all we have is now. An overemphasis on time is part of the illusion that confuses humanity.

One proof that time isn't really real is the changing nature of time. Consider how long an hour seems while waiting in a traffic jam versus watching an exciting movie. Notice how the journey toward a destination seems to take longer than the trip back home. Older persons report an accelerated perception of time as they age. In this New Age of heightening consciousness, many notice time seems to be passing more quickly. These are examples of how time reveals its illusory nature.

Believing in the supremacy of time sets us up for suffering. If I thought my life was limited to about 80 years or less, every passing day would be scary. Knowing that time is eternal eases the discomforts that accompany life's stages. I'm only in my early 40's but, despite excellent holistic health habits, baldness, gray hairs, crowned teeth, and hearing loss have already set in. I almost had a cow when I recently found my first white pubic hair—talk about hitting you where it hurts! Knowing that time is illusory and that our Real Selves continue infinitely makes these changes easier to bear.

Humanity's lack of understanding about the relative reality of time also contributes to rage and confusion about suffering. If time is real, life often seems unjust and chaotic, especially when a child dies. Why can't *everyone* live to a ripe old age? One answer is that *Soul time* is quite different from Earth time. Souls know time doesn't exist and there is only the Eternal Now moment. Souls may even purposely *plan* to learn their lessons quickly and return Home again ASAP.

From a purely physical perspective that emphasizes time, the death of a 5 year old is a great tragedy; only from an enlightened, timeless Soul-perspective does it make sense. Five or 95 Earth-years are just the blink of an eye in Soul-time. Feel the peace that accompanies shedding your old misconceptions about the supremacy of time.

Past life regression subjects have described time in a unique way. Their Soul group interactions on the Other Side are like an eternal poker game and, periodically, a Soul says 'Don't deal me in this hand, I'm leaving for an Earthly incarnation. I'll see you all shortly.' Many years in Earth time may be like just a few minutes in the Spirit World. Soon the Soul returns from Earth's classroom and says 'OK, I'm back. Deal me in.'

Eternity is difficult to comprehend; a great Hindu metaphor helps. The Himalayas are solid granite; imagine that a dove with a silk scarf in its beak flies over the mountains every one thousand years and lightly brushes the peaks with the scarf. Consider how long it would take for the silk scarf to erode them completely flat. That's just one day of the cosmic cycle.

I recently experienced a golden moment during which the illusory nature of time and space was temporarily revealed. It was a perfect spring day with blue skies, cool breezes, and the ground covered with wild flowers. While walking on a mountain ridge, I looked up and saw two hawks soaring directly overhead. My perceptions suddenly shifted when I looked ahead again. Although the shift probably lasted only 60 seconds, it seemed much longer and felt sacred.

A large leaf blew through the air in front of me but in slow motion. All colors appeared more bright and vivid and the wild flowers seemed to be singing springtime songs of joy. I felt totally at one with all nature and knew this timeless Oneness experience was a more accurate perception of reality.

Perhaps you've experienced time seeming to stand still while you were immersed in the timeless present. Time in nature, meditation, serving others, creative work, and favorite hobbies allow us to experience the eternal now moment. Access timeless states regularly to remember that time—like death and physicality—is only relatively real.

Manage Your Time

Now that we know there's no such thing as time, let's discuss how to manage this relatively illusory phenomenon. Time management strategies help carve out opportunities for optimal development of body, mind, and spirit. Most persons are so busy they can't find time to live a balanced life. Take the time, make the time to enjoy life fully.

Many persons are chronically overworked, fatigued, and grumpy; they lack energy to keep up with the rat race, let alone realize and nurture their Inner Divinity. As you increasingly discover your Eternal Self, the nature of life's game changes. Enlightened Souls don't waste time playing power games or obtaining excessive material goods.

My friend Kent, a massage therapist, tells of clients who say "I'm willing to do *anything* to get healthier and happier!" He responds, "Are you willing to spend 60 minutes a day meditating, praying, stretching, and exercising?" Usually the answer is an incredulous "Are you kidding? Who has that much time?" What are *your* priorities?

In *Real Moments*, Barbara DeAngelis, Ph.D., shares wisdom from an anonymous writer: "First I was dying to finish high school and start college. And then I was dying to finish college and start working. And then I was dying for my children to grow old enough for school, so I could return to work. And then I was dying to retire. And now, I am dying... and suddenly I realize I forgot to live."

Don't be like so many individuals who belatedly find they've missed out on happiness, great relationships, and fulfilling lives. In this era of heightening consciousness, more persons are remembering and reordering their priorities. Take time to play and enjoy leisure time on a regular basis.

Henry S. Canby said "We live in the midst of details that keep us running around in circles and never getting anywhere but tired... (the answer is) to find out what we really want to do and then cut out the details that fritter away what is most important. *Live deep instead of fast.*"

We never know how long we have in this lifetime to share our special gifts with the world. In past incarnations, we each no doubt have left important tasks undone, vital messages left unspoken. Vow to not let this happen again. Balance fulfilling all life's demands *and* enjoying the passage of time.

Until recently, I had been so serious about my mission that it hurt other aspects of my life. Watching part of a Bengal's football game helped awaken me to this imbalance. Cincinnati was leading at halftime and our quarterback was laughing with some other players. I suddenly felt angry: it had been many years since Bengal fans had much to cheer about. I felt the players should stay serious and focused until the game was over and won.

Upon analyzing my feelings, I realized I had stumbled onto an old unconscious rule that "You shouldn't have fun until the game is over!" My puritanical rule stemmed from my upbringing, societal expectations and perhaps past life frustrations. I came into this lifetime *determined* to assist a greater awareness of love and light in all. But if I was always serious, I would turn off lots of people and miss out on the fun of the journey.

Two years ago, a rolfing therapist told me I was exhausted at my core. Although I could and did work all day most days, I was running on empty. I wasn't happy or balanced and this negatively affected every aspect of my life. Now I work hard *and* play hard; both are important to win the marathon race we Lightworkers have accepted to run.

To know ones Soul and live from that perspective requires leisure time. "Creative laziness" is essential for getting and staying balanced; we *deserve* to enjoy life and live fully. Those on the path are willing to live more simply and earn less in return for more leisure time; we really can't afford *not* to. We need to periodically kick back and enjoy the ride.

E.B. White said "Every morning I awake torn between a desire to save the world and an inclination to savor it. This makes it hard to plan the day." If we don't savor the world, what's the purpose in saving it? It's important to play, have fun and enjoy life. Unless you become like children, you shall not inherit (realize, experience, enjoy) the kingdom of Heaven.

It's tricky but possible to fulfill your various roles while following your Soul's calling. Only you can intuit the right balance for yourself; suggestions include:

- it's OK to say no; you can't be all things to all people
- watch only minimal, high quality TV and movies
- exercise with or while talking to family or friends
- avoid social/community events you feel *obliged* to attend
- early to bed, early to rise creates extra quality time
- limit the number of extracurricular activities your family enjoys; children need time to be kids and parents weren't created to be shuttle drivers
- benefit from consistent holistic practices; e.g., just 20 minutes of meditation and 30 minutes of exercise done regularly produce extra energy and effectiveness

Shield Yourself

Although God is All, some life forms don't recognize that yet. As such, there is apparent negativity and "evil" from which to *shield* or protect ourselves. I say "apparent" because "evil" has no real power over Souls firmly aligned with God. Until we become more fully realized, however, negative energies can impair our balance. Evil spirits, negative persons, and our own "stinkin thinkin" can create disease and disharmony.

Norman Shealy, M.D., founder of the American Holistic Medical Association, says there are "sappers" and "zappers." "Sappers are the folks who cannot get enough, like a great hole that will never fill. You can give and give, and it is still nowhere near enough. Usually, they are people who are quite depressed." "Zappers" are indiscriminately angry; they let it fly, so to speak. You can feel in your body where you've been zapped—usually your chest or belly. It's not personal but it still hurts.

To shield yourself from negative people, cross your arms across your chest and abdominal area or simply walk away. Before meditating or doing energy visualizations, pray for and affirm that you are shielded with the Light of God and Christ. Imagine this Light pouring outward from the solar plexus area, forming a shield of white Light in front of you that protects you from negativity, "evil", and "darkness." Visualize this Light extending all around your body, forming a protective *cocoon*.

Shaking off negative energies is especially important for health care practitioners who do body work on diseased and tense individuals. Tingling and pressure in the hands and arms after touching a particularly negative person signals the need for shielding and shaking techniques. Shake your hands briskly as if you were trying to flip water off your hands. Washing the hands in cold water also helps remove imbalanced energies.

The "Lion's Breath" is a yoga breathing technique that removes potentially harmful energies and prevents them from accumulating. Take a deep breath in, then forcefully and quickly exhale through the opened mouth. Repeat 3 times. As always, *prevention* is the best approach; use the various shielding techniques daily, more often when overstressed.

Reduce Financial Stress

Excessive material possessions generate stress, worry and more work; the more things you have, the more you have to lose and deal with. Precious time may be wasted because of too many possessions. On the other hand, becoming prosperous and enjoying good things *in moderation* is part of a balanced life.

Remember "Greg" who set off across the country to follow his dream and promote his music? After a year of touring, he was broke, discouraged, and depressed. Every thing that could have gone wrong did and he didn't have adequate capital reserves for these challenges. That's why impeccable warriors do best to prepare for *total success*. Create space for Soul growth *and*, at the same time, have sufficient financial prosperity to stay the course.

The movie *Defending Your Life* depicted the afterlife review as including the question 'how did you treat yourself? Did you enjoy the comforts of life you deserve? Or did you shrink from prosperity because of fear and lack of self-love?' Money is not a root of evil; excessive love of or preoccupation with money is. It's OK to enjoy a comfortable life-style.

BUT, don't try to keep up with the Jones'; they're up to their eyeballs in debt and stressed out. Many persons have unwittingly become economic slaves by following Madison Avenue advertisements. Minimize exposure to TV, radio, and printed advertisements that make you buy things you don't need. Don't be brainwashed into believing you need the latest, biggest and best to be happy.

Many work their lives away in pursuit of "the good life" only to die just before or soon after they reach it. Shop-aholics try to fill the void in their lives by getting that brief jolt of feeling important and being in control. There are better and less expensive ways of reaching these goals.

The more material possessions you have, the more you have to maintain, pay taxes on, and replace when broken. Don't become a prisoner to consumerism and waste your precious time pursuing the illusion of material happiness. The person with the most toys doesn't win. Practice *balanced consumption* based primarily on what you *need* so you have time to really live.

Excessive material possessions can be an impediment to Soul growth. *Traveling lightly* is a key to realizing and acting in accordance with your True Nature. Don't waste another incarnation on the pursuit of too many possessions. Several years ago, I built a large office building and my debts totaled nearly $500,000. From a business standpoint it was a smart move; from a Soul perspective, I was miserable.

That investment "painted me into a corner" for a number of years and removed flexibility and space for following my Soul's urgings. It was a valuable lesson for me—and, hopefully, others. Find the balance between living well and having a Soulful life.

Spinning

Spinning balances and accelerates energy vortexes in the chakras or key energy centers of the body. I first experienced spinning 17 years ago at a holistic health conference. I began the session as a skeptical psychology graduate student making clinical notes about seemingly strange people. After the Sufi dancing, I felt in love with all in attendance and put away my notebook. The whirling dances helped awaken my Soul and facilitated a firsthand, heartfelt experience that we are all one big family.

Spinning is used in Sufism, by Australian Aborigines, by dancers at Grateful Dead concerts, by Tibetan yogis (as described by Peter Kelder in *Fountain of Youth*), and is recommended by Pleiadians ("star people") in Marciniak's *Bringers of the Dawn*. Rumi, a prolific Moslem author, created his poems while spinning. For more proof about the importance of spinning, watch a child laugh with joy after spontaneously whirling around and around.

The technique is simple. Before beginning, affirm and pray for what you intend to manifest in your life; align yourself with Divine will and state your desire to grow in love and understanding. You don't want to accelerate negative energies so shake off any negative energies using one or more of the shielding techniques.

Start with just a few spins and *slowly* work up to 21 times (Kelder) or 33 times (Marciniak). Spin *to the right* (clockwise) if you're *above* the equator; spin to the left (counterclockwise) if *below* the equator. Don't wear shoes and spin on a flat open space for optimal balance and safety.

Hold your arms out to the side and watch your right thumb as you spin. (Left if spinning counterclockwise.) Or, place your palms together, thumbs up, with your arms extended in front of you. Always look at your thumb(s) while spinning to prevent becoming dizzy.

When you are ready to stop spinning, place your feet shoulder width apart for stability. Bring your palms together and against your chest. Keep your eyes open; the room may momentarily spin around at first. If you feel dizzy, you're spinning too much too soon. Stand still for a minute before moving to anchor the energy and make sure you're steady on your feet.

Serious spiritual students who are "going for the One" in this lifetime might try spinning 33 times, three times per day as discussed by Marciniak. A friend who has few responsibilities and lots of time for spiritual growth felt no noticeable difference when spinning that much. On the other hand, spinning that much when my life was overly busy and imbalanced was a bad combination.

I felt more impatient, frustrated and discontented. The heightened energies revealed a vision of the future with a simpler life-style and more time to live, learn, teach, and write. I was so excited that I wanted to immediately sell everything and become a balanced human being, seminar speaker/counselor, author, and student of Truth.

Such a major transition required time and patience so that technique was "not yogic" for me at that time in my life. That much spinning resulted in disharmony and difficulty for my family and my self. I now spin 33 times once per day and balance my spiritual growth with my other responsibilities while moving toward my dream ASAP. As soon as the transition is completed, I'll be a lean, mean, spinning machine at 99 times per day again.

Yoga

Sri Swami Satchidananda wrote "Know that it's not the Self that needs Yoga. It's always tranquil. But the limited mind goes through these practices to expand and see the Self clearly. Then, when the Seer sees his Self and rests in his true nature, he sees the *real face* which is never disturbed. You are the image of God. You are the Infinite by yourself... Remember the goal: Aim at something great. All of you can be Buddhas, Christs, Mohammeds, great sages, and saints."

Yoga, meaning "yoke or union", is a powerful path to realizing the Divinity within and all around. Webster defines yoga as "a discipline by which the individual prepares himself for liberation of the self and union with the universal spirit." Yoga is a thousands of years old science from the East that wise persons will use regularly.

Body positions and meditation have been used by various religions over time to better apprehend the unity of all things. Greek Orthodox mystics used silent contemplation to become deified by Divine energies. Jewish Kabbalists sat in solitude and concentrated on the light of the Shekinah (God's presence on Earth) above their heads.

Labels tend to limit, demean, or mislead; if we must use labels, I'm a Liberal or Universal Christian who believes many paths lead to God and Christ. I see no conflict between Eastern techniques like meditation or yoga and the teachings of Jesus. In fact, some claim that Jesus traveled and learned esoteric Eastern techniques during the "lost years" between ages of 12 and 29. (APPENDIX)

I pray daily to God and Christ for guidance, clarity, and direction. This trusting attitude has allowed me the latitude to explore different paths to enlightenment. If you've been wondering about yoga or other techniques, follow your heart and Soul. Proceed slowly and use your common sense. Pray that every aspect of your life will be of good and God, of love and light. Then learn, expand, and transform into the radiant and powerful Divine-Human you were meant to be.

There are a number of excellent yoga programs. (See RESOURCES and APPENDIX.) I practiced the five "rites" described in *The Fountain of Youth* for years; these are simple but powerful and require only 15 minutes. For the last couple years, I have used "Integral Hatha Yoga" as taught by Swami

Satchidananda. This 75 minute program includes prayer, yoga postures, deep relaxation, breathing techniques, chanting and meditation.

No Tobacco Products

Nearly 1/2 million Americans die each year from tobacco related diseases. As a respiratory therapist, I saw thousands of persons suffering needlessly and dying horribly and prematurely because of cigarettes. Several patients begged me just before they died to warn others about the dangers of smoking before it was too late. The end stages of chronic lung disease are a living "hell".

It's very difficult to remember your Soul and follow your dreams when you're hacking, wheezing, and suffocating to death. Suffering *can* transform a person for the better but there are much more harmonious paths; it's your choice.

Health issues aside, smoking and other self-destructive habits show a lack of love and respect for self, loved ones, and the Creator. When we truly love ourselves and others, we take care of ourselves. When we realize our bodies are the temple of God and the spirit of God dwells within, we treat our bodies with love and respect.

Nicotine is as physically addictive as heroin so compassion and professional help are needed. Hypnotherapy in combination with a gentle, gradual weaning program has been most effective with my patients. I recommend weaning at a rate of 2 to 5 cigarettes per day for a 3 to 4 week period, depending on the length and severity of the nicotine addiction.

For example, if a person smokes one pack of cigarettes per day, wean from 20 to 15-18 per day for 3 to 4 weeks. Then reduce to 12-15 for another 3 or 4 weeks and so on until stopping completely. This graduated weaning approach of tobacco cessation minimizes physical and psychological withdrawal.

To assist *removing* cigarettes from your life, *add several healthy practices. These include:*
- aerobic exercise 5 days a week
- take 10 slow deep breaths at least times four times a day
- take excellent vitamin and mineral supplements

- create different patterns not associated with smoking, e.g., if you always smoked after a meal, get away from the table and take a short walk or other fun activity

Sun-breathing

Pir Vilayat Khan, head of the Sufi order in the West, taught me about sun-breathing at a holistic conference in 1980. This approach that literally fill us with light energy is also used in yoga practices. Eye doctors rightly caution looking directly at the sun; however, sun-breathing is a very precise exposure for a short duration. I have used this technique for 17 years without adverse reactions.

Sun-breathing involves looking at *just the sun's central orb* for only 15 seconds per eye, once a day. Make a fist with just a pinhole of light showing through the space between the palm and fingertips. Close one eye and look through this pinhole with the other eye. Adjust your fingers so you can see just the core of the sun but not the bright rays that emanate from its periphery.

The light should not be unpleasantly bright but should appear as soft multicolored rays of light inside the palm of your hand. This energy is absorbed by the pineal gland and is said to contribute to optimal wellness of body, mind, and spirit. "Breathing" in this light energy may also help prevent SAD (seasonal affective disorder.)

While we're on the subject of sunlight, *moderate* exposure to sunlight is a healthy practice. Overexposure in the sun or tanning booth increases risk of skin cancer and looking like aged leather. Enjoying sunshine in moderation is an important component for health, feels great, and is fun! As the late John Denver reminded us, sunshine on our shoulders makes us feel happy and high.

Only Dopes Use Dope

Drugs and alcohol *occasionally* provide a glimpse of higher states of consciousness. Being "under the influence" is the best way most persons know to change their state of mind. While artificial highs may allow a peek of Heaven, the user always comes down. Historically, most persons in the West have not been aware of "natural highs", of non-drug paths to euphoria and peace.

We each are searching for our way back Home and have vague memories of our true Spiritual Nature. We miss our eternal "parents"—Mother/Father God—and our Soulmates from the Other Side. This longing creates an inner anxiety, confusion, and emptiness that cries out to be filled.

Life's problems cannot be solved by swallowing, injecting, or snorting various substances. Given the high potential for substance abuse, it's better to pursue more natural paths to higher consciousness. Those dedicated to Self-realization will definitely want to avoid the pitfalls of illegal drug use and alcohol abuse.

From a metaphysical perspective, drug and alcohol abuse can cause serious spiritual problems. When they "die", addicts on Earth carry those addictions to the Other Side and will have to deal with those issues again. Addiction is also one cause of "possession" or "haunting" by ignorant and confused spirits. Although this admittedly sounds "Twilight Zonish", here's the model.

Souls still addicted in spiritual dimensions can only cop a buzz by hanging out *with or inside* an addict in the physical plane. That is, Souls with addictions get their fix by being in the aura or energy field of one who is actively abusing. "Ghosts" are Souls who can't or won't stay on the Other Side because of a shocking death, an excessive attachment to the physical, or for revenge motives. Psychics have described seeing more and more malicious spirits surrounding a person as he or she gets more and more drunk.

For all these reasons, get high naturally and please don't use drugs or abuse alcohol.

Read Widely

"The mind, once expanded, never returns to its original size."
—Oliver Wendell Holmes

Many authors and poets throughout history and from varying cultures have written about the mysteries of the Soul. The
timeless nature of classical literature attests to the essential
wisdom of their words. Notice how many great writers are listed
with those who believed in reincarnation.

A wide knowledge of eclectic information and various phi-
losophies expands your grasp of reality. Open your mind and
broaden your horizons with literature; read topics that are exciting to you. I've been fascinated lately by books about UFO's
and channeled entities. I may not agree with or understand
everything I read but I learn something from every new re-
source.

For example, I've long grappled with the question of why
innocent children suffer tragically. In *Bringers of the Dawn*,
star people explain "You will find that events do not come out
of the blue. Some of you believe that you create your own reality but that others do not create theirs—especially little babies
who have all kinds of things happen to them or children who
are abused."

"It is a difficult concept for many of you to grasp that seemingly helpless children or starving people also create their own
reality. Whenever you buy into the victim mentality, you send
people the idea that they are powerless and you make that
probability one for yourselves. You must learn to honor other
people's dramas and lessons. Realize that the newspaper is not
going to tell you about the potential for change that exists for
all of those involved in a particular scenario."

"So, please, with any newspaper event or world drama in
which it looks as if people are hopeless victims, honor them
and honor yourself by saluting that they created their own reality. It may not be a reality that you need to learn from or
anything you feel a need to participate in... others must go
through the realms of density to bring them to light. Sometimes the greatest enlightenment lies in the greatest catastro-
phes and the greatest difficulties."

I am cautious about channeled sources but this information felt right and rang true *for me*. We learn by venturing
forth and exploring different aspects of life, including reading
widely.

Over the years, I've studied and/or attended many different denominations and religions. This has helped transform me into an *Universal Christian*. I see the Spirit of God and Christ reflected in all sincere paths; as such, I can't fathom a God who demands adherence to any one religion or set of beliefs. Awareness of and participation in different spiritual approaches reminds us that all roads lead to the Divine.

For at least one half hour before bedtime, read positive and inspiring literature. Just as "you are what you eat," you are also what you put into your mind.

Drumming and Vocalizing

"It isn't hard to find the truth. What is difficult is holding on to it, sustaining it. To maintain that truth we do self-inquiry, we meditate, we chant, and we constantly remember God."
—Swami Chidvilasananda

Sound and rhythm strengthen our connection to Prime Creator. Repetitive sounds include chanting, singing, and toning. African, Sufi, and Native American drumming and singing have helped open my heart and Soul. At this point in my spiritual growth, drumming and sound are as meaningful teachers as reading and talking. Check it out!

Western societies have traditionally considered ceremonial, ritual, and earth healings as superstitious and demonic. It's an age old control technique. Label anything you disagree with or don't understand "occult" and many people will blindly believe it. From my perspective, Eastern and Native spiritual understandings are closer to "the truth" than many Western religious teachings.

If anything is demonic, it's the way Western cultures have forced their religions, hang-ups, sugary junk foods, alcohol, cigarettes, armaments, and diseases on third world persons. Many Native Cultures were already harmonious with Mother Earth and the Great Spirit. Mistreatment because of different skin color, religion, and culture is a sad chapter in history. But hope! Most Native persons have forgiven the past and their sacred circle is open to all.

Repetitive rituals with drumming and chanting create a spiral of energy and a healing aura for all life in the area. Spiritual ceremonies ground and uplift energy and recall our Spiritual Source. Earth peoples don't worship the moon, animals, and other aspects of nature but, rather, recognize them as various facets or faces of the Creator. Ho! (Amen)

After a Native American ceremony by the ocean with 200 relatively enlightened persons, that part of the beach was palpably energized into a *sacred spot*. A friend saw a stooped, elderly man walking slowly down the beach. He stopped at the sacred site and paused for a long time, looked around, slowly bent down and picked up some sand in his hands. Then he suddenly straightened up and walked quickly down the beach while intermittently waving his hands high in the air. Another happy feet recipient of the energy vortex created days before!

I couldn't resist sitting, meditating and doing yoga there the rest of the week and experienced a miracle each day of the week. On the first day, a great blue heron taught me a telepathic lesson. I was power walking down the beach and started to pass the bird when a powerful thought/voice told me to sit down and be still. I usually don't interrupt my aerobic workouts but was impressed by the strength and clarity of this communication. For five minutes, the heron waited completely motionless in the water.

Just as I started to get impatient and thought "what lesson is this teaching?" suddenly, the heron struck its beak into the water and caught a small fish. A clear lesson presented itself in a nanosecond: "Be *patient*, Mark. Consider how long the heron waited for just a morsel of seafood. How much more patient can you be given your goals to help, teach, and serve others." And that was exactly what I needed to hear at the time.

On the second day I saw the Spirit Being with Elaine as already discussed. That night, two hundred of us sang, chanted, drummed, prayed, and stated our affirmations aloud. As the ceremony ended, I walked to the water's edge to express my gratitude to Creator for such a moving and powerful experience. As an afterthought, it occurred to me how magical a shooting star would be—like icing on the cake. At that moment, a bright shooting star appeared from upper right to lower left in the sky; a moment later, another appeared from upper left to lower right.

On the third day I saw my first UFO as I'll describe later. On the fourth day, several dolphins beached themselves right in front of our condo. A group of persons explored how to get dolphins back into the water after physical means alone didn't work. Prayer and group energy work did the trick and the apparently healthy dolphins remained in the ocean after this interaction.

On the fifth day, after meditating at length, I opened my eyes to find a great blue heron just a few feet away. It was moving its wings, head, and legs in rhythmic gestures unlike anything I had ever observed before while watching these beautiful creatures. Avian yoga?

On the sixth day, we watched a complete lunar eclipse and had another nighttime beach gathering. After midnight, when only a few of us were still present, the moon appeared to be pulsating like the throbbing of a heartbeat. A luminescent blue halo appeared around the moon and expanded outward; later, a reddish ring of light was also visible. In all my years of watching the night sky, I had never seen anything like it. I was convinced the moon is a living, conscious creature.

What a magical week! It was unlike any I've ever experienced and was no doubt created, in part, by the group drumming, chanting, and Native ceremonies.

Imagine—and get ready for—the entire planet vibrating with higher energies of Love and Light. To assist that transformation, use drumming and vocalizing at home and with spiritual study groups. We never know which spiritual outreach will achieve critical mass and usher in a New Age for all humanity. See RESOURCES for sources of recorded spiritual chants and songs.

Bodywork

"Bodywork" is important for Lightworkers who are helping and healing themselves, others, and our planet. Bodywork includes chiropractic adjustments, massage, reiki, rolfing, touch for health, therapeutic touch, hydrotherapy, aromatherapy, polarity, reflexology, and energy balancing using crystals, color, sound, and light. Other body/mind/spirit practices include body awareness movements, hypnotherapy, martial arts, tai chi, qi gong, and yoga.

Bodywork approaches offer many potential benefits. More and more persons are exploring "alternative" ways of reaching their fullest potential. Lightworkers, especially, can benefit by using bodywork approaches to assist their inner and outer work. Many on our planet are so filled with fear and ignorance that they can't yet fathom the good news that all life is One. Bodywork helps reverse that process.

An exciting, unprecedented spiritual revolution is underway. Humans Beings are in the midst of becoming, as C.S. Lewis put it, *little gods* and co-creators with God. It is time for humanity to realize its vast potential and shake off the interferences that have held us back for so long. It's time to "see the light" that shines from within and all around—the Divine Light in all life.

When regularly utilized along with other holistic health practices, bodywork techniques assist deep relaxation and heightened awareness, a firsthand experience of that silent space or peace within. These approaches help us *know* we are an integral part of the Great I Am Consciousness. Bodywork helps us follow the Biblical injunction to 'Be still and know I am (we each are part of) God.'

In *Bringers of the Dawn*, the Pleiadians state "We recommend to all of you that you receive bodywork. Bodywork simply involves bringing energy from outside the cosmos into your body, infusing it with your other bodies—mental, physical, emotional, and spiritual... the nervous system is the key to opening your ancient eyes and see, and for you to remember who you are, where you come from, and where you are going. The nervous system must be able to take the electrical current into the body, transduce the grid energy, fit it inside the body, and let the body evolve and nurture itself on this high energy that is consciousness."

They continue "Information is stored in bone and stone. Bodywork serves to bring about a release. You have used the tissue and muscle of your body as armor to cover up your skeleton. This tissue has compacted and buried itself and kept what is in the skeletal form from rising to the surface. You want to access information that is within bone, for bone is where the story is held, while the blocks are held in tissue. You must go through all of these layers to get to the truth inside your body... When you experience some sort of bodywork or crystal work, or you create any kind of movement to higher ground, you get a bigger picture."

For many important reasons, include regular bodywork as part of your wellness program.

Meditations for Manifesting

This meditation, taught to me by Dr. Wayne Dyer, is the reemergence of an ancient technique for which humanity is now ready. Before meditating, mentally affirm what you would like to manifest and co-create in your life. The power of *will* and *intention* are amazing when channeled properly and applied regularly.

My first affirmation is "peace and joy, love and light for all persons everywhere." My second is "that all people enjoy total success and Heaven on Earth now." The third is "I am an outstandingly successful Divine-Human—a great husband, father, family member, friend, author, teacher, doctor, healthy athlete, and spiritual seeker/server." I mentally note the changes I would like to manifest in my life, *always* with the condition they are according to God's will and for the greatest good of humanity. Then I give thanks to God and the Heavenly Host for assistance in realizing these goals.

After stating your intentions, focus on bringing energy up from the 2nd chakra (below the navel) to the 6th chakra (the third eye) as you inhale. Imagine a channel between these two energy centers that allow procreative and pleasure energies to manifest in a higher good for all. The mantra for the morning meditation is "AHHH," the sound of *creation* audible in different names of the Divine such as God, Allah, Ram, Krishna,

Buddha, Wanka Tanka (Native American), and Kahuna (Hawaiian).

As you inhale, visualize energy flowing from the 2nd to 6th chakras. As you exhale, imagine this energy *bursting forth* from the "third eye", creating your desires that are in alignment with Universal Law. Say AHHH aloud during several exhalations, then more softly, then silently for the remainder of the 20 minute meditation.

The evening meditation is the same except the mantra is "OM", the sound of *gratitude* for all our blessings. The OM mantra thanks Mother-Father God and the Heavenly Host who assist and guide us.

Use this meditation twice each day for 30 days and notice the increase in physical, mental, and spiritual wellness. Read *Everyday Miracles: The inner art of manifestation* by David Spangler for an excellent discussion of the concept of co-creating. Manifesting "has much more to do with incarnation—with shaping ourselves and our world—than with acquisition." This is not just a parlor trick or power technique to get what you want. Your outcomes will be proportional to the selfless Spirit of your goals.

Hell No

Conventional wisdom has taught we were born on a certain date, will live a number of years, then die and after judgment day live for eternity in Heaven or "hell." That sounds like a kindergartner's fairy tale to me now.

A good friend just completed a health care mission in a third world country. The mission was organized and funded in part by an evangelical denomination. Sounds like a praiseworthy project, doesn't it? Villagers hiked for many hours over rough terrain to receive dental and medical care. Once they arrived, however, my friend was shocked to learn of the fundamentalist's hidden agenda.

Travel weary natives, some in intense pain, were grouped and assigned an evangelist who showed them a large picture of (a white skinned) Adam and Eve. "They disobeyed God by eating an apple so everyone since then is born into sin. You all will burn in hell forever unless..." Then they showed a huge picture of (also white skinned) Jesus. "This is God's only son. If you accept him as your personal savior, you won't go to hell. Whoever loves Jesus, raise your hand!"

The villagers nervously looked at each other in puzzlement. My friend felt that most raised their hands just to shut these ethnocentric zealots up and get health care. There actually was a color-coded system to track who did and who did not raise their hand. Those who didn't "get saved" after the first sermon were confronted by other members of the Jesus squad until all souls were redeemed.

The oddest aspect of this sad spectacle is that well-educated Americans really believe God works this way. What *fear* these well-intentioned but dreadfully confused "missionaries" must feel inside by believing in such a vengeful and arbitrary deity! This story will hopefully help you break through past misconceptions about "hell" and see common fear tactics as misguided ignorance.

To those with open hearts and minds, Heaven and "hell" are more accurately understood to be states of consciousness instead of places someday in the future. This view lends a new freedom accompanied by a heightened sense of self-responsibility and awe of God's Great Design. Heaven and "hell" are states of mind, body, and spirit that we choose or earn by our every thought, word, and deed. God doesn't judge us or put us anywhere; She always wants only the best for all but allows us the freedom to choose.

Ralph Waldo Trine, author of *In Tune With The Infinite*, stated "The word heaven means harmony. The word hell is from the old English hell, meaning to build a wall around, to separate; to be *helled* was to be shut off from." Just as a poor student is *held* back in school, so is an immature Soul held back or separated from God and knowledge of ones True Nature. Held back not by God but by oneself; as soon as we choose to know God and our Inner Divinity, we are lovingly welcomed and assisted.

In Matthew 25:46, "These shall go away into everlasting punishment", the earlier Greek *Kolasin* meant "cutting off" instead of eternal tormented punishment. Those who sin and ignore their spiritual inheritance cut themselves off from a happy life but God has no time/space limitations for His sheep to return. The word "hell" also means grave, pit or death; while in spiritual immaturity, we are *obliged* to die and be reborn into grosser physical realms to learn lessons the hard way.

Bishop Kallistos Ware said "Hell is not a place where God puts us: it is a place where we put ourselves. The doors of Hell, insofar as they have locks, have locks on the inside." Psalms 139:7-8 states "whither shall I flee from thy presence? If I ascend up into heaven, thou (God) are there: if I make my bed in hell, thou art there." Even when we are in a self-appointed temporary "hell", God is always there, waiting patiently to bring us Home.

In Jeremiah 7:31 and 32:35, God rebukes those who would cause their sons and daughters to pass through fire, "a thing that I had not commanded and that had not come up into my heart." If it never came into God's heart, surely His plan doesn't include wide-scale eternal burning.

Becoming spiritually mature involves understanding the meaning of Jesus' words that the Kingdom of Heaven is within and at hand. An inner heavenly state can always be enjoyed despite ones outer circumstances. As our Souls continue to advance, we have more sublime incarnation choices and aren't, by necessity, required to repeat difficult lessons. We are no longer *held back* but can graduate to higher realms.

Contrary to popular belief, we do not become instantly enlightened after passing over; "death" is not a panacea. A "nonspiritual" person on Earth will not be adequately prepared for heavenly realms on the Other Side. Immature Souls may experience a *temporary hell*, require rest, healing and counseling until they are ready to accept a higher frequency of Love and Light.

As discussed, persons who were addicted at the time of "death" may have the same addiction on the Other Side. Heaven would seem like hell to someone who is imbalanced in any way. That's why temporary "hells" may be experienced in spiritual dimensions or on Earth by persons who are overly attached to drugs, money, sex, golf status, or anything in excess.

Realize that Heaven and "hell" are states of being that can be changed in a heartbeat. Know that there are proven techniques of spiritual wisdom that will make the transition to Heaven much easier and quicker.

Lessons From Nature

Nature is another manifestation of the Divine, a very healing and instructive aspect. Spend time in nature regularly to recharge your physical, mental, and spiritual batteries. Listen to nature's wise teachings. Walk in nature and watch sunrises, sunsets, stars and moon.

Time in nature assists discovery of ones hidden potential and Inner Divinity. This *inner knowing*, the greatest "proof" you are an Eternal Soul, surfaces when you become quiet within. Ones Infinite Self is apparent when you feel and think clearly amidst nature's beauty.

Shuffling barefoot in water, grass, sand, or dirt removes negative energies and collects more positive, grounded ones. Children instinctively know this, that's why their shoes are off whenever possible. When people "grow up", they forget important practices like walking barefoot, spinning and meditating to keep centered and vibrant.

Some persons claim to have experienced delightful nonhuman beings in remote areas of nature like Finhorn. Fairies, gnomes, elves and little light beings love deep woods that are free of negative energies. Although this may sound farfetched, it is one explanation for persistent legends of "little people"—like leprechauns—in various cultures.

Perhaps the "imaginary friends" some children have aren't so imaginary after all. When considering the breadth and diversity of God's creation, it's presumptuous to think humans are the only non-animal specie that inhabit Earth. These little beings will instruct those who ask for assistance and quietly use all their senses in nature's classroom.

Native cultures depict ones *multidimensional self* as human, animal, plant and spirit combined. In dreams and deeply relaxed states facilitated by polarity work, I have experienced life from the perspective of a hawk and an oak tree. Being in nature *initiates* us to our kinship with all life and the totality of who we really are. I love hugging trees, talking to plants, and getting "grounded" by working and being outdoors. I highly recommend doing the same.

Animals are also great teachers; we discern these lessons best when we are centered and peaceful. I perceive their teachings as subtle, clear thoughts that occur even when I'm thinking about something else. One example occurred after our long-time family cat, Friskie, was killed by a car.

I had intended to meditate, do yoga, and write that morning before going to the office. Instead, I consoled my children and had to deal with Friskie's body. I briefly considered putting her body in a trash can; the ground was hard, I had other things to do, and trash pickup was later that day. No one would know the difference. But *it just didn't seem right*; I felt Friskie wanted her body returned to the Earth.

I was immersed in digging, sweating, and thinking about being late for work when a series of gentle, lofty mental messages interrupted my thoughts. The first seemed to be an expression of gratitude from Friskie's Life Force for burying her body in the ground. Next, I received a clear lesson that it's OK to make plans and set goals but that I should be open to life's flow and unexpected changes.

Just as my morning's plans didn't work out, other goals had not panned out recently either. These teachings indicated that both were for a good reason and special blessings would be forthcoming. When doors don't open like I think they should, the counsel continued, maybe I should look elsewhere.

Throughout the day, subtle thoughts continued coming in despite my mind being on totally different subjects. These came in a disassociated way that I had only previously experienced in very deep relaxation. At one point, I was adjusting a patient when I received a clear mental picture of Earth from above, as if seen from a spaceship. The picture zoomed in and I saw my home, practice, family, and life from a different perspective.

A calm thought/voice suggested that what I had been viewing as excessive stress and responsibilities were really blessings, options, and opportunities. I saw through my fears and worries and realized how many beautiful blessings I really had.

These visions and insights occurred in a split second, then I returned to normal waking consciousness and resumed practicing.

Later, another suggestion surfaced that, instead of selling my entire practice, perhaps the flow was to find a partner and practice only 3 days per week. Then I would have more time for writing and teaching yet could continue to care for my patients. This was prophetic of how things did work out within that year.

The next teaching surprised me: "You teach others about their true Spiritual Identity but why are you afraid you'll always be trapped in physicality? Remember that one day you'll be completely in the Spirit Realms again. Don't be too homesick or discouraged by the density on Earth."

In the last "transmission," I perceived Friskie bidding me farewell and thanking me for all my kindness to her. Perhaps these subtle communications were made possible via heightened energies she experienced during her transition back into Spirit.

Iasos says that Beings in the Elemental Kingdom manifest energy into physical patterns and include all physical forms from electrons to plants, human bodies, rivers, planets, and beyond. Elemental beings increase their size as they evolve; Earth is an ancient Elemental.

Elementals "are under obligation to materialize whatever they pick up from the thoughts and feelings of mankind. This relationship was intended to facilitate the remanifestation of 'heaven on earth' but as humanity's thoughts and feelings fell into general imperfection, these elemental beings were obligated, against their preference, to outpicture this mass imperfection—resulting in all the nature extremes of tornadoes, hurricanes, volcanoes, earthquakes, and the polluted oceans and atmosphere."

Appreciation and love of all Nature, including your body elemental will assist establishing an inner and outer Heaven. For all these reasons, take time to get quiet in nature and learn valuable spiritual lessons from plants, animals, nonhuman forms, and other elementals.

Tibetan Rites

Read *Fountain of Youth* by Peter Kelder for a fascinating account of "rites" or yoga techniques used by Tibetan yogis. These "lamas" or priests usually live robustly past 110 years of age; yoga is one of their secrets to long robust lives.

The rites accelerate and balance chakra energies that—like any energy waves—have optimal frequency, amplitude, and direction. When functioning optimally, we radiate energy and realize our True Nature as vibrant and vital parts of life. When these energies are blocked or imbalanced, we become energy deficient, ill, anxious, unhappy, and die prematurely.

The rites have a holistic effect, that is, they benefit body, mind, and spirit. Physically, soft tissues (muscles, tendons, and ligaments) are stretched and strengthened. Yoga postures also exert internal pressures on organs, thereby toning and massaging internal viscera. The mind becomes more healthy with balanced energy flow and increased oxygenation via deep breathing. Most importantly, spiritual energies are awakened and harmonized.

I practiced the rites daily for three years and found them to be of great benefit for only a 15 minute investment of time. Kelder's book can be read in a couple hours and is an extremely interesting discussion of how we can exceed limiting barriers.

Uplifting Music

The tone, volume, and rhythm of music can elevate the Soul or cause a headache. Kirlian photography and energy research have documented improved plant growth and more harmonious auras in response to inspiring music. Great music calms and transforms us. Classical music, particularly *baroque* pieces by Beethoven, Brahms, Mozart, Tchaikovsky, and Vivaldi, have endured partly because of this effect on our Timeless Selves.

More recent artists whose music soothes and heals the Soul include: Steven Halpern, Jeff Lantz, Enya, Tim Wheater, Iasos, Cecilia, Robert Gass, Herb Ernst, Georgia Kelly, and Chris Snidow. A group of persons who had experienced NDEs selected the music of Iasos as being most like the music they had heard on the Other Side.

Music from Native cultures triggers ancient memories that it's time for all persons to realize they are One. Examples include Carlos Nakai, William Eaton, Peter Kater, Rick Roberts, Medwyn Goodall, Gabrielle Roth, and Brooke Medicine Eagle.

Recommended contemporary acoustic music includes: Yanni, Fresh Aire, Tangerine Dream, Andreas Vollenweider, George Winston, Craig Monticone, Christopher Franke, Tony O'Connor, and artists on the Narada, Windham Hill, and Cloud 9 Music labels. I listened to these various artists while writing *Toward Heaven On Earth* and appreciated the sublime energies and beautiful musical background.

After lunch on my 44th birthday, I enjoyed my usual midday ritual: prayer, spinning 33 times, the pillar of light meditation, and a 20 minute nap. After falling asleep and while snoring, I dreamed I was hiking up a steep mountain with another person. My old and feeble companion was covered with a hooded cloak and I alternately had to carry, push, pull, and prod this stooped figure up the mountain side. I cut through briars and we repeatedly fell down and slid on loose rocks but after a long struggle, we finally reached the top.

I turned to the mystery person and pulled back the hood to see—myself. I realized that the burdensome person represented the "negative" aspects of myself: fear, worry, regret, etc. The climb symbolized my life up to the present moment. My empowered and disempowered selves then hugged and instantly merged into, alternately, a strong person, a hawk, and a being of light.

I began to joyfully run across a grassy plateau and, encountering a ditch, effortlessly jumped it. Soon, another larger chasm appeared and I easily soared across it. Then a huge canyon loomed ahead; without hesitating, I leaped across it, totally sure I could traverse that vast gulf. At that moment—while still deeply asleep—the song "I Believe I Can Fly" by R. Kelly began playing as if on a heavenly sound system.

Tears literally came to my eyes as I soared high and far, viewing beatific scenes that represented the many blessings and opportunities ahead in my life. My life mission and dreams were clearly identifiable and obviously attainable. After a while

I gently landed and gave thanks, fully ready to go forth as an enlightened and unstoppable spiritual warrior.

I'll never forget that birthday present, especially the part when the music kicked in. I use inspiring music throughout my seminars to enhance opening to love, light, and life. Regularly enjoy music that can assist *your* spiritual unfoldment: "I believe I can fly, I believe I can touch the sky, think about it every night and day, spread my wings and fly away, I believe I can soar, I see me running through that open door, I believe I can fly..." I believe you can fly, too!

Alternative Healing Approaches

It's difficult to experience Heaven on Earth when suffering from serious health conditions that persist despite—and sometimes because of—conventional medical treatment. Invasive medical treatments like radiation, chemotherapy, and drugs with side effects make it difficult or impossible for natural healing to occur. More conservative and preventive health care measures may help without destroying the body's equilibrium.

Healing techniques should be evaluated objectively regardless of profit considerations. The health care industry has reached $1 trillion per year in the U.S. Big business interests have controlled much of what has passed for "health care." Unfortunately, an overemphasis on drug and surgical approaches has detracted from open minded, well funded explorations of less profitable but potentially beneficial natural cures.

Last year, *USA Today* stated 180,000 deaths and $14 billion uncompensated costs from "the annual toll of medical harm." The October 1995 AMA's *Archives of Internal Medicine* estimates the costs associated with "negative therapeutic outcomes" to be between $30 and $136 billion a year. The authors commented "Preventable drug-related morbidity (illness) and mortality (death) represent a serious medical problem that urgently requires expert attention."

Medical drugs interfere with normal body functioning, have dozens of potential side effects, often don't help, are expensive, turn off important bodily signals, and divert addressing the *underlying causes* of disease. Chopra says "Whether we like it or not, a symptom is something the body wants to express—it is a message—which drugs suppress. If multiple drugs are prescribed for each symptom, new imbalances begin to pile up."

Newer and safer approaches are needed but a wide range of expert opinions exists for both orthodox and alternative therapies. I call for *unbiased* government and independent studies to define what constitutes optimal health care. That will happen only when enough consumers and voters demand it; until then, you must educate yourself.

Natural health care issues to consider include:

* *chelation therapy* to reduce clogging of blood vessels and remove excess heavy metal toxicity
* *homeopathic remedies*, long used in Europe as much or more than conventional medical approaches
* *herbal remedies* used for many centuries by various cultures to assist healing without major side-effects
* *mercury amalgam removal*, a hotly debated topic in dentistry needing objective scientific research
* *avoiding* mandatory and experimental *vaccinations* when other health factors are optimally met
* *alternative AIDS treatments* that address root causes of life-style habits, impaired immunity and latent infections
* *parasite removal* and internal detoxification programs; animals are regularly deworming, what about humans?

See APPENDIX for further reading about these admittedly controversial but potentially important health care topics.

Experience Your Own Birth and "Death"

Birth was not your beginning, only another transition in Eternity. The Real You preexisted your present body and will survive bodily decay. "Death" is not a punishment but an important, exciting experience. Recall a time in your life when you experienced the greatest peace, joy, and enthusiasm—then multiply it by a million. That's what leaving the body is like for Souls who have been cooped up in physicality and spiritual amnesia.

Visualizing your own birth and death is an immensely instructive experience. Most people work best with "deadlines";

remembering you have limited time *in this incarnation* motivates you to get on with it. Imagining your own birth and death
takes away much of the death anxiety that haunts so many.
You're then freer and braver to follow your bliss and live well.
Self-actualizers get over death of loved ones more quickly because they know it doesn't really exist.

If you feel emotionally strong enough to experience this
technique, affirm that you always are protected and assisted
by God and Christ and surrounded by Love and Light for higher
spiritual growth. Become deeply relaxed and centered. Tape or
have someone read the following instructions so you can fully
experience the technique.

"Using all your senses, glimpse your real Home where part
of your multidimensional Self always abides. Recall a sensory
cue that reminds you of your Heavenly Home in another dimension: smell a fragrance, hear angelic music, see beautiful
light displays and celestial nature settings. Take a deep breath
and remember you never really fully left Paradise. This will
empower you to experience your Earthly sojourn more calmly
and courageously.

Now picture your Soul just moments before birth into this
lifetime. Visualize your True Self as white light, pure energy
or formless Love with varying colors like a candle flame. Recall the moment when your Soul agreed to complete union with
your physical body.

Now, do a short life review—as if watching a film of your
life in fast forward. See yourself being born, crying, crawling,
walking, and growing. Review highlights that remind you of
the phases throughout your life—the first day of school, ado-
lescence, your first kiss, sports events, church confirmation,
special awards, graduation, and so on.

Make sure you also include a recollection of important *spiritual* milestones. Recall when you first glimpsed the good news
that you are an Eternal Soul. Remember the moment when
you just transiently recalled that your Essential Self is one
with the Creator. Revisit the time when you perhaps even
briefly remembered your Soul's mission. Now, reconnect with

those special times when you loved and assisted others self-lessly.

Picture other milestones as you mature through young adulthood: your first job, important friends and family, mar-riage, becoming a parent, and entering middle age. Regardless of your current age, evoke images of growing older, getting white hair, having grandchildren, retiring, noticing bodily degenera-tion, and preparing for passing on.

Next, visualize yourself several moments before dying. Notice your appearance, age, and surroundings. The more de-tailed and clear the image, the more beneficial the experience will be. Who is with you? What are you dying from and how prepared are you for the transition? Picture your Soul leaving the body and moving toward the Light. Using imagery com-monly described in NDE reports, imagine what you see, feel, and hear as your Soul leaves the body.

Impassively visualize your body being prepared for burial or cremation. Deeply realize it's just a shell that you've out-grown. Notice the curious objectivity you feel as your True Self views the now lifeless body to which so many persons are overly attached.

Now imagine your funeral or memorial service. How do your friends and family *really* feel about you? What are people say-ing and remembering about your life? What about your life endures beyond death: your business and financial accomplish-ments or your kindness and service to others? Picture your Soul as it looks down on the whole situation and sends reas-suring messages to grieving loved ones. Feel your Self sending peace and joy, love and light to all those in need.

Finally, picture your body's final resting place. If you were cremated, where are your ashes scattered? What words and thoughts were expressed as your remains were interred? If you were buried, what would you like the monument stone inscrip-tion to be? Hear your Soul expressing gratitude to the physical body for being its vehicle for a time.

Spend as long as you like at your grave site, reviewing your life and remembering your Soul's mission. What final gifts can you relay to those on Earth before you return to your spiritual

Home Base? Again, share the Love and Light—now so obvious to you—with those suffering in confusion, fear, and spiritual darkness. Send more teachings, blessings and assistance to those on Earth.

Now that you can see clearly through the illusion of birth and death, you *know* for a fact there are never any final good-byes in God's Plan. When you are ready, imagine the Real You gently letting go of the physical realm. Feel your Infinite Self being lovingly transported to the next realms for further adventures: loving, learning, enjoying, and serving God in all Its manifestations.

Now that the 'birth and death' visualization is completed, realize that it was just an exercise in your mind. If you found aspects of aging and dying that were disconcerting, it's not too late to do something about it. You still have time to make *better choices* and create improved outcomes.

If you felt peaceful about your visualization, that suggests you are on the right track and need only continue to commit to constant, never-ending improvement. Today is the first day of the rest of your life; resolve to live your remaining days in a way that you'll be *proud* to review someday when you actually pass on.

When you're ready, slowly let your consciousness return to the waking state. Affirm that you will feel completely relaxed, rested, and peaceful. Leave all tension, negativity, worry, and fear behind. Pray that these efforts toward spiritual growth will be recognized and assisted as you grow toward ever greater spiritual peace, love, and understanding. Wiggle your toes and fingers and slowly open your eyes."

You may use this technique as often as you like. It is especially useful in group work when followed by sharing of insights afterwards.

Order Your Affairs

People who know they are "dying" are counseled to prepare ahead; settling ones affairs is prudent advice when "death" is imminent. Similarly, the transition toward becoming a realized Soul is enhanced by having ones Earthly affairs in order.

Have a will, durable power of attorney, and living will prepared. Maintain enough life insurance so your family is taken care of should you graduate sooner than expected. Write out and sign your preferences for funeral services and interment. Let significant others know where important documents are kept. Completing these tasks frees up energy for living fully today. Now you're prepared for passing on, whenever that may be.

If you had only 24 hours to live, what would you want to say to loved ones? Then say it so you won't have any regrets should your passing be unexpected. Express your love and discuss important matters like death and dying while things are calm. This is especially important for children or adults with high levels of death anxiety.

Start slowly and gently, though. One friend tried to discuss "death" openly for the first time with his anxious 72 year old mom. Her reaction was "Why are you talking about this? What's wrong with me?" She became so upset that she experienced (created) chest pains and called the ambulance to be hospitalized. All physical tests were normal. Now *that* is death anxiety!

Live as if you will reach age 100 *and* as if today is your last day on Earth. Maintain a happy medium. For example, some persons waste countless hours keeping their homes compulsively perfect inside and out. That's overdoing it. At the other extreme are slobs who need to streamline their living environment. The outer reflects the inner. Organizing your outer life creates room for Soul growth and inner changes.

Take time to really enjoy life, fulfill your roles, do spiritual practices, and follow your Soul's mission. Spend a few hours per week organizing and cleaning living spaces and storage areas. Separate items into four groups: throw away, give away, recycle, and keep. If you haven't used or worn it for a year, consider the first three options. Your quality of life will likewise be more simple and uncluttered.

Life-Scripts

Our language, values and beliefs shape our decisions, actions and, ultimately, our destinies. Most of us are walking around with unconscious negative scripts, bits and pieces of faulty programming from the past that aren't true. Negative internal dialogues effectively hypnotize us into confused, disempowered beings. Those committed to reaching their highest potential will want to invest time to examine and reprogram their tapes.

One technique is to *watch your language*. Remove the words "I'll try, I can't, I should, and maybe I could." Use "I'll do it, there's always a way, I choose to, and I know I can" instead. Also avoid *global statements* and false generalizations such as "*no one* likes me", "*everyone* has it better than me", "you always put me down" or "the world is a mess." Small improvements in semantics eliminate barriers to total success.

Identify six *power virtues* that guide your life no matter what challenges you may face. Mine are: courage, determination, joy, passion, faith, and love. These are the traits that will predominate in your life *if* you anchor them in. Read these aloud using an expressive voice while in peak state: "My power virtues are…!"

Asking great questions is another key to total success. Many people repetitively ask bad questions that reinforce their problem. For example, a depressed person might frequently ask "Why am I tired and down all the time?" We move toward our most dominant thought so it's best to ask questions that trigger positive solutions. A better question would be "How can I feel more energetic and happy every day?" Then the awesome computer-brain will set out to solve the new question.

Other examples of poor questions are "How can I get *everyone* to like me?", "Why does *everything* go wrong for me?" and "How can I make my life *perfect*?" Better positive questions are "How can I love myself and be a good friend?", "What's great— or could be great—about my life?" and "How can I constantly improve and do my best?" Adaptive questions are positive, realistic, and focus on what you can do to improve things instead of depending on someone else.

Identify your *primary life question*, the driving issue that underlies your life's purpose. This question reflects one of the specific purposes your Soul came to Earth to achieve. What issue is so important to you that, if you didn't accomplish it, you feel part of you would die inside?

My *old* primary question was "Why is there so much suffering and sadness on Earth?" There was a time when that question was adaptive; it led me to find answers to life's ultimate questions. The suffering and death I saw in this and, perhaps, past lives drove me to understand why. But by continuing that focus, I literally created those feelings inside myself. It also contributed to humanity's mass delusion that there is lasting sadness and suffering.

My *new* primary question is "How can I help myself and others enjoy Heaven on Earth *now*?" This question stimulates my internal abilities to work toward solutions instead of repetitively focusing on the problems. It addresses my perceived Soul mission and makes me feel resourceful and empowered instead of overly identified with suffering.

To identify your primary life question, first become centered and deeply relaxed. Pray and affirm that your Higher Power will assist these efforts. Let your mind drift over your life and review key moments; allow images, words, feelings, and other clues to arise. What has been your life's primary focus? What riddles have you been trying to solve? What question haunts you and is so pressing that if you don't answer it, you feel your life has been wasted?

Now write down your old primary question:

_____

_____

Your old primary question probably has negative or limiting aspects. How can you improve it? What is a better primary question that is attainable, positive, and solution oriented? Write it out now:

_____

_____

Now you're ready to extinguish the old and condition the new. To *scramble* or extinguish the old, assume down physiology and quickly repeat your old question 10 times using a *mocking voice* as if your old question was incredibly silly. Then repeat it using a Mickey Mouse or other *cartoon character* voice. Finally, say it *backwards* quickly 10 times.

Anchor your new primary question in *peak state* (stand tall with shoulders back and head high, breathe deeply and speak in a determined voice. Recall empowering feelings and past victories. Recall your power cues. Play your peak state music as you dance, cheer, and jump around for at least 30 seconds. You're in peak state!) Boldly state your new question 10 times using your entire body. Emphasize your new life-directing question with hand gestures, accentuate key words, and say it like you mean it.

Another technique for positively reprogramming your self is to develop a *positive incantation*. The principles are the same as above; many persons are subconsciously programmed for failure because of what they repeat to themselves. Listen carefully to yourself and others speak; you may be shocked at how often you put yourself down and repeat what you *don't want*. For example, some people who are trying to lose weight repeatedly say: "I'm so overweight. Everything tastes so good. I don't really like to exercise. My family members are all overweight. I guess I just inherited fat genes." Anyone would be out of shape if they repeated this negative mantra to themselves!

I had unconsciously developed a *negative incantation* (in-*CAN'T*-ation) about not smiling. Here was "my story" why I rarely smiled: "I was born without two front permanent teeth and had gaps after my baby teeth came out. I was so excited when I finally got false teeth in sixth grade but then a boy laughed at me and said my teeth looked like a donkey's. And at my school, you had to be tough and tough guys didn't smile. And then there's those last three past lives in war torn settings. Because of all this, I don't smile easily."

I had unconsciously developed a loser's limp—a set of self-limiting stories about why I couldn't smile easily. I was negatively hypnotized to think I didn't know how to smile. And that hurt my total success. First impressions are so important; by not smiling, people thought I was aloof, arrogant, and un-friendly. My lack of smiling hurt my relationships and professional success. Most of all, not smiling made me feel sad and morose. Confronting all these negative ramifications created sufficient *leverage* to make me change. I realized that not smiling created more pain in my life than changing this habit would.

Now I'm a person who smiles easily and naturally; I *made the decision* to become a person who smiles and took action steps for that to happen. I practiced smiling in front of the mirror. I modeled others who had a nice smile. I asked my loved ones to remind me to smile. I noticed that smilers with imperfect teeth looked better than non-smilers with perfect teeth. And I wrote a *smiling* incantation: "I've remembered my Soul, my heart is free, it's time to let my Light shine; *smiling* and happy is the way I'll always be now that I know we're each Divine!"

Whenever you become aware of old negative incantations, scramble and extinguish them as previously described. Then selectively focus on your *positive incantations* (in-*CAN*-tations) that work best using action verbs, a rhythm, and words that are personally meaningful to you. My new positive *life* incantation is "It is time to remember there's an exquisitely perfect Divine design; I enjoy peace and mirth while experiencing Heaven here on Earth!"

With this information in mind, write your positive incantation:

_____

_____

Recite your positive incantation aloud for at least 5 minutes each day while exercising. Remember to use your entire physiology and a confident, determined voice. Can something this simple work? *Do it* and see for yourself.

Readers, *stay with me* and remember to remain in peak state when mastering and practicing these techniques. I know this is not light reading but these approaches are time-tested and unbelievably powerful when used as described. *Please* take the time and energy to master and apply these principles. You deserve it!

Having created your positive life incantation, you are one short step away from assembling your *life-mission statement*. Corporate mission statements have been a hot item for several years; individuals can also benefit greatly by clearly designing and repetitively reading it. Your mission statement need not incorporate rhymes or rhythm.

My mission statement is "I, Mark Pitstick, see, hear, feel, and *know* the purpose of my life is to be totally successful, enjoy Heaven on Earth, and help many others do the same!" (On my correspondences, a shortened version reads "Assisting transformation toward personal and global Heaven on Earth.")

Spend some quiet time and think about what is most important in your life. How can you succinctly describe your mission and special calling? Get your initial impressions on paper and work with it over several weeks just as an artist works until it's just right. As always, enthusiasm, determination, and body movement increase the degree to which you *own* and personify this statement. Repeat *with passion* daily for two weeks and at least once per week thereafter.

Another powerful technique is to identify the *values and rules* that drive your life. Unconsciously developed inappropriate rules make it difficult to experience the emotions you desire in your life. One woman said she felt loved only when "everyone loved her all the time"; this rule obviously made it impossible to feel loved. A CEO said he felt successful only when he made $3 million per year (he *only* made $1.5 million) and had a 6% body fat (his was 9% which is very low). His unrealistically high standards prevented him from *feeling* successful even though he already was.

While in a clear, empowered peak state, generate a list of your top 10 *towards values*, those emotions or traits you want to increase in your life. What is most important to you in life and what are the characteristics that will help you achieve those goals? Common "toward values" include: love, cheerfulness, passion, vibrant health, fun, adventure, courage, commitment, gratitude, faith, peace, patience, confidence, intelligence, freedom, service, happiness, respect, creativity, chal-

lenge, attractiveness, honesty, learning, and vibrant energy.
Write yours out now:

1. _____   6. _____
2. _____   7. _____
3. _____   8. _____
4. _____   9. _____
5. _____   10. _____

The key is to develop rules that make it *easy* to feel these
positive towards values every day. For each value, write a sentence with the formula: "I experience _____ *anytime* I
_____ or _____ or _____ or _____. For ex-
ample, one of mine is: "I experience cheerfulness *anytime* I smile
or think of loved ones *or* see another person happy *or* breathe
deeply *or* remember God's love." These rules make it easy and
automatic for me to feel cheerful each day. Using this formula,
write your 10 towards rules:

1. _____
   _____

2. _____
   _____

3. _____
   _____

4. _____
   _____

5. _____
   _____

6. _____
   _____

7. _____
   _____

8. _____
   _____

9. _____
   _____

10. _____
    _____

The next step in this process is to identify your *"away from"* values and rules. These are negative emotions and traits that you want to extinguish. Common "away from" values include: fear, unhappiness, regret, failure, guilt, sadness, complaining, procrastination, embarrassment, anger, depression, worry, discontentment, boredom, and frustration.

Write down 6 "away from" values you want to extinguish.

1. _____   4. _____
2. _____   5. _____
3. _____   6. _____

The key is to make these negative traits *very difficult* to experience. The formula is: "I would experience the illusion of _____ *only if* I were to consistently and inappropriately believe _____ instead of _____.

For example, "I would experience the illusion of failure only if I were to consistently and inappropriately believe it is possible to fail instead of remembering that I learn from every event so there is no such thing as failure!"

Using this formula, write out your "away from" rules:

1. _____
_____
_____

2. _____
_____
_____

3. _____
_____
_____

4. _____
_____
_____

5. _____
_____
_____

6. _____
_____
_____

On a big piece of paper or a poster, write your power virtues, new primary question, positive incantation, mission statement, and towards and away from values and rules. Read the page while in peak state and *with passion* for 14 days, then once per week as long as you want to be totally successful. Review and modify your sheet four times per year, preferably at the onset of a new season. These are the "secrets" that incredibly successful people use to reach outstanding levels of accomplishment in every area of life. They'll work for you IF you regularly and actively read, upgrade, and embody them.

Pillar of Light Meditation

This technique, as described by Marciniak, accelerates and balances the twelve chakra centers, energy vortexes for various life focuses. Each has a particular location indicated in parentheses and include: the 12th (in deep space of the Universe), the 11th (Milky Way galaxy), the 10th (in our solar system), the 9th (between the Earth and the moon), and the 8th (about a foot above the head.)

These chakras represent potential higher levels of influence by our *multidimensional selves*. That is, your physical body is just one part of the totality that comprises your Real or Cosmic Self. Part of your energy may manifest, serve and learn elsewhere in the Universe while your body is on Earth.

The 7th or crown chakra (crown of the head) is the center for *cosmic consciousness*, those energies that recognize God is All and a perfect Divine Plan operates in the cosmos. The 6th chakra (over the *third eye*, the spot just above and between the two eyes) entails *higher powers* of intuition, wisdom, and "paranormal" abilities. Tears shed without really crying may reflect opening of the 6th chakra center.

The 5th chakra (throat) is the center for *planetary consciousness* and speaking your truth. Getting "choked up" may indicate activation or blockages here. Humanity's collective energies are rising more into this level, thus the *speaking out* about various abuses that were once hidden and not discussed.

The 4th or heart chakra (center of chest) is the bridge between the lower and upper energy centers in the body. The heart center contains energies associated with all types of *love*, from platonic to unconditional. While being activated or blocked, pressure over the sternum—like your heart is breaking—may be felt.

The 3rd chakra (below the sternum, over the solar plexus) is associated with power, fortune, and fame. The 2nd chakra (just below the navel) contains energies relating to pleasure by any means. The 1st chakra (perineum, behind the genitals) is the site of energies associated with survival of death and concern for sufficient safety, food, water, and shelter.

While relaxed in a quiet setting, pray that the Light of God and Christ heal and harmonize all chakras. Picture a pillar of white Light flowing into each chakra from twelve to one, balancing and optimizing energies at each center. Imagine this beam of Light flowing down your legs and feet, connecting and grounding you with Mother Earth. Then picture the Light flowing through the third chakra (solar plexus) to form first a shield, then a cocoon of Love and Light around you, shielding you from negativity, darkness, and evil.

Enjoy this calm healing Light for several minutes and affirm that you are opening to your *True Nature*. Intend that this Light heals and nourishes every cell in your body. Send this Love and Light out to all people everywhere. Affirm that God and Her Heavenly Helpers love, guide, and assist you always.

Daily practice of this meditation helps you realize this is not just an imaginary exercise for those in "la-la land." It instructs that we are *always* bathed in God's Love and Light; some just haven't remembered or acted upon that truth yet. Use the pillar of light technique to increasingly incorporate Cosmic Energies from God and benefit from His ever-present emanation of Love and Light.

Persistence

Giving up too soon is a major cause of unfulfilled potential. Walt Disney was rejected 302 times before he found a bank willing to finance Disney Land. Extraordinary achievers often fall short of their goals numerous times but don't give up. You never know how close you may be to your goal when you feel like giving up. Discouragement is a signal you need to recharge and try a slightly different approach.

A difficult lesson about persistence occurred several years ago when I gave my first seminar after the release of *Balanced Living*. The very reasonable $5 fee went toward refurbishing our city's historic Majestic theater. We publicized the event by radio, TV, newspaper, and flyers and hoped for a full house of 300 people.

The big day finally arrived, ominously, as the first warm sunny day of spring. Not a good sign. I figured maybe only 200 would attend because of the great weather. Show time approached and the crowd was *very* sparse; I still hoped for a late rush to reach the 100 mark. Two minutes before show time and only a handful of people. Maybe the crowd had encountered heavy traffic or trouble parking.

Ten minutes past starting time, only 15 people were there; half of them were close friends and family members. I wanted to crawl away and never give seminars again. I felt humiliated, angry, and very discouraged. But the show must go on. I somehow did my best and worked through to the intermission.

In the backstage bathroom, I was still in shock about the turn out. What could be worse? I quickly found out. As I urinated forcefully, I discovered, to my horror, that my wireless microphone was still on. Hope springs eternal: maybe the audience didn't hear it. I peeked through the curtain and saw people rolling with laughter. They heard.

I could see a little humor in it all but was mostly bummed out; then my friend Paul came backstage and made me laugh with his own story. He had promoted a bluegrass concert but only 8 people, including 4 family members, attended. The other four were dye-in-the-wool music fans, though, and told the band "Boys, if you're good, we'll listen all night!" After the first song, those four got up and left. That helped some.

Now, four years later, I can appreciate many lessons from that trying day:

- Never give a seminar on the first warm sunny Saturday afternoon in spring in northern climes.

- Small Appalachian towns aren't hotbeds for seminars about higher consciousness and holistic health yet
- Many persons aren't interested in reaching their fullest potential. A seminar on Elvis sightings, JFK's sex life, baseball cards or drag racing would have fared better.
- When following your bliss, be prepared for disappointment and don't be discouraged when encountering obstacles.
- Don't let external responses like small audiences prevent you from being true to your mission. Continually improve your program and focus on those who do benefit from it.
- Such experiences are humbling and temper the ego

Not everyone can draw crowds of thousands, be a star, or have an impact on the multitudes. We each can, however, listen to our inner voices and follow that calling wherever it may lead. If we reach only one other person, who knows how far reaching those positive repercussions might be.

I shared my "Majestic story" with Michael Price, a trainer with Tony Robbins. He told of a friend who gave a seminar expecting 1000 people but only 15 showed up. The speaker decided he would give that seminar *as if* 1000 were in attendance. After the inspiring talk, an audience member introduced himself as the CEO of a large company and invited the speaker to address the company's 1000 employees.

One very special aftermath of my Majestic talk occurred with "Ed", an audience member with terminal cancer. Ed became a patient after hearing my discussion of NDEs, our true Soul Nature, and other spiritual verities. His condition was too advanced to respond to holistic health measures but we had several fine talks about survival of consciousness after "death" and a magnificent Divine Design despite appearances to the contrary.

When he passed on, I visited the funeral home. Ed was beloved by many and the line of visitors was long. Ed's wife, Jean, saw me and motioned for me to come up by the casket. It was the first time I had line cut at a funeral but she insisted. She proudly introduced me to her family and shared Ed's special experience just before his passing.

Ed had been in a coma for three days and was very near death when suddenly he became alert. He couldn't talk but kept smiling and pointing out the window up to the sky. When Jean started to leave to get a drink of water, he hoarsely gasped "Don't leave me." She reassured him that she would never leave. He smiled, pointed excitedly again toward the sky and said "I love you", closed his eyes and passed on. Jean felt that our talks had decreased Ed's fears, prepared him spiritually, and assisted this wonderful transition experience. I would now gladly suffer through a thousand humiliations to help just one person in such a special way. I'll persist with my mission until the day I pass and thereafter through Eternity until I'm assigned to a new job.

Reach peak state daily and review your goals and dreams. Fueled with an unstoppable desire, you won't become discouraged easily. Remember that all successful persons meet with repeated obstacles but persevere. Add *persistence* to your list— along with patience and surrender to God's will—of "must have" traits for total success and achieving your Soul's dream.

Lessons From Suffering

"When one door closes, another opens. But we often look so long and so regretfully upon the closed door that we fail to see the one that has opened for us."
—Alexander Graham Bell

A greater plan than we can imagine is always at work, *especially* when suffering and tragedy are involved. God does not make us suffer; our Souls—in alignment with Universal Law and in accordance with God's will—purposely *choose* life events that will foster optimal Soul growth. That is the crucial question to ask yourself in the midst of tragedy—what spiritual lessons can be learned from this? Everything happens for a reason although we may not comprehend it at the time.

One way humans worsen the suffering in their lives is by not forgiving or letting go of past negative events. The Aborigines said "All humans are spirits only visiting this world. All spirits are forever beings. All encounters with other people are experiences, and all experiences are forever connections. Real

People close the circle of each experience. We do not leave ends frayed as Mutants do. If you walk away with bad feelings in your heart for another person and that circle is not closed, it will be repeated later in your life. You will not suffer once but over and over until you learn. It is good to observe, to learn, and become wiser from what has happened. It is good to give thanks, as you say, to bless it, and walk away in peace."

In *Tying Rocks to Clouds* by William Elliott, Elisabeth Kubler-Ross, M.D., says "Most of our suffering is self-imposed. Some people have to suffer because they made somebody else suffer before. They want to have a clean slate. They want to make up for some boo-boos they've made earlier." The law of karma is swift and sure. Unless we repent and ask for forgiveness, we have to pay for our mistakes and learn the hard way. Suffering is one way to *atone*, to remember we're "at one" with all life.

Another major cause of suffering is forgetting our True Nature and believing the *illusion* that "death" and tragedy have the last word. When we *really remember* we are timeless extensions of the Creator, fear and worry vanish. When we can't see through the illusion of physicality, we suffer.

Richard Bach says "Don't be dismayed at good-byes. A farewell is necessary before you can meet again. And meeting again, after moments or lifetimes, is certain for those who are friends." This is a tough one to remember, especially in the midst of suffering, dying, and death.

As I write this, my family is at a funeral home paying their respects to one of my daughter's classmates. While playing in gym class, "Mandy" suddenly collapsed and died. This lovely, friendly, and helpful child was gone without any farewells. Why? And how can we make sense of such a seemingly tragic and untimely death?

In *Angel Letters*, Sophie Burnham shared the story of a woman whose daughter was critically ill: "As I prayed, an understanding came to me. This small child that I loved so much was not 'mine.' She belonged to something much higher and stronger than I, and if she and God had decided it was time for her to leave, there was nothing I could do but be thankful for the time that I had been able to share with our little angel and feel blessed to have had her in our lives. This understanding came with a rush of peace and love that I cannot begin to describe. I felt a light in the room, I opened my eyes and saw a white glow, almost like a cloud around her bed. I felt mesmerized by the light and the feeling of love."

Kubler-Ross says "suffering (unfortunately) provides very little growth for most people. One of my (spirit) guides said to me, 'When I'm born again to a human body, I want to die of starvation as a child.' I'm very blunt, very outspoken, and I said, 'You're really a jerk! You would choose to be born to die of starvation! What kind of an idiot are you?' He said with incredible love, 'Elisabeth, it would enhance my compassion.' I got goose pimples! That taught me a lesson. Suffering has many faces. I'm sure many, many millions of people who suffer have chosen suffering in order to grow."

In *The Celestine Prophecy*, James Redfield wrote "We must assume every event has significance and contains a message that somehow pertains to our questions. This especially applies to what we used to call bad things. The Seventh Insight says that the challenge is to find the silver lining in every event, no matter how negative."

The task is to see the "world as a mysterious place that provides everything we need if we get clear and get on the path." He says that Souls choose, with clarity and purpose, to enter dysfunctional, abusive situations. They do so to break the cycle, to heal, and to awaken themselves and others. A higher life perspective can be gained by becoming deeply relaxed, then accessing the Higher Self and asking "Why did I suffer in that particular time, place, and way? What is the Soul lesson and insight I am to learn?"

Important lessons are gained from suffering. Spiritual wisdom holds there are no accidents and no tragedies despite apparent evidence to the contrary. Marlo Morgan says Divine Oneness planned no suffering to any living creature, except what the creature accepts for itself. Of Aboriginal beliefs, she writes "each individual soul on the highest level of our being could, and sometimes did, select to be born into an imperfect body; they often came to teach and influence the lives they touched... All diseases and disorders, they believe, have some spiritual connection and serve as stepping-stones if Mutants would only open up and listen to their bodies to learn what is taking place."

"Spirit Woman said that members of the tribe who had been murdered in the past had selected prior to birth to live their life to the fullest but, at some point in time, to be a part of some other soul's enlightenment test. If they were killed, it was with their agreement on an eternal level and only indicated how truly they understood *forever*."

This week, a depressed mother threw herself and her three children off a 14 story building. Maybe the children's Souls volunteered to suffer or die to teach important lessons to humanity. Instead of shaking our heads about how crazy some people are, let's address the root causes of poverty, mental illness, spiritual ignorance, hopelessness, and fear. Let's give their suffering more meaning by learning and changing for the better.

Weiss states "It is true that overcoming obstacles and difficulties accelerates spiritual progress. The most serious lifetime difficulties, like severe psychiatric illness or physical disability, may be signs of life progress, not regress. In my opinion, it is often the very strongest souls who have chosen to shoulder these burdens because they provide great opportunities for growth. If a lifetime can be likened to a year in school, then lifetimes such as these can be likened to a year in graduate school. This is probably why difficult lifetimes are more frequently recalled during regressions. The easier lifetimes, the 'rest' periods, are usually not as significant."

Metaphysically, Earth is overpopulated because so many Souls want to be where the action is. From a spiritual perspective, we are living in a very exciting, once in an eon, opportunity to raise planetary consciousness and Light over darkness on a galactic scale. Edgar Cayce said that most children born in this time period are enlightened Souls without karma to settle. They have volunteered to suffer in order to *trigger* a collective remembrances of who we are and why we're here.

Melvin Morse, M.D., in follow up studies of children who had a near death experience, found they experienced profound transformative lessons. They learned that life has a real purpose. They "revere life and see the intricate connections throughout the Universe." Eight years after their NDEs, Dr. Morse found these teenagers to be exceptionally mature, with excellent family relationships, and without behavioral, sexual, or drug problems.

The comforting lesson from Dr. Morse's research is that if these children learned so much from a few moments of nearly dying, how much more do those who actually pass on experience? Perhaps even "premature death" and suffering have an important purpose and meaning. Maybe things are not always as they seem.

Dr. Dyer says "It's important to realize that there are no accidents in our intelligent Universe. Every event, situation, and person in your life has something to teach you, which is why you need to express gratitude for everything in your life... Try not to judge God. Know that hurricanes, tornadoes, crime, and poverty are as much a part of the Divine plan as are sunny days, calm seas, and compassion and prosperity. Your desire to improve conditions is also a part of the plan. So, concentrate on *that* rather than on why certain conditions seem 'wrong.'"

Heaven and Hell Revisited

"It can in no sense be said that heaven is outside of any one; it is within... and a man also, so far as he receives heaven, is a recipient, a heaven, and an angel."

—Emanuel Swedenborg

Jesus spoke of Heaven as a place within, not a physical location: "nor will they say, 'Lo, here it is!' or 'There!' for behold, the kingdom of God is in the midst of you" (Luke 17:21) When pressed for details, Jesus likened the kingdom to leaven, a mustard seed, and a pearl of great price. None of these sound as if He were describing a place in the sky.

In a recent *Christian Century* issue, N.T. Wright wrote that the end time in the book of Revelation "isn't about humans being snatched up from earth to heaven: but, rather, when "the holy city, New Jerusalem, comes down from heaven to earth. God's space and ours are finally married, integrated at last."

As Jesus taught us to pray "Thy kingdom come, on earth as it is in heaven."

During a recent flight, I thought how, as a child, I used to think of Heaven as way up there somewhere and "hell" as deep inside the Earth. But astronomers have peered into deep space and geologists have plumbed the earth's core with no physical findings of either. Perhaps we've been looking in the *outer* for what resides in the *inner*, in the visible for what is invisible.

In the past, many could not fathom that Heaven could be experienced in the here and now; such a celestial state was imagined as somewhere, someday but certainly not on this "satan-controlled" planet and not in these tumultuous times. Heaven and "hell" are primarily levels of consciousness and God has no space or time limits to keep anyone from experiencing Heaven and escaping "hell".

Freeman tells of a "preacher" who began his sermon to troubled and delinquent children with "Are you prepared to spend eternity in hell?" Freeman's reaction was "Preacher, where do you think I am now, sitting here listening to you?" He continues "Dante, from whom the medieval Christians got most of their notions about the place, said that the sign above hell's gate reads, 'Abandon hope, all ye who enter here.' It should have read, 'Abandon reason, all you who believe in such a place.'"

Many persons and theologians agree. God is not a monster who would consign or allow any person to suffer in "hell" forever. That's a concept only an unenlightened human could imagine. God *is* love, goodness, mercy, peace, and understanding. A Being of this caliber doesn't need an eternal place of torture in Its plan for salvation and perfectibility of all.

"Evil" is not as widespread as some might think. The Western world has a long history of "demonizing" those who disagree or differ from them. Elaine Pagels, professor of religion at Princeton and author of *The Origin of Satan* says that the earliest Christians made their opponents out to be the devil— first Jews, then Romans, then other Christians who differed from the fledgling orthodoxy.

She states "It's important for those of us who grew up with the Jewish and Christian traditions to know how they structure the way we think, especially when we are thinking politically and socially... Associating heretics, pagans and Jews with the powers of evil has been a massive theme in Western history."

This practice has continued through modern times, e.g., against gays, other races, opposing denominations, and different cultures. Could *fear of differences* have fueled so many divisions and so much misunderstanding? Have humans unwittingly created evil and "hell" when, in fact, life was meant to be like Heaven? And are enough persons finally awakening—remembering—that God and Love are All?

Heaven and "hell" are a reflection of our energies at any point in time especially at the time of passing. Those who strongly believe in "hell" and judge themselves as evil may experience temporary hell-fires until they are ready for a more loving state. An atheist who believes there is nothing after death may experience just that for a time. A more enlightened Soul might experience a peaceful transition like walking from one room to another.

Someone like Hitler may sleep for eons before his Soul can face the pain he inflicted on others. But Hitler was badly abused as a child; how much pain must a child withstand to be twisted into a torturer? God understands the big picture. So even this epitome of Earthly evil has a chance for redemption whenever he truly repents and desires to know God. God's love and forgiveness are without limit. If I can imagine a Soul like Hitler's being salvageable, certainly God can.

In *Journey of Souls*, Michael Newton, Ph.D., states "All my case work with the spirits of my subjects has convinced me there is no residence of terrible suffering for souls, except on Earth. I am told all souls go to one spirit world after death where everyone is treated with patience and love. However, I have learned that certain souls do undergo separation in the spirit world... These souls don't appear to mix with other entities in the conventional manner for quite a while."

We have the ability to choose Heaven or "hell" in each new moment, no matter what the past. Some use the law of karma as an excuse why they can't act differently. A drug addict might lamely claim it's his karma to be a junkie and live a hellish existence. But no matter what the past held, each person has the freedom to act appropriately this time around. An addict's karma may be the opportunity to overcome drug dependency, erase negative patterns, and help others avoid drugs.

Mary T. Browne, in *Life After Death*, tells of a woman with a serious birthmark covering most of her face. Mary commented to her spiritual teacher, Lawrence, "Must be very difficult karma for that young woman." He responded "No, she is at peace with herself... She has great soul beauty. Anyone who spends time with her will see the inner person. She has served others by her dignity and lack of self-pity. Yes, it was her karma to incarnate with this birthmark. It is her personal choice as to how she deals with this. Her behavior is creating new good karma every moment."

No one is destined to suffer hellishly but some are so afraid and confused that they repeatedly make poor choices. Realizing each person is a maturing Soul is a major step in minimizing "hell-experiences" for ourselves and others. Dehumanizing or demonizing others who act differently only intensifies polarities and reinforces negative societal trances. These are the roots of "hell" that are being increasingly addressed and understood.

In *Life After Death*, Sir William taught "Think of a moment when you were in a total state of peace of mind. This is heaven... We can find heaven on earth. It is right in front of us. It lives within our hearts. We just need to love each other. It really is quite simple." Read *In Heaven As On Earth* by M. Scott Peck, MD, for an excellent and thought provoking novel about this topic.

Rev. Freeman says "It's not that I don't believe in heaven and hell. It's just that I don't believe in them as future eternal dwelling places... I don't believe there are a heaven and hell such as the traditional churches have imagined—dwelling places in the next world, to which we are transported when we die, there to remain through everlasting —in a fiery pit if we were bad, in an angelic city if we were good."

He continues "Heaven and hell are states in you and me. The gulf between them is no wider than a thought. I know people who spend every day in heaven and people who spend every day in hell... The kingdom of heaven is among the heaven-hearted, wherever they are, and that is the only place it will ever be." Earth can also be like Heaven, that's the way it was meant to be.

So let any residual fears about "hell" go now. And remember that you don't have to wait until you die to experience a relative utopia. Heaven is dwelling in the presence of God. You can enjoy Heaven on Earth now and help transform our entire world toward the same. Know that it's possible and it's time to demonstrate that potential.

Meditation II

The recent Harvard "Spirituality & Healing" conference noted: "For more than 25 years, laboratories at the Harvard Medical School have systematically studied the benefits of mind/body interactions. This research has shown that when a person engages in a repetitive prayer, word, sound or phrase—and when intrusive thoughts are passively disregarded—specific physiologic changes ensue. Metabolism, heart rate, breathing frequency all decrease and distinctive slower brain waves appear."

"These changes are exactly the opposite of those induced by stress and can help reduce hypertension, palpitations, insomnia, infertility, premenstrual syndrome, chronic pain and the symptoms of cancer and AIDS. In fact, to the extent that any disease is caused or made worse by stress, to that extent is this physiological state an effective therapy."

Later research established that people experience increased spirituality as a result of eliciting this state regardless of whether or not they used a religious repetitive focus. Spirituality was defined as "experiencing the presence of a power, a force, an energy, or what was perceived of as God and this presence was close to the person. Furthermore, spirituality was associated with fewer medical symptoms." Meditation, anyone?

Components for successful meditation include:
- Find a quiet spot where you won't be bothered by the telephone, excessive noise, or interruptions. Program your mind to ignore outside noises.

- Meditate early in the morning before most of the world awakens and starts the rat race. Prana/chi/life-force is more abundant or accessible before dawn. Getting centered and peaceful is more difficult later in the day when millions of electronic devices and brains are broadcasting negative, erroneous messages.
- Sit with the spine straight. For some, the classic half or full lotus position works well; for others, sitting on a chair with feet on the floor is more comfortable. A pillow or two folded just under the "buttock bones" assists a proper upright posture.
- Place your hands on your thighs, palms up with the thumb and index fingers touching lightly.
- Use diaphragmatic breathing. Let the abdomen move downward and outward as you inhale; gently pull the abdominal muscles upward and inward as you exhale.
- Breathe at a slow, rhythmic pace through the nostrils; breathing through the mouth causes dryness that may interfere with a peaceful, quiet experience.
- Let the jaw and facial muscles relax completely; your lips may just touch or part slightly.
- With eyes closed, shift your gaze to focus on the 6th chakra, just between and above the anatomical eyes.

These steps set the stage for meditation and, with practice, establish a foundation for bodily comfort so the mind can become quiet and the Soul can shine through. In the beginning, meditation is more of a discipline than a spiritual experience. The ego will come up with a thousand reasons why you don't have time to meditate for 20 minutes. *Just do it*. The many benefits of meditation will soon become self reinforcing.

One very powerful but simple meditative approach is to *very slowly* mentally recite uplifting spiritual passages like the prayer of St. Francis, the 23rd Psalm, the Lord's Prayer, or other favorite spiritual passages.

Most meditative techniques use a sound or "mantra" to assist reaching the quiet mind. Research by Harvard's Herbert Benson, M.D., author of *The Mind/Body Effect*, suggests that the particular sound is secondary in importance. Some Eastern culture teachers hold that "bija" mantras, given by meditation instructors only after adequate preparation and commitment, have more power.

(Parenthetically, skeptics may question the ethics of selling techniques of enlightenment. Most persons in the West are motivated by money; paying for any product motivates the buyer to really use it. Spiritual teachers also have an overhead and living to make; they should be reasonably compensated for their time and information.)

Recommended common mantras include the sounds OM and AH. Depending on your spiritual path, you may want to use: God, Jesus, Allah, Buddha, Ram, Krishna, Mother Mary, Moses, Peace, One, Great Spirit, OM Shanti (Sanskrit for Divine peace), Shalom (Jewish for peace), Dog (if you're dyslexic), or any other word that reminds you of the Above One. Use the mantra in three phases: first aloud for a few minutes, then more quietly until just moving the lips without sound, and finally with just silent mental repetition. Mentally repeat the mantra with each exhalation or with both inhalation and exhalation.

As you breathe, focus your attention on the nostrils or back of the throat and just notice the breath rising and falling. "Breath meditations" omit the mantra and just focus on the breath. Proper breathing is an integral part of optimal meditation; breath is the connection, the junction point between mind, body, and spirit.

Let the breath and mantra proceed by themselves naturally and effortlessly. With practice over time, the entire process will become graceful and easy—the most peaceful and blissful time in your life. Chopra says "Meditation is not at all a way of making your mind be quiet; rather, it's a way of entering into the quiet that's already there, buried under the fifty thousand thoughts an average person thinks every day."

Early attempts at meditating may go something like this: 'breathe, say the mantra, oops—I'm thinking, breathe, say the mantra, oops—I'm thinking again.' And so on. I'm a very analytical person; my early "meditations" were 20 minute thinking sessions with only occasional attention on the breath and mantra.

The key is to be patient and continue meditating every day. In time, it becomes a highlight of the day, an oasis of peace and quiet amidst life's hectic demands. With practice, a subtle but very important distinction will become apparent. Thoughts will still come and go (although less often) but you'll be in touch with your True Self that isn't doing the thinking. Thoughts will drift through like fleecy clouds instead of barrages of incessant static.

Whenever you become aware that thoughts are occurring, gently return to the breath and mantra. This is a key point for successful meditation. Anytime you realize you're not focused on breath and mantra, simply return to that focus. You may think the mantra only once before drifting into a deep reverie or space. Whatever needs to happen, will.

Don't delay experiencing inner peace by chastising yourself for thinking during meditation. Self-criticism is just another ruse by the ego to remain the center of attention. The ego/thinking mind/personality are real and important but only relatively so. The ego's fear is that it will cease to exist.

With meditation, the ego continues to function but in harmony with the Eternal Self, allowing us to become Divine Humans. We then can function well in the physical world while remembering this Earthly sojourn is just a fleeting thought in the Mind of Spirit. Experiencing our Inner Divinity prepares us for any eventuality that occurs. We are then truly in but not of the world.

A subject that repeatedly surfaces during meditation may indicate an imbalance that needs addressed and adjusted. Intra-psychic material, layers of negative thinking and repressed emotions may be released over time. Inspirational ideas may also come to your attention. I keep a notepad by my meditation area so I can jot down new insights and ideas after—not during—the meditation.

Several techniques used in conjunction with meditation assist diminution or removal of reoccurring negative emotions. If repetitive mental interruptions occur in the middle of a chant or meditation, *name* the emotion (sadness, anger, lust, guilt, fear, resentment, etc.) three times, then continue meditating.

Clarifying and identifying the recurrent emotion assists pranic healing.

Another approach is to *number* your negative emotions; when you notice them surfacing, instead of experiencing heavy feelings, just lightly note "there goes old #2 again." A last suggestion is to offer your relatively minor sufferings up in honor of those *really suffering*. This opens the compassionate heart to those worse off, helps us realize our many blessings and strengthens our connection with the One.

Meditation is an effortless process when we listen to our bodies and take time to relax and reflect. I fondly remember sitting for long periods in rocking chairs with my Grandma Marsh. She drifted off in a natural reverie and required a moment to refocus when I interrupted her porch meditation. One of the blessings of the senior years is having the time and space to just do nothing. Even brief centered moments with the Inner Self lessen the fears that accompanies aging and approaching "death."

Meditation may seem weird or foreign to some. Part of the resistance is due to deep seated racial, religious, and cultural prejudices. Even today, some "churches" preach that meditation, yoga, and Eastern religions are the work of the "devil." Adherence to such ethnocentric, ignorant, and prejudicial thinking has kept humanity confused and fearful.

You must decide for yourself whether to try something different or new. Some of the most spiritual and loving people I know practice meditation and yoga. Those who wish to *know* they are Eternal Souls and experience Heaven on Earth would be wise to do the same.

An older, very conservative gentleman attended a recent series of yoga and meditation classes I taught. I had an uneasy feeling that he thought the classes (and I) were kooky. After several weeks, he approached me with tears in his eyes, "I just wanted to tell you that the yoga and meditation have brought me more relaxation, peace, and joy than I ever experienced in my entire life."

Are you ready to go out on a limb and try something new? Our Souls have eternity to get it right but we only have so long in this particular incarnation. Will your Soul return Home having remembered and accomplished its mission? Consistent meditation will greatly assist your success.

Deflect Religious Misconceptions

We have for too long been taught untruths or half-truths in the guise of the Truth. It's time to heal old wounds caused by erroneous teachings, to deflect past misconceptions, forgive all, and enlighten humanity. Past institutions and teachers usually did their best while those who purposely distorted the Truth deserve our forgiveness.

If you were taught bizarre notions about God, realize that offending information was incorrect just as your heart and Soul whispered. Armstrong describes an increasing atheism in Europe and notes that some find the idea of no God an improvement over the strange images we have been led to believe are the Truth:

"Those of us who have had a difficult time with religion in the past find it liberating to be rid of the God who terrorized our childhood. It is wonderful not to have to cower before a vengeful deity, who threatens us with eternal damnation if we do not abide by his rules... We imagine that the hideous deity we have experienced is the authentic God of Jews, Christians and Muslims and do not always realize that it is merely an unfortunate aberration."

Religious misconceptions certainly created feelings of confusion, fear, and skepticism for me. Dogmas that never made sense to me, even as a youngster, included:

- God will send (or allow) many persons to suffer in a fiery hell forever
- God would commit atrocities—vengeful punishments by flood, fire, and plague—as described in the Bible
- God knew humans would sin so pre-planned a chance of salvation through the torture and murder of His only son
- all other religions are wrong, inspired by "satan", and a fast track to an eternal "hell"
- Christian missionaries must teach "the gospel" and save the souls of all pagan (non-Christian) people.

If many large congregations in huge buildings believed all this, why didn't I? My youthful mind felt guilty and afraid. I remember praying "Please don't let me go to hell, help me believe all this even though it doesn't make sense." Over the years, I've discovered many others who felt the same but never shared their disbelief. Who would want to be a doubting Thomas or a traitorous Judas?

Many of us were taught "death" was the big moment that precedes either Heaven or "hell" for eternity. Talk about a pressure situation! No wonder death anxiety is such a pervasive and significant fear in our culture. Imagine the emotional stress from believing we have only one lifetime and then either unimaginable pleasure or unspeakable torture *forever*.

During massive "church" building campaigns, creative thinkers devised *a third possibility*, "purgatory," for Souls who didn't quite meet the criteria for either Heaven or "hell." Souls in purgatory supposedly remained in limbo until monetary offerings induced enough priestly prayers to lift them into Heaven.

I vividly remember the funeral of my paternal grandfather, not a saintly man but not a bad guy either. There apparently was some question whether he would make the big leagues or languish in purgatory forever. Offering plates were sent around to lubricate the priest's generosity in praying for his Soul. (In retrospect, church members were the ones who needed the lubrication.) The plates quickly filled with $20 dollar bills from families who didn't have it to give.

I asked one of my relatives what this was all about. "The priest", he explained, "is going to try to pray Grandpa's soul out of purgatory and up to heaven." Even at my young age and despite all the church's official looking power trappings, I realized what a scam it was.

Many others have rejected orthodox religious teachings that were purposely or inadvertently distorted. Historian Karen Armstrong states that by the first century A.D. many "intelligent and thoughtful people turned to them (Platonist philosophers) for an explanation of the meaning of life, for an inspiring ideology and for ethical motivation. Christianity seemed a barbaric creed. The Christian God seemed a ferocious, primitive deity, who kept intervening irrationally in human affairs." The Platonist "needed no grotesque salvation by means of a crucified Messiah."

Prominent Christian "church fathers" have led the way in teaching fear, ignorance, and violence as a way of life. Pope Innocent VIII (what a misnomer) launched the great witch craze in 17th and 18th century Europe. Anti-Semitism, fears of sexuality, an obsession about "satan" and his supposed powers, and the church's repressive nature and appetite for power all contributed to the torture and murder of many thousands of men and women.

Armstrong describes Martin Luther, 16th century German religious reformer, as "a rabid anti-Semite, a misogynist (woman hater), (who) was convulsed with a loathing and horror of sexuality and believed that all rebellious peasants should be killed. His vision of a wrathful God had filled him with personal rage."

John Calvin inspired the Puritan revolution and was very concerned with the social, political and economic aspects of religion. He had theologian Michael Servetus executed for the heretical writings expressed in *Christ the Savior*. Armstrong describes Servetus' beliefs: "the 'Son of God' was not a statement about Jesus' divine nature but simply meant that he was especially loved by God. He had not died to atone for our sins but was simply a teacher who 'showed and taught the way of salvation.' As for the doctrine of the Trinity, that was simply 'a monstrosity,' an imaginary fiction that was 'repugnant to reason.'"

These same ideas occurred to me as a youth; I guess Calvin would have had me killed too. The facts are clear: religious teachings of today were mightily influenced by very powerful and very fallible men. The words of Great Masters who founded religions have been rewritten and misinterpreted over the years. Current religions are a mishmash of truth and fiction compiled from older religions, oral traditions, power plays, mythology, and misinformation.

Freeman states that the Persian religion Zoroastrianism greatly influenced Judaism, Christianity, and Islam. Some Persian religious beliefs that might sound familiar include:

- A Divine Creator who made heaven and earth
- An evil opposition by the leader of the devi's, a term remarkably similar to "devil"
- Heaven for those holy enough and hell for the wicked
- A trumpet blowing angel signaling the dead to rise
- Three messiahs, all born of virgins
- The millennium ending with Judgment Day

The Zoroastrian description of hell, kinder than some current versions, only lasted for an age, after which fire would burn the wickedness out and then all would share in salvation. Freeman states "Many Christian thinkers believe that our idea of an eternal hell was mistakenly imposed on us when early translators used words like *everlasting* and *forever* where the original authors of the Bible had meant the end of the age. In fact, in some modern versions of the Bible, this phrase is used again."

Another example is Mithraism, an ancient Persian religion that predated Christianity. Followers of the god Mithra celebrated his birthday on December 25 and believed this god died but was later reborn. These examples illustrate that today's religions are a combination of fact and fiction. Pray for Divine guidance and direction, then feel free to trust beliefs from your heart and Soul.

Many persons don't realize that Christianity has been a constantly changing and widely debated process since the time of Jesus. The Gospels are not necessarily "the gospel truth" and were written decades or even centuries after Jesus lived. Many of the books in the New Testament had multiple authors and Biblical scholars have argued over which books or parts of books are most authentic.

For example, the First Council of Nicea in 325 AD and future councils changed the original Bible. The *Apocrypha* or hidden writings are books of Christianity that were rejected from the Bible. For additional Biblical information that may have been kept from widespread knowledge, read *The People of the Dead Sea Scrolls* by John Allegro.

Hundreds of years of violent arguments among bishops resulted in settling upon 27 pieces of writing as 'genuine revelation.' The Catholic and Protestant Bibles include different Old

Testament books. Numerous councils and fierce battles shaped what many persons take to be the ultimate in "God's word". As such, human errors and prejudices have been inserted over the years.

Benefit from organized religions and their combined history, wisdom, and strengths. *At the same time*, however, trust your own inner voice and feelings. What if—after prayer, meditation, and study—you consistently get answers different from those of established dogma? I say trust yourself. The Truth is a dynamic and flowing process. Answers that made sense several thousand years ago may or may not be the wisest counsel for you now.

An overweight patient recently asked me about weight loss information. I suggested the *Fit for Life* approach and outlined the principles that include eating only fruit until noon. She responded, "But doctor, I'm a 'Christian' and your advice isn't based on Scripture. The Bible doesn't say anything about eating only fruit till noon!" In shock, I responded "Does the Bible say it's OK to drive a car?"

Combine common sense and appreciation for your Soul's wisdom with respect for religious teachings. If your church has sufficient flexibility to allow and encourage that, great. If not, you may want to consider another approach. Don't let past religious misconceptions stand between you and God.

There's a place for each viewpoint along the spiritual journey. My brother is a deacon in a Baptist church; we don't see eye to eye on some theological matters but we've agreed to disagree while loving and respecting one another. Persons with varying beliefs can find common ground while being tolerant of differences.

Benefit from the wisdom of the Koran: "Do not argue with the followers of earlier revelation otherwise than in the most kindly manner—unless it be such of them as set on evil doing—and say 'We believe in that which has been bestowed upon us, as well as that which has been bestowed upon you: for our God and your God is one and the same, and it is unto Him that we all surrender ourselves.'"

Spiritually Uplifting Films

In Marciniak's books, Pleiadians admonish us to watch little or no TV because electronic media are used to spread messages of fear and confusion. Even "positive programming" can relay undetectable subliminal negative energies. They say that harmful broadcasts by ill-intentioned ETs are transmitted even when the TV is turned off and people with televisions should keep them unplugged except when in use.

This admittedly controversial information, together with more conventional warnings, constitutes ample reason to watch only minimal and high quality programs. If positive films can uplift us, what effect do negative and violent films have? Recent research has demonstrated negative TV viewing increases sadness and anxiety among viewers who internalize unrelated worries. I sometimes have nightmares after watching violence on TV or movies. Sexually explicit scenes often replay in my mind; when I see an attractive female, I'm more likely to envision her as a fantasy sex object than a unique human being and child of God.

Having said all that, well produced combinations of film, music, and theme *can* touch our hearts and Souls. While viewing films with uplifting and spiritual messages, I experience pressure over the sternum, get choked up and have tears in my eyes. These sensations suggest that the fourth (heart), fifth (throat), and sixth (third eye) chakra energies have been activated.

At the 1996 Academy Awards, Christopher Reeve called upon the film industry to address social issues and make a positive difference in our world. His examples of quality films that "have enlightened us, challenged us, and given us the opportunity to learn" included: *Lorenzo's Oil, Boyz N' The Hood, Philadelphia, Thelma & Louise, In Cold Blood, In the Heat of the Night, Coming Home, The Grapes of Wrath, Norma Rae, Silkwood, Platoon* and *Schindler's List.*

Selected family and children's films provide consciousness raising and wholesome entertainment. Examples are: *The Little Princess, The Secret of Roan Inish, The Dark Crystal, The Land Before Time, Charlotte's Web, Fluke, Angels In The Outfield* and most movies produced by Disney. *Touched By An Angel, Promised Land,* and *Highway to Heaven* are examples of enlightened TV.

I marveled as the movie *Pocahontas* highlighted the many positive attributes of Native Americans—what a change from the old cowboy movies! European "settlers", who used to be portrayed as the good guys, were more accurately depicted as plundering racists. And it all ended on a positive note, emphasizing the ever-present potential chance for peace.

Quality films stretch our imaginations and draw instructive parallels to current challenges. Examples include *Oh God I and II* , the *Star Wars* trilogy, *Field of Dreams, Resurrection, Made in Heaven, Powder, Back to the Future, Shine,* Heaven *Can Wait, Stargate, Ghost, Joe Versus the Volcano, Being There, My Dinner With André, What About Henry?, Defending Your Life, Star Trek* movies, and the perennial classic *It's a Wonderful Life.*

Divine-Humans

Throughout history, theologians have debated whether God is a personal or transcendent Being. Some depict the Creator as a loving, caring Father/Mother with personal attributes. Others recognize the vast, transcendent nature of our Source and describe It as Energy, Life Force, and Universal Law. Both views are necessary to fully appreciate the vastness of the phenomena we call God.

And both views have room to include you and me in the equation. From the personalized view, we are children of the Most High, His beloved Creation. In the transcendent model, we each are extensions of the Infinite just as each drop of ocean water is part of the ocean. Appreciating our oneness with God helps us understand both our nature and responsibilities more clearly.

Armstrong captures the crux of the matter as she relates a Nazi death camp story by Nobel Prize winner Elie Wiesel:

"One day the Gestapo hanged a child. Even the SS were disturbed by the prospect of hanging a young boy in front of thousands of spectators. The boy who, Wiesel recalled, had the face of a "sad-eyed angel," was silent, lividly pale and almost calm as he ascended the gallows. Behind Wiesel, one of the other prisoners asked: 'Where is God? Where is He?' It took the child half an hour to die, while the prisoners were forced to look him in the face. The same man asked again: 'Where is God now?' And Wiesel heard a voice within him make this answer: 'Where is He? Here He is—He is hanging here on this gallows.'"

Armstrong comments "The horror of Auschwitz is a stark challenge to many of the more conventional ideas of God. The remote God of the philosophers, lost in a transcendent *apatheia*, becomes intolerable... The idea of a personal God, like one of us writ large, is fraught with difficulty. If this God is omnipotent, he could have prevented the Holocaust. If he was unable to stop it, he is impotent and useless; if he could have stopped it and chose not to, he is a monster. Jews are not the only people who believe that the Holocaust put an end to conventional theology."

God was there in the form of every person present yet none stepped forward to halt the murder. Closer to home, how many of us have remained silent in the face of various injustices? *Imagine*, then co-create a world in which more of us remember our Souls and act as if all Creation is One. Cruelties and injustices will diminish, then cease as more and more persons live according to the truth that they are all of one Spirit.

God doesn't make atrocities happen; humans do and humans can prevent or reverse them. Prime Creator has endowed each of us with an inner Christ Light and awesome powers. The Supreme exists throughout the cosmos *and* within each of us but He/She/It is not a puppeteer. We always have the freedom to choose right over wrong. Acknowledging this truth is too much for some; knowing we each are God's hands on Earth is a fierce responsibility. It's easier to praise or blame God for everything that happens.

Perhaps the little boy *volunteered* to bring humanity one step closer to Heaven on Earth via his suffering. Maybe it's not a coincidence that the boy looked like a "sad faced angel." He may have been an advanced Soul who had the strength to bring in such a sad but powerful lesson. Maybe teachings of that horrible magnitude were needed to awaken humanity to reexamine past patterns.

Let's resolve to learn from all past sufferings and swear their pain will not be in vain. Let's learn from history, forgive, and go forward in unity, peace, love, and harmony. God has both transcendent and personal attributes and so do we. Human Beings are becoming gods or, more accurately, are remembering they always were inseparable from the Creator. As such, we each have the power to act courageously even in the face of adversity.

Some say we volunteered for this mission on Earth *to explore the dark side*. This view depicts God as an ever-expanding Being that is still exploring Itself. Some of God's energy was manifested into Souls who agreed to be pioneers—to find out what happens when there is free will, temptation, and temporary amnesia about our True Nature. An Earthly incarnation is a lofty and exciting opportunity; as such, we each have tremendous joys and responsibilities as Divine-Human explorers.

Levar Burton put it beautifully "Now, here's the wild thing about being a human being: God decided to conduct an experiment. God said, 'Let's create a scenario in which we will experience ourselves as consciousness through the most amount of density possible. We will immerse ourselves in an experience of physical density, and the game will be to remember that we are God—despite being in physical forms.' I know that I agreed to come in and create for myself and others triggers to the knowledge that we are God."

Channeled information from beings not on Earth provides a unique perspective. Because of its controversial nature, temper channeled input with other information and *your feelings*. Marciniak claims to have channeled wisdom from Star Beings who are assisting Earth in becoming as it was designed to be, a beautiful and peaceful oasis, an intergalactic information exchange center. The Palaedians say we are entering an Age of Light, when the past dominance of darkness and ignorance on Earth will shift toward greater Love and Light.

They say there was a power struggle about 300,000 years ago and the "dark forces"—those *not* aligned with Love and

Light—have had their way on Earth ever since. This sounds a lot like the Christian concept of "satan" being in control on Earth for a time. Ours is a "free will zone"; darkness has been allowed and will teach valuable lessons. God is in all things and is always expanding and growing.

When we see with expanded consciousness—through the eyes of Horus—we remember humans are co-creators with Prime Creator. We then take our rightful place as powerful beings instead of worshipping others and mistaking ourselves for dog crap. The Palaedians say that wanting to have something to worship is a frequency control of Earth; we should listen to ourselves *and* wise teachings.

Fear, the Palaedians reassure, is part of the plan. We should get used to it, learn from it, and have courage. "Fear will always play a part in your evolutionary process, so get used to it. Do not feel that fear is bad... Begin to say 'I will transmute this fear. I will understand that it is part of the plan. I will understand that it can serve me.' Remember, your power and your ability to create reality through your will ends where your fear begins... life is meeting fear."

"Prime Creator brought this Universe into being with the components of free will so that free will could lead to chaos and then to a realignment of energy and a realization of the Creator within all things." So take heart. Darkness has taught important lessons but has had its day. We each play an important role in bringing Light to the fore now and it's time to remember that role. It's OK to feel afraid, just don't let fear stop your mission. There is a beautiful rhyme and reason inherent throughout the Universe even though it doesn't seem like it at times.

Synthesize Polarities

Acknowledge the polarities in life and remember that a greater good often results from so-called difficulties. A patient who recently suffered an auto accident discovered this truth. She started chiropractic care because of her symptoms from the injury (a "bad" event). As a result of treatment and holistic health education, she reached a level of well-being she had not enjoyed in many years (a "good" event).

Life is often like that. When seeming "tragedies" strike, keep your eyes open for the blessing. There's a greater good to every misfortune; it's a universal law even though the positive outcome may not be apparent immediately. This eternal truth lends hope and courage when the going gets tough.

Our world has been filled with polarities: positive-negative, love-hate, good-bad, faith-doubt, and so on. Wise teachers say it could not have been any other way: humanity needed polarities to learn important spiritual lessons. Maturing spiritually has many benefits, including a realization that the yin-yang of polarities is all part of the plan. As more and more of us ascend into higher dimensions of consciousness, perhaps such lessons will no longer be necessary.

Rabbi Schacter-Shalomi says "People generally want God to be the God of the good. They don't realize that the same Source that is the Source of what we call good is the Source of evil. The Source of what we call the beautiful is the same Source of the ugly. In fact, it is the Source of Allness. When we start picking and saying we like "'this' better and 'that' less, we are making division between good and evil."

One of polarity's teachings is the importance of synthesizing—or at least respecting—differing views. For example, current cultural transitions have heightened the polarity between "New Age" and "fundamentalist" groups. I have learned much from each camp; they're both barking up the same tree. Differing semantics and lack of dialogue are two factors contributing to this needless division.

While walking in nature, my brother excitedly told me about the Billy Graham crusade coming to his town; I told him about my recent New Age spiritual retreat. We listened to each other and acknowledged the importance of our individual focuses. It's OK that we're not clones. Neither path is better, just different and perfectly designed for optimal growth. Differences don't have to be barriers. Get the picture?

Now, enlarge, brighten, and zoom that image in. Most importantly, remember we all are Souls in the process of realizing our True Nature; this is the perfect backdrop for respecting and reconciling varying stances. Fundamentalists are understandably concerned about an erosion of values that they feel accompanies more liberal viewpoints. Those in the New Thought or human potential movements criticize the close-mindedness of more conservative approaches.

Throughout history, those with opposing views have been cast as enemies—even devils. Now is the time for a more loving and understanding stance. Like my brother and I, all persons can walk together despite their differences. We can accept and respect areas of disagreement while learning from and cooperating with each other. Remembering our essential Oneness as the family of God is a good start.

Remembering we each are Souls at various stages of spiritual understanding diminishes the impact of polarities in our world. There are no bad guys or gals; just Souls trying to remember who they are, why they're here and where they're going. Realizing that helps us love one another instead of polarizing into "us versus them." This is especially important with those we dislike, those who remind us where we have unfinished work to do.

As more and more persons remember their birth and world visions, a critical mass will be reached and love will shine more brightly than fear. A more enlightened humanity will realize the importance of *unity despite diversity*. With more conscious goals and strategies, all people can contribute toward a common dream—Heaven on Earth and the reign of peace and goodwill.

In *The Tenth Insight*, Redfield stresses the importance of loving others with differing views and those who commit negative actions. Seeing them as enemies only strengthens their negative resolve and gives them something to fight back against. "Image enemies" are created and compulsive trances are reinforced. Haven't we danced to this same old tune long enough? It is time for humanity to *hold the vision* that we each are awakening Souls instead of fearing that our world is falling apart.

Maintain your optimism and stay centered. Identify and believe in your own intuitions, those fleeting mental images of how you want your life to evolve. Remember that your individual adventures are occurring within a greater context of human awakening. This grounds you, holds your positive intentions, and ensures success. Our individual hopes summate into a collective force that goes forth to bring about the end we envision.

The Great Invocation

This prayer is designed to be used by triads of spiritual seekers who repeat it each morning upon rising. I visualize myself, Jim and Dorothy holding hands while sitting in a circle as beams of Light shine on and flow between us. I recommend this powerful approach to spread light, love, and power to all persons everywhere. (I personally alter the gender biased language but have printed it in the original form.) See RESOURCES to contact the center for more information.

THE GREAT INVOCATION

"From the point of Light within the Mind of God, let light stream forth into the minds of men. Let Light descend on Earth. From the point of Love within the Heart of God, let love stream forth into the hearts of men. May Christ return to Earth. From the center where the Will of God is known, let purpose guide the little wills of men—the purpose which the Masters know and serve. From the center which we call the race of men, let the Plan of Love and Light work out. And may it seal the door where evil dwells. Let Light and Love and Power restore the Plan on Earth."

Discover the Christ Within

Jesus remembered his *birth vision* and contributed mightily to an enlightened *world vision*. He brought light to the darkness of his day and saved us by sharing his spiritual wisdom.

One of my patients is a "fundamentalist" minister and a close friend of the family whose house blew up. I asked how they were coping with the death of one child, the severe burning of another, and the loss of everything they owned. He said they were doing remarkably well and considered it a concrete example of how the "body of Christ" uplifts others through prayer and support. A chill ran through me as I felt the love and power he described. I was reminded that each denomination has important messages and strengths to contribute.

His words also had great impact on me because he used the term "Christ" instead of "Jesus." This distinction is a *bridge to understanding* between every denomination and religion. Jesus, the Master from Nazareth, demonstrated his Divine-humanity and taught enlightened precepts. In the years since his death, many different denominations have been formed and wars have been fought in his name. Some adherents say that unless others accept *Jesus* as their personal Savior, they will suffer in hell forever. This message understandably alienates and confuses many.

A very different meaning results when the word "Christ" is used. The term *Christ* describes the point at which God's Spirit meets humanity and manifests in Divine-Humanity. This Christ Consciousness is in everyone, not just Jesus, and is just waiting to be realized and used. Knowing or accepting *the Christ within* is necessary for salvation from fear and spiritual ignorance. When we ask Christ and God into our lives, we open ourselves to the full experience of who we really are.

No religion has an exclusive claim on this Christ Spirit and it is known by many different names. The Creative Spirit that made and sustains the Cosmos doesn't care what we call It, just that we call. The concept of Christ Consciousness is a key to peace and understanding among the world's religions. The Christ Spirit spoke most clearly through Jesus, Buddha, Mohammed, Confucius, Lao Tsu, Moses, Native teachers, and other Spiritual Masters.

This same Christ Light will shine through each of us when we *open to* and express the indwelling Christ. Dr. Errico says the original Aramaic for "the word or logos" meant "energy of mind and wisdom." "The Christ" meant "the anointed one who is full of wisdom." We each have that potential to live out and look forward to.

Great Spiritual Masters have been deified and worshipped while concretized institutional religions were built around them. In doing so, many people have missed their messages. Certainly, Spiritual Teachers deserve honor, respect, and emulation. But to put them on a pedestal, to consider them—*and only them*—as God on Earth, misses their teaching and vision.

Richard Bach, in *Illusions*, comments "Strange thing about that is he didn't quit when they first started calling him Saviour. Instead, at that piece of bad news, he tried logic: OK, I'm the son of God, but so are you! The works that I do, you can do!' Anybody in their right mind understands that." Relegating Jesus to a position far above us provides an easy excuse from acting more like him. After all, as some churches have pointed out so many times, we are only lowly, worthless sinners.

I believe the message of Jesus has been mightily misunderstood. If he read one of the many versions of the Bible, he might recognize a few lines as his actual words. In the passage referred to by Bach, John 14:12, Jesus is quoted as saying "He that believeth on me, the works that I do shall he do also; and greater works than these shall he do because I go unto my Father."

These don't sound like the words of "the only Son of God" but teachings from a Master who knew and demonstrated his Inner Divinity. The word "on" can also be translated "as" or "like." Jesus was saying we each have the same potential and possibilities, not if we *believe he* was the only Son of God but when we *realize we each* are beloved and powerful sons and daughters of God.

I recently found a 'testimonial card', fittingly, on top of a urinal. It read "If you never know me... you won't miss *anything*. But if you never know Jesus... you will miss *everything*." That little card, presumably designed to save souls, succinctly captured everything that is wrong with some religious approaches.

From this perspective, the bearers of these cards—and, presumably, all other humans—are complete zeroes, nothings, and wastes. There's nothing to gain by meeting anyone but (drum roll, please)... Jesus! And if you never know him, you're doomed to hell forever! Well, the Jesus and God I know would find such a strong-armed tactic laughable if it weren't so spiritually misleading and blasphemous. And if you were Jesus, would you want someone to leave cards like that about you on urinals?

As described in *The Unknown Life of Jesus Christ*, Nicolas Notovitch purportedly discovered a very old Buddhist document describing the travels and studies of a young man, Issa. Issa departed for Asia at age 13, studied with Hindu and Buddhist masters, taught for a time, and returned home to Palestine at age 29. The remarkable similarities between Issa and Jesus make some scholars wonder if they are one and the same. *The Jesus Mystery* by Janet Bock and *The Lost Years*, a documentary film by Richard Bock, recite the "Legend of Issa."

This information supports the idea that Jesus incarnated from the highest Soul level *and* heightened his oneness with God through spiritual study and practices. The life of Jesus in the Mid-East 2000 years ago is one instance of the Christed One that has manifested at different times in varying guises and places. We each have the same inner Christ Light and connection to Prime Creator but few persons suspect, cultivate, or demonstrate it. With spiritual practices, a sincere desire to know God, and time, we too can attain high levels of Soul growth and mastery.

This viewpoint is in sharp contrast with one that is commonly taught: 'the only Son of God came to Earth only one time, was understood by only a few dozen persons, suffered a horrible death, and will return one day to lead true believers in him to Paradise while everyone else fries throughout eternity.'

That model leaves a lot of people in "hell" and is, in my opinion, a tad myopic. Almighty God can do better than that. There are many diverse spiritual paths for the wide variety of human perspectives and cultural settings. The Christ Spirit is behind each of these truths.

Theological historian Karen Armstrong states "There has been much speculation about the exact nature of Jesus' mission. Very few of his actual words seem to have been recorded in the Gospels... the doctrine that Jesus had been God in human form was not finalized until the fourth century. The development of Christian belief in the Incarnation was a gradual, complex process. Jesus himself certainly never claimed to be God."

He also never claimed that he had come to atone for the sins of mankind. The theology that the crucifixion of Jesus was an atonement for some original sin of Adam did not emerge until the fourth century. Noting the increasingly popular Buddhist notion of a *bodhisattva* who endured rebirth in order to rescue people in pain and darkness, Armstrong states "the notion of Christ's sacrificial death was similar to the ideal of the *bodhisattva*, which was developing at this time in India. Like the *bodhisattva*, Christ had, in effect, become a mediator between humanity and the Absolute, the difference being that Christ was the *only* mediator."

"There is a potential danger here. The innumerable Buddhas and the elusive, paradoxical *avatars* all reminded the faithful that ultimate reality could not be adequately expressed in any one form. The single Incarnation of Christianity, suggesting that the whole of the inexhaustible reality of God *had* been manifest in just one human being, could lead to an immature type of idolatry."

Contemporary Biblical scholars differ widely in their assessment of what can and cannot be known about the historical Jesus. Many admit that the final word about the details of his life must be taken on faith. Barriers to knowing with certainty the exact events include:

1. the lapse in time between actual events and the recording of them into written word

2. changes in translation and interpretation between languages and over time. There are currently hundreds of versions of the Bible, each with different nuances

3. debate and voting in various church councils about what should and shouldn't be included in the Bible

4. the zealousness, albeit perhaps well-meant, of a new religion that had to fight to survive amidst other established and more powerful religions

The iconoclastic (examining established beliefs) "Jesus Seminar", a group of Biblical scholars , asserts that little of the New Testament can be proven or trusted. The Seminar's books, *The Five Gospels* and *The Acts of Jesus*, argue that historical analysis of the Gospels exposes most of them as inauthentic. They recognize the points listed above and state that most

Christians' picture of Jesus is "an imaginative theological construct, into which have been woven traces of that enigmatic sage from Nazareth—traces that cry out for recognition and liberation from the firm grip of those whose faith overpowered their memories."

A debate among theologians about these matters has existed for hundreds of years but most churchgoers have been unaware of this fact. Rudolf Bultmann, the foremost Protestant scholar in the search for historical clarity, called for Christians to focus on the Jesus of faith, stating "we can now know almost nothing concerning the life and personality of Jesus." He and other respected Biblical scholars called for a halt in the historical search of the Bible because of the paucity of proof and corroborating data.

When I learned all this in theology school 20 years ago, I was initially upset and wondered if any part of any religion was true. I was like a kid who learns there is no Santa and then wonders what else has been misrepresented. Some respond to this lack of verifiable information by becoming agnostics or atheists. Others choose a particular religious group and put their blind faith in those tenets.

There is, however, a third response. Since even the experts don't agree, we each have the opportunity and responsibility *to decide for ourselves*. From this extremely freeing and exciting position, more and more persons are choosing to synthesize available data and then decide for themselves. This liberating response is the beginning of becoming an Enlightened Being, of realizing our formidable inner Divine potential.

We are then free to follow our hearts and Souls and worship God as we see fit. We can shrug off past control mechanisms and set about the business of realizing Heaven within and all around. Then, I believe, we can best hear and act upon the wise teachings of Lord Jesus. Not because one book or religious group says so but because we've realized and actualized *the truth* just as Jesus did.

Over the years, I have read widely, asked lots of questions, searched diligently, and kept an open mind. I have prayed daily that I might discern God's will for me and serve as an optimal channel for His work on Earth. My understanding of the truth continues to change over time. My fundamentalist brethren would call that "backsliding"; I call it growing toward an ever greater spiritual maturity.

Here are some of my current beliefs and understandings about Jesus and Christ:

- Jesus the Christ *saved* many from spiritual ignorance— not eternal "hell"—by teaching spiritual wisdom and demonstrating life after death.
- The Soul in Jesus, now known as Sananda in some circles, continues to teach and save on a Universal scale.
- The Soul that incarnated as Jesus 2000 years ago has also manifested in different bodies in different times.
- The notion that God had a plan to sacrifice His only son to redeem mankind from a bogus original sin stems from archaic sacrificial practices and is insulting to God.
- Jesus is not the only son of God and he never claimed to be. This precept was concocted many years after his death to maintain Christianity's survival among larger and more powerful religions.
- Jesus was one of—if not *the*—greatest Masters on Earth but Divine-Humans of that caliber don't keep score or have egos that demand top ratings or sworn allegiance.

It is time for enlightened spiritual understandings based on present day understandings, ancient teachings, *and* our own perceptions of the truth. The good news that I have learned through Jesus' teachings is: the Christ Light is already inside, just waiting to shine through. We each are special Souls who are awakening to the truths that he tried to teach but that, to date, few have heard or internalized.

Relationships

Relationships are one of the best and toughest paths to Self-realization. Yogis who fast, remain celibate, take vows of poverty, and live in caves have selected a difficult course. But that's child play compared to being a "house holder", a term used in India for one who pursues the spiritual path while having a job, raising a family, maintaining a home and all the concomitant responsibilities. Now *that* is an arduous path!

Some say Soulmates are the ones who can push our buttons the best and who drive us crazy at times. Others believe that everything flows effortlessly and peacefully with Soulmates. Either may be true at different times depending on the agendas of the Souls involved. If I need to increase in patience and understanding, what better way than living with three females who have synchronized hormonal cycles? Who said God doesn't have an interesting sense of humor!

The issue of relationships becomes very interesting when we remember we each are Eternal Souls. Relationships are not coincidental or unimportant. Think of the thousands of persons we encounter in our lifetimes; why do we form close and lasting relationships with one person but not another? We have to deal with recurring negative relationships sooner or later. Why not now?

Don't be "held back" and experience a "hell" of lower quality living because of unresolved relationship issues. Serious spiritual seekers will make optimal relationships a priority. *Love is the key* and relationships provide a life long workshop for giving and receiving love.

If persistent problems plague your relationships, consider the Soul or karma aspects in addition to usual counseling considerations. Remember that roles may have been reversed or quite different in past incarnations. For example, your rebellious son may have been your stern mother in an earlier life. Look *beyond* the usual dynamics and discern patterns that may need addressing. Past life regressions under hypnosis can assist healing relationship problems by letting go of past life conflicts.

One way to discern if you're relating to a Soulmate is to recall the first time you met in this life. Remember the description of memory triggers or cues that are planned just before Souls return for new incarnations? In reviewing my first meetings with loved ones, time seemed to stand still for a moment. My brain seemed to whir faster than usual as if trying to comprehend the various energies and feelings. I felt happy inside as our eyes met and we held the gaze longer than customary or comfortable during first meetings.

One of Dr. Newton's clients told of a memory trigger at age seven involving a silver pendant. The pendant of a neighbor lady shone brightly in the sun and the woman smiled at him. They became fast friends and, describing the event from the Soul's pre-incarnation perspective, he said "I will know her only a short time before we move, but it is enough. She will read to me and talk to me about life and teach me to respect people."

As one progresses toward greater personal growth and heightened consciousness, relationships may encounter a new type of stress. One person may be actively involved with spiritual and holistic health improvement while the other couldn't care less. The relationship may suffer if this gulf widens and interests remain markedly different. The rapidly changing partner may be in an overzealous or self-actualizing phase while the more orthodox partner may be content with the status quo.

People *hear the call* in different times and ways. Spiritual wake-up calls may be misinterpreted as a marital problem, mental illness, or life-stage crisis. Until I solved my "creative discontent dilemma," I wondered if my wife and I had grown apart, if I was going through the "foolish forties" or if I was just burnt-out. More persons will be experiencing "calls to action" as the time arrives for them to let their Soul's Light shine. For those desiring optimal Soul growth, life's dynamics will heat up until we agree to share our special gifts that contain the keys to realizing Heaven on Earth.

In a loving relationship, both persons have an appreciation for individual differences and needs. If problems surface, nourish the relationship, communicate often, and have patience. If, however, counseling and mutual efforts don't improve a chronically unhappy and unrewarding relationship—move on. Life is for loving; too many have wasted their lives "sticking it out."

A major key to healthy relationships is to see the Divinity in each other. Relationships based solely on lower chakra energies of physical attraction, dependency issues, and money are breakups waiting to happen. The body may grow old and the mind feeble but, viewed through eyes of love, the Soul's beauty always shines through.

Relationships are a perfect opportunity for seeing the Divine in everyone. Recall your first loves and how you were thrilled to look deeply into each others eyes, the windows of the Soul. The problem is, most people limit opening their hearts to just a few others. Then they're crushed when the relationship ends by death or parting. Make a habit of looking deeply, even if only for a moment, into the eyes of everyone you meet. You'll be pleasantly surprised to find the Beloved in everyone.

When first encountering 4th chakra energies, perhaps during "puppy love", we may erroneously think love is something we can lose. As we grow into higher awareness, we realize love is inside and all around us. Love does not come from another person nor can it be lost since we *are* Beings of Love. Then, whether in a relationship or not, we're always enjoying an internal state of Love.

When a relationship does end, remember there is more than just one "true love" with whom to enjoy life. Love deeply but don't "put all your eggs in one basket" and set yourself up for heartbreak. Just as diversification is wise in financial investing, keep a varied "portfolio" of beloved friends and family. Then, when a relationship ends, you won't be left feeling so lonely, although, as you now know, you're never alone.

I learned this the hard way 23 years ago. My first love was an inordinately large part of my life. We were young and I had an unhealthy over-dependence on her that, naturally, drove her away. After our breakup, the pain was so intense that I awakened at night with a wet pillow from crying in my sleep. That was the only time I have even briefly thought of suicide as a way to ease my pain.

My old self died that summer but other exciting doors opened as I reexamined all aspects of my life. In the long run, the *loss* led to many blessings and lessons that I wouldn't have learned otherwise but what a painful way to grow! I italicize 'loss' because we never really lose true Love, one of the constants in life. We can have meaningful relationships with loved ones despite their physical absence for whatever reason.

For example, I was intently reading X-rays when suddenly I felt my late Grandma Pitstick's presence and saw her in my mind's eye. Then I experienced the following in the flash of a second: I saw the last two houses she lived in, small rentals but sufficient for her needs. I saw her at her old jobs as a school cafeteria cook and a caretaker for a priest. A series of verbal messages came through in first person, as if she were talking to me:

"I was always taken care of and things always worked out. I had to keep working but I enjoyed helping other people and brightening their day. You will be watched over in the same way but your service will be teaching and guiding others. Trust your Soul's calling, don't worry, and make your move!"

This experience occurred as I was preparing to finalize selling half of my practice. Although I had long yearned for this transition, the imminent prospect of greatly reducing my income and making vocational changes was a little scary. I felt a deep peace after this event; I *knew* I would be supported just as Grandma had been.

Skeptics might consider this as simply a message from my subconscious mind while my cerebral cortex was studying films. However, the rapidity of the communication, the first person narrative, the sudden and inexplicable sense of her presence, and the ensuing peace make me feel it was a reassuring communication from the Other Side, an ongoing relationship despite physical distance.

Brian Weiss says "It is through relationships that we learn to express and receive love, to forgive, to help, and to serve. From the experiences that some of my patients have in the 'between life' state, I have come to believe that we actually pick our families for each lifetime before birth. We chose to live out the patterns that will afford us the most growth with the souls that will most effectively manifest these situations in our lives. Very often, these are souls we have met and interacted with in many ways in other lifetimes." If we picked each other, let's love and appreciate one another and—when it's time—let go lightly, remembering the Truth.

The older I get, the more I value loved ones. I deeply love my family and friends and, during trying times, know that they are providing the perfect environment for Soul growth. Real friends and family are there to listen, share, and enjoy. Loved ones are worth their weight in gold and are a key ingredient for spiritual progress.

Judge Not

Jesus admonished us, "judge not, that you be not judged. For with what judgment you judge, you shall be judged". Those seeking spiritual enlightenment will want to avoid judging others. We can't fully understand another person until we've walked a mile in their moccasins. Live by the Golden Rule and refrain from putting value systems on someone else who may have an entirely different agenda and Soul purpose.

Avoiding judgment is also wise for our own good. As the words of Jesus indicate, the law of karma acts surely and swiftly. When we judge others, we attract unfair judgment from others and ourselves. As a youth, I used to think that if we judged others, God would judge and punish us in retaliation. Now, I believe we bring harsh judgment *on ourselves* through universal laws of cause and effect.

Great Being *is* love, forgiveness, understanding, and compassion. God doesn't need to smite or punish, humans do a fine job of that themselves. We temporarily suffer via "the cosmic boomerang" effect: we reap what we sow; what goes around comes around; if we want to dance, we must pay the fiddler. So, please, if nothing else motivates you, avoid judgment of others to save yourself grief.

Criticism is a first cousin to judgment. If you want to become an effective world change agent, focus on gratitude versus criticism and judgment. *A Course In Miracles* suggests "I will judge nothing that occurs today." For just today, resolve to view every aspect of life uncritically. Just like a recovered alcoholic, do this one day at a time. Dropping judgment is an important key to remembering the ever-present potential for Heaven on Earth. When we focus on the good—instead of the frailties and dissimilarities—in ourselves and others, the world reveals itself as the Utopia it really is.

Spiritually immature persons judge and have prejudices based on relatively insignificant matters such as skin color, gender, age, sexual preference, religious beliefs, body size, hair style, cultural background, disability, socioeconomic status and political affiliation—have I missed any? Basically, many humans are *afraid* of anyone who is different from them. Insecure persons who haven't yet remembered their Oneness with all Creation lash out when threatened.

For example, discrimination and violence against women continues on an appalling scale. Consider these chilling facts from the Spring 1996 *Noetic Sciences Review*:

- a woman is raped every 6 minutes in the U.S.
- 98% of Pakistani women are beaten by their husbands
- in Bombay, India, 95% of fetuses identified as female were aborted in 1994
- 80 million women in Africa suffer from genital mutilation
- estimated loss in female lives by physical neglect of girl children is 60 to 100 million worldwide *annually*
- women account for 70% of the world's poor and illiterate
- women comprise only 10% of the world's lawmakers at any national level

We have, in part, certain organized religions to thank for this persistent misogyny. Although both early Christianity and Islam were marked by equality of the sexes, both later degenerated into gender discrimination that persists in many quarters to this day. Karen Armstrong noted that early Christian church fathers like Augustine, Jerome, and Tertullian castigated women with words that occasionally sounded deranged.

For example, Tertullian wrote about women: "do you not know that you are each an Eve? The sentence of God on this sex of yours lives in this age: the guilt must of necessity live too. *You* are the devil's gateway... *You* so carelessly destroyed man, God's image. On account of *your* desert, even the son of God had to die." Is that bizarre or what?

Augustine, who castrated himself to be "a eunuch" for God, questioned why He even created women. Just more historical examples of the imbalance and ignorance in the core teachings of some churches. It is time to evaluate objectively these prejudices in the light of modern day, nonjudgmental thinking.

The movie *Powder* addresses the theme of discrimination beautifully. Born with albinism, Jeremy suffers an unbelievable amount of rejection and abuse just because of his skin color—or, actually, lack thereof. To a racially prejudiced deputy

who hates (fears) Jeremy, the sheriff said: "I didn't think anyone could be *too white* for you!"

All forms of prejudice are still common and deep-rooted.
The good news is that more and more persons are seeing the
inhumanity and ignorance involved in all forms of discrimination. Important advances against gender discrimination have
been made. A leading southern U.S. church group recently ex-
horted members to rise above past racial bigotry. These are
steps in the right direction but there is still a long way to go.

I'll discuss prejudice against homosexuals at length because
of ongoing debates about gay rights. I just read another dis-
criminatory attack on gays in a religious right publication that
tries to dictate morality under the guise of concern for "family
values." A well-known 'holier than thou' leader urged a letter
writing campaign condemning IBM because of the company's
recent policy of extending benefits to partners of gay employees. IBM should be applauded—not criticized—for their Golden
Rule oriented policy. The recent "church" boycott against Disney
is largely about gay rights.

Rationalizations for discrimination against gays are just
another variation of bigotry we've seen too many times. Misinformed and self-righteous "moral authorities" have made similar arguments in the past against racial equality, women's
rights, and interfaith and interracial marriages. Same song,
different verse. When will humans learn to focus on the logs in
their own eyes?

Homosexuals suffer an astonishing amount of judgment and
prejudice from those who should know better. Labels and inac-
curate characterizations are part of the problem. The term "homosexual" only describes ones sexual preference; some erroneously believe the term conveys accurate information about a
person's morality and character.

Over the years, I've become friends with a number of people
who happen to be homosexual. They are, without exception,
among the most intelligent, sensitive, creative and loving persons I've known. The solution to healing all forms of prejudice
is obvious. When we get to know someone well, we realize we
are much more alike than not. We each are brothers and sisters, children of the same Source, and truly One.

Part of the problem is there's a catch-22 that inhibits understanding between gays and heterosexuals. Getting to know each other better would help homophobes realize that homosexuals are much like anyone else except for their sexual preference. But many homosexuals are understandably reluctant to "come out of the closet" for fear of unfair discrimination or retaliation.

The gays I know agree across the board: they certainly would never whimsically choose a life-style that is so attacked and ridiculed by others. Even some immediate family members and "close friends" reject gays when they finally come out. Increasing research suggests that sexual preferences are shaped by genetic, neurological, and biochemical differences. If this is so, expecting a homosexual to change is like asking someone to change their skin color or baldness pattern.

The American Psychological Association has long considered homosexuality to be a valid life-style preference and not indicative of any psychopathology. Even "Dear Abby" states "I have always believed that one's sexual orientation is genetically predetermined before birth. Homosexuals have, for too long, suffered because of fear, ignorance and prejudice. Homosexuals are born—not made."

When I watched film footage of homosexual marriages on the news, I saw children of God who happened to love members of the same sex. They were excited, crying, hugging, and laughing just like any newlyweds. Those trying to block marriages, benefits and job rights of gays might want to look within and remember our unity.

New light on issues of homosexuality emerges with an understanding of reincarnation. Individuals who have been females during many past lifetimes may still primarily identify with being a female even though they chose a male body in this life. Conversely, Souls who have repeatedly incarnated as males in the past may still feel like a male despite currently having a female body. This may partially account for so-called "gender confusion" issues of the many persons who don't fit neatly into heterosexual "norms".

Dr. Newton says "Regardless of the circumstances which lead souls to make gender choices, this decision was made before arriving on Earth. Sometimes I find that gay people have chosen in advance of their current lives to experiment with a sex that was seldom used in former lives. Being gay carries a sexual stigma in our society which presents a more difficult road in life. When this road is chosen by one of my clients, it can usually be traced to a karmic need to accelerate personal understanding of the complex differences in gender identity as related to certain events in their past."

Those whose fear and judgment are so strong that they would deny basic freedoms to others will be ashamed of themselves when they review their life after passing on. Perhaps in future lives their Souls will choose to be a minority or target of discrimination so they really learn how wrong and hurtful they were.

The good news is, it's getting better all the time. A Caucasian couple I know felt called to have another child although her three children were in their 20's. When they couldn't conceive, they adopted a Korean baby boy. When I first met him, I was inspired by their loving gesture that will, among many other benefits, decrease racial prejudice.

As more and more couples adopt or intermarry racially, differences in skin color will be realized as a relatively minor and unimportant detail. Tiger Wood's immense popularity is especially timely: as a multiracial, one man planetary citizen, he represents a new age in which differences are respected and appreciated.

There is no separation in God's Creation. Let's not judge but, rather, focus on improving ourselves. Live and let live. When viewed through a heart of love and understanding, prejudice based on any differences is unconscionable. Non-judgment and respect of others who are different is a key to accelerating humanity's evolution of consciousness.

Home Altar

Begin each day with quiet time at a home spiritual "altar" or worship area. Mine consists of a small table with pictures and statues of some of my spiritual teachers: Jesus, Buddha, Paramahansa Yogananda, S.S. Satchidananda, Neem Karoli

Baba, Ram Dass, and Maharishi Mahesh Yogi. Candles and incense remind me of the Light and Fragrance of God's Kingdom within and all around.

This special setting reminds me I am a spiritual being having a physical experience *and* a physical being having a spiritual experience. Having a little corner for spiritual growth is a potent aid for remembering the good news that sets us free. It sets the stage for feeling closer to God through prayer, chanting, yoga, breathing exercises, drumming, singing, and meditation.

Levar Burton stated "I experience God with a thought, a breath, or an activity of puja (ritualistic worship). Anything can be a trigger that causes me to remember God—and that I am God. One thing I do is to create altars wherever I am. They trigger my stopping and acknowledging the presence of God in my life."

In the movie, *The Little Princess*, the devastated young girl coped and marshaled her Life Force by drawing a circle and sleeping inside it. Native cultures have long used the sacred circle as a power symbol and configuration for seating during ceremonies. I walk around my room three times in a clockwise direction, holding burning incense, and chanting OM. These rituals feel right and help create a sacred environment as I remember my Spiritual Essence.

Beings of Energy

An electromagnetic field is within and around all life; humans are bioenergetic beings. This Life Force is even in rocks and other apparently "inert" forms; matter is a manifestation of energy. Russian researchers of Kirlian photography said, "All living things—plants, animals, and humans not only have a physical body made of atoms and molecules but also a counterpart body of energy" which they termed the Biological Plasma body.

In one experiment, plants that had been in the same room were separated. When plants in one room were cut up and destroyed, the energy fields of the unaffected plants in another room showed intense changes. Changes in human Kirlian fields have been demonstrated after treatment with homeopathy, acupuncture and chiropractic treatment.

Chiropractic adjustments help balance physiological and more ethereal forms of energy just as yoga assists kundalini energies to flow throughout the body. Some patients see white light immediately after an adjustment. On a number of occasions when I was really intent on healing, I've seen a pale green or violet light extending an inch or so beyond my fingertips. On other occasions, vertebrae have noticeably moved when I just lightly touched the skin.

The Chinese view humans as having four components: mental, structural, biochemical, and electrical. Humans are beings of electricity with a flow of bipolar electromagnetic power that runs and heals the body. This mysterious force is variously termed chi (China), ki (Japan), prana (India) and vital force in the Western world. The Chinese postulated 4000 years ago that the basic cause of disease is imbalance in energy flow which causes abnormal system function and, ultimately, overt pathology and premature death.

Each of us has a unique energy field that reflects our Soul level and current state of health and happiness. "Dottie" has seen auras all of her life and, as she grew up, was surprised to discover that everyone doesn't see them. Last year, she and her husband, Joe, came to our spiritual study group and described the auras of 25 people. After the session, she asked if we might talk privately because she had seen something in my energy field that she didn't want to share in front of the group.

She asked if I had a sense of mission—almost an obsession—that I was to help transform our world for the better. Had I experienced this vision early in life and felt it was something I was called to do? After I replied in the affirmative, she excitedly told me that I had an energy field she had seen only four times in 60 years. She described a uniquely textured golden hump of light from the back of my head to my mid-back that emitted sparkles of white light.

The other three persons each had a similar sense of mission—a special calling they *knew* they must accomplish. She said my Soul had undergone training and experiences that many Souls on Earth had not yet. My calling was to teach higher understandings to assist peace on Earth. If I did not follow this mission, she added, I would soon suffer physically and mentally till I got with the program. But she saw me making the necessary moves and launching my programs "sooner than you think."

This was fascinating input from a person I had never met, yet who seemed to know my inner most dreams and visions. Our meeting occurred when I was struggling about how and when to make major life changes. It was a greatly appreciated validation that I wasn't just following a silly whim but was sensing a higher calling. These levels of passion are detectable by gifted, sensitive persons.

Their wise counsel was not just for me but for everyone who has felt a gentle tugging or perhaps a major upheaval in their heart and Soul. God doesn't give us dreams without the means to carry them through! Remember this and follow your vision. Work through your fears; develop the courage, clarity and commitment necessary to implement your dreams.

Knowing we are, in truth, Infinite Beings of energy, love and light is an immensely freeing and empowering realization. Energy fields and auras more accurately reflect the real nature of life than do solid bodies. Einstein's theory of relativity proved mathematically that $E = m(c$ squared$)$. That is, energy equals mass times the speed of light squared.

Put another way, *matter* (solid stuff) when accelerated at a sufficiently great speed is interchangeable with energy (invisible life force). Quantum physics has advanced this research, positing that matter and energy are not discrete phenomena but overlapping entities. When asked to paint a picture of reality, this view describes an interplay between formless energy and formed matter with a dynamic, ever-changing cusp between them.

I first realized the implications of this in an undergraduate chemistry class. The professor emphasized, "You think your hand and the table are distinct objects. In reality, there is a mutual flow of atoms between the hand and table so there is no concrete separation between the two." The significance of this truth momentarily mesmerized me and I seemed to dimly remember having known this before. (Unfortunately, I also only dimly remembered the material when exams came.)

I became excited as my mind raced with this new piece of the puzzle. If there is no separation between my hand and the table, then—as spiritual masters have been trying to tell us for eons—all creation *is* literally One! Chopra states that each of us have molecules in our bodies that actually were once in the body of Jesus or any great spiritual teacher. An energy flow and subatomic interplay between me and another "solid" object implies the same relationship throughout existence. Science had proven and corroborated ancient spiritual truths!

Energy cannot be destroyed but only changes state. For example, the potential energy in a piece of wood changes to heat energy when it is burned. The essence of the wood is not destroyed but merely changes. Ashes remain and the freed thermal energy radiates in all directions.

At "death," the Life Force moves on and the body returns to its constituent minerals but this does not constitute an end, merely a transformation. Life is a constant series of changes. When we acknowledge our True Nature as Eternal Beings of energy and manifestations of the Creator, changes in physicality (birth, aging, "death") are seen as inconsequential shifts in form.

Our fundamental nature is a spark of the Divine; we are particles of energized units that originated out of one unit— the Maker. This is why bioenergetic healing will be a major focus in the future—it addresses a more fundamental level in the prevention and treatment of health disorders. See APPENDIX for further reading about various body and energy work techniques that harmonize and balance energy patterns.

Trust Yourself

"If the doors of perception were cleansed, everything would appear to man as it is, infinite."

—William Blake

Trusting yourself is a giant step toward perceiving reality clearly. We each are, in truth, Eternal Souls who possess a remarkable inner wisdom. Questioning rules that don't make sense is an important part of Soul development. Trusting internal voices of intuition and knowing is one of the most powerful paradigm shifts we can make in our lives.

Trust your feelings. We each have a wise inner voice, an internal sense of what is best for our optimal being. The Soul will speak clearly if we listen and follow its urgings. As musician Sting reminds, "Let your soul be your pilot, let your soul guide you, it'll guide you well." Walt Whitman said "reexamine all you have been told at school or church, or in any books, and dismiss whatever insults your own soul."

Yet, in our bustling material world, few persons seem in touch with their inner knowing. Many tune out their Soul's pleading for creativity, play, space, peace and growth. Some virtually imprison themselves to an unhappy life void of the essentials for harmony and total success.

I recently spoke with an acquaintance who is president of a large industry. I hadn't seen him for a year in which many company difficulties had occurred; he looked ten years older and had developed white hairs and wrinkles. When I asked how he was coping with a trying year, he *said* the right things: "I don't take it personally, it's part of the job." But his body and posture said otherwise.

The business world, in particular, makes life-choking demands that require denial and make it difficult to know or trust oneself. Layers of denial eventually create enough unconsciousness so that even extreme unhappiness, fatigue, poor relationships and frequent illness don't register that something is wrong. Alcohol, drugs, excess TV, and unbalanced lower chakra pursuits complete the formula for being comfortably numb but undeniably miserable.

It's always amazed me how well smokers and other substance abusers deny their problem. In between coughing up chunks of lung tissue, smokers can rationalize why they don't quit now: they could quit anytime, it's hard to quit, they've been smoking for so many years, and their grandmother who never smoked still died of cancer. Substance abusers who have lost job, family, and health still vehemently deny that their addiction has any bearing on their problems—it's just "bad luck."

Many see through these pitiful denials yet don't address how *they are addicted* to behaviors and beliefs that prevent total success. Few persons really love their jobs and have sufficient time to enjoy life. But playing the material-world game sucks them into putting off their heart and Soul's longing till "someday, then I'll..." That's why many lead lives of quiet desperation without clarity about who they are and what they really want to do when they grow up.

We best realize our Divine-Human nature when we trust ourselves and follow our inner urgings. Past teachings have led us to distrust and deny our inner wisdom in deference to "those who know best." It's time to recognize that we've been misled by those who don't have always our best interests at heart. Control groups (big businesses, governments, and churches) profit when the masses are afraid to explore and trust their own answers.

Here's a small example that helped me trust myself and freed up personal power. Even as a child, I thought neck ties were stupid and could never understand why they were worn. My theories were: a phallic symbol (don't tie them too short!); a carry over from priestly vestments; or a sign of who was willing to play the game by others' rules.

In my early years as a professional, I wore ties because all the books on "dressing for success" said I should. I attended one seminar where nearly everyone in the room was wearing a blue or gray suit, pale blue shirt, and maroon (a "power color") tie. We looked like a bunch of mindless idiots who had sold our individualities and Souls in the pursuit for success. And we were.

At some point, I gave away the wool pants (too hot), the suit coats (too confining), the ties (choking and too short) and the wing-tip shoes (what's the deal with all those little holes anyway?). Business consultants told me I would lose 15% of my patients if I wore a beard and another 30% if I didn't wear a white jacket and a tie. I kept my beard, wore casual pants and golf shirts, and doubled my practice by following my bliss.

Fortunately, more and more persons are awakening to control issues and living the lives *they*—not someone else—have imagined. In the business place, 'down dressing' and meditating or jogging at lunch are becoming more common than a suit and tie, power lunch, and double martini. Others are taking the entrepreneurial plunge and becoming their own boss in a more rewarding *lifework*.

A patient, Pam, was chronically ill, fatigued, over burdened with four children under age six, and couldn't afford health care. I did everything I could to assist her plight and gave her professional discounts and extra treatment and education time. After several months of care, it was time for a re-exam with spinal videofluoroscopy. Pam said she couldn't afford it and might be pregnant *again*.

I asked if she were using any birth control measures. She responded that she was a member of a religion that doesn't believe in birth control. "Do they believe in chronic illness, fatigue, and not being able to afford basic health care?" I asked. She didn't get that one. Then I murmured something about old men who wear dresses and have never even married, let alone had children, but counsel others about life-style decisions.

The maxim "question authority" seemed apropos for Pam. Her instincts had to be screaming "this is crazy!" yet she continued to let archaic advice from a very wealthy and powerful institution shape her "life" choices. (I put "life" in quotation marks because she didn't have a clue about what a quality life was.)

I'll never forget one Sunday evening in a church that tended to be a tad fundamentalist. A visiting "revival preacher" was speaking that night; the congregation, all church regulars, went to church three times a week and had already participated in the morning service. After a long and boisterous sermon, it was time for the altar call.

"Whoever wants to get right with God, *come on down!*" (He obviously was a 'The Price Is Right' fan) No one moved; everyone there was already tight with God. "Whoever wants to give their life to Jesus, come to the altar." People were tired and we all had been "saved" multiple times. But this jerk was not going to be denied. His next tactic was "If you love Jesus, come on down." People looked wearily at each other; this was cold-hearted. Of course we loved Jesus but what a manipulation.

Many persons came to the altar on that one. But a few of us had dug in our heels. Enough is enough; this Bible thumper was downright insulting. Then it got *really* ugly. "My friends, God loves you more than you will ever know. BUT, don't make God bring a tragedy into your life so you'll come to Christ! Do you want your loved ones to suffer? Is that what it will take for you to make a decision for Jesus?"

Almost everyone went to the altar on that one. The revival was a success and the preacher's ego was intact. He had filled the altar rail and prompted yet another massive wailing, jabbering, and beseeching spectacle. But a couple of us freethinkers sat defiantly in our pews, absolutely smoldering. In reflecting back, that man did me a huge favor; from that moment on, I trusted my heart and Soul. Never again would anyone manipulate me with fear and guilt.

Now that you know the Real You is much greater and wiser than any power structure or Madison Avenue con job, trust *your* beliefs and accept *your way* of living. It's OK to be unique, different, odd, eccentric, and listen to your own drummer. As Robert Frost said, "Two roads diverged in a wood, and I—I took the one less traveled by, and that has made all the difference."

In *Bringers of the Dawn*, star beings teach "We cannot emphasize enough to you that you must stop listening to society. This is going to be the hardest task for you to do and the biggest break for you to take. You have the societal self and the spiritual self, and you must decide which one is sacred. Which one is your source of authority? Let your intuitive self become your authority."

They continue, "Life is like a restaurant. Learn how to order what you want from life like you do in a restaurant and then trust that, because you ordered it, it will be put before you... Look at the divine nonchalance you have when you order things in a restaurant. That is how you order up life. Get clear on what you want, order it and be done with it. Don't keep calling up spirit to see if they got the order or give advice on how to fill it. You ordered it. Trust that it will come."

UFOs and ETs

While considering whether to include this section, I attended a holistic seminar in Gulf Shores, Alabama. While watching the sky, a solid silver streak suddenly appeared in a clear blue sky. I figured it was a jet vapor trail although the streak was much more solid and silver than usual.

As for its sudden appearance in a clear sky, I reasoned the jet had been flying toward me, then turned directly in front of me. I looked away for a second and when I looked back, the streak was gone. Only blue sky appeared whereas a jet would have left a slowly dissipating white trail. Had I just seen my first UFO?

In 1917, during the miracles at Fatima, Portugal, over 100,000 people saw unusual UFO-like events on five different occasions. As described by Joseph Pelletier in *The Sun Danced at Fatima*, a flat silver disk, revolving on its own axis, sent forth shafts of multicolored light. The disc plunged erratically downward causing thousands of believers and disbelievers alike to fall to their knees, publicly confessing their sins before the world ended. The disc suddenly stopped and rose slowly into the sky, finally disappearing into the sun.

After investigating for thirteen years, the Catholic church reported "This phenomenon, which no astronomical observatory registered and which therefore was not natural, was witnessed by persons of all categories and of all social classes, believers and unbelievers, journalists of the principal Portuguese newspapers and even by persons some miles away, facts which annul any explanation of collective illusion."

University professor and UFO expert, Ronald Westrum, stated "The government has known for years that we are being visited by aliens, and that is one of the first things they probably tell the president when he takes over the Oval Office. But if Bill Clinton got up and said we've been tracking this for 50 years and it's real, it's very powerful, and we don't have any weapons that will work on it, well, it would not be a very smart thing to do, politically."

Over the past two decades, he and a group of scholars have studied reams of data and concluded that something or someone is abducting people from their homes. It's time, he says, for mainstream science to start taking this seriously. He cites a 1992 Roper Survey that found about one in 50 Americans randomly polled had experienced symptoms of an abduction. Westrum says "These are not psychopaths and they are not publicity seekers. "

Distinguished journalist C.D.B. Bryan, author of *Close Encounters of the Fourth Kind: Alien Abduction, UFOs, and the Conference at M.I.T.*, attended the Abduction Study Conference headed by Dr. John Mack, professor of psychiatry at Harvard Medical School. Bryan wrote, "I am struck by how my perception of the abduction phenomenon has changed: I no longer think it is a joke... And, based as much on what has been presented at the conference as on the intelligence, dedication, and sanity of the majority of the presenters, I cannot reject out-of-hand the *possibility* that what is taking place isn't exactly what the abductees are saying is happening to them."

Virgil Armstrong, author of *The Armstrong Report*, is a retired Army Intelligence Officer who claims to have participated in the first intact UFO capture at Sands Proving Grounds in 1948. He states that there have been over 13 million UFO sightings, over 2000 contact cases, and at least 26 alien ships captured. The first spacecraft was taken to Wright Patterson Air Force Base surreptitiously by traveling at night and setting up road detours.

Air Force and Navy veteran Milton W. Cooper, author of *Behold A Pale Horse*, claims that he and other military personnel saw various spacecrafts on land and at sea. While on watch in a submarine, he and others watched an aircraft-carrier sized spacecraft repeatedly fly out of the ocean and into the clouds. He states that a massive government cover-up has existed for decades and that many witnesses have been harangued, institutionalized or murdered.

If ETs do exist, why don't they make their presence known on a wider scale? Probably because humanity hasn't been emotionally or spiritually prepared for the possibility of aliens with technology far superior to ours. Just consider the mass panic that followed the radio production of *War of the Worlds* by H. G. Wells.

Fortunately, films like *ET*, *Close Encounters of the Third Kind*, and the *Star Wars* trilogy have presented a positive slant on ETs. Exciting benefits for Earthlings and beings from elsewhere can be gained through sharing and cooperation. I believe enough humans are now sufficiently prepared for widespread contact and mutually beneficial interaction. The collective human consciousness is ready to admit the obvious— Earth's inhabitants are not the only life forms in the cosmos. Double duh.

Why would I discuss another controversial topic and what does all this have to do with Heaven on Earth? There are several reasons why it's important to know the truth about UFOs and ETs. It's tremendously ethnocentric to believe our planet has the only life forms among the Universe's some 50 billion galaxies, each with a similar number of stars. Such narrowmindedness fuels other limiting beliefs such as prejudice, hatred, greed, war, and religious and national superiority.

Government claims that UFOs don't exist makes people doubt their senses and the government's veracity. Are we to believe that millions of normal people—like you and I—are delusional and incapable of seeing the truth? Double messages like "UFOs don't exist!"/"but millions have seen them!" contribute to humanity's collective schizophrenia.

Establishing there are other life forms in the cosmos also broadens our perspectives about a number of topics:
- the ideas of reincarnation and multidimensional selves are easier to imagine if other varied life forms exist
- we realize that orthodox institutions may not have the definitive truth for all people
- we increasingly open to the uniqueness and diversity on Earth and in the vast cosmos
- deciding whether certain channeled sources of information exist and are reliable; if other intelligent life exists, might they try to communicate with us?
- we trust our intuition more as we learn life is not as simple, as predictable as we once thought

Just a few hundred years ago, most people believed the world was flat and the Earth was the center of the Universe. Scientists who presented conflicting evidence were disgraced or killed. Independent thinkers—artists, writers, healers, and political dissidents—who disagreed with state and church power structures were tortured and killed. These were the "dark ages" from which humanity has partially emerged.

Humanity is now ready for another quantum leap in enlightenment, a new era of peace, love, and understanding. Let go of past fears, misunderstandings, and limiting beliefs. Achieving this requires an open mind and the courage to think for yourself. Study about ETs and UFOs and then decide what *you* feel is right. The payoff is more freedom, power, and knowledge of the Truth.

In *The Gods Of Eden*, William Bramley provides much fascinating evidence for his claim that, throughout history, humanity has been plagued by and interfered with by malevolent ETs. He originally set out to investigate why wars and strife have persisted among humans. To his surprise, he found substantial evidence for the theory that ill-intentioned nonhumans have maliciously meddled in Earthly affairs.

If this sounds too far out for you, read Old Testament passages that don't make sense unless ETs exist. For example, in Genesis 6:4, who were these "giants in the earth in those days" and "sons of God" who took daughters of men as wives? Were there other players besides God and descendants of Adam and Eve? If so, who were they and where did they come from?

Especially examine passages that describe "God" and His despicable acts upon innocent men, women, and children. Suggested readings to convince you that your childhood intuitions were right ("a loving God surely wouldn't do such things!") include:

• Genesis 19:1-17. A description of the destruction of Sodom and Gomorra, usually depicted as just dues because of homosexuality. But are we really to believe that so many men, young and old, sexually desired these two males over two beautiful virgins whom the father so generously offered to the crowd? Or was the multitude interested in "knowing"—*investigating*, not in a sexual way—two strangers who had awesome powers that enabled them to fly and destroy on a grand scale? Would a just and loving God destroy *all* the people in these towns?

• Exodus 13:21-22. "God," who had just murdered all the Egyptian human and animal first born, appeared "in a pillar of a cloud by day" and "a pillar of fire by night"; does the Supreme Being really operate this way or did Biblical writers confuse God with malicious gods, ETs who used their powers for rampant destruction?

• Exodus 14:24 "in the morning watch the Lord looked unto the host of the Egyptians through the pillar of fire and of the cloud, and *troubled* the host of the Egyptians." (Troubled means killed all of them by drowning.) Looking through this device "in the morning watch" sounds more like a high-tech military maneuver than actions of our Cosmic Creator.

• Exodus 40:34-38. The daytime appearing "cloud" that could be *taken up* appeared as "fire" by night. Does this sound more like crude descriptions of space ships than the Ultimate Ground of All Being?

• Ezekiel 1:1-28 describes his "visions of God." Does this sound like the Source or ETs with hover craft and space gear?

• I Samuel 5:6-12 describes "the LORD" destroying and smiting men with emerods, itches, scabs, and blotch in "their secret parts." (Sounds like a fate worse than death to me) Plague outbreaks have been described as being preceded by ships in the sky spraying a stinking mist. Our all-loving Heavenly Father at it again?

Bramley says UFOs have been described since earliest recorded time. "The religions of ancient Mesopotamia, Egypt, and the Americas were dominated by the adoration of humanlike 'gods' from the heavens. Many of those 'gods' were said to travel about in flying 'boats' and 'globes'. Ancient claims of that kind are today the basis of the modern 'ancient astronaut's' theory which postulates that a space age race had once visited Earth and had involved itself in human affairs."

Custodial ET overlords, says Bramley, purposely created pestilence and destruction to control and confuse early humans. This kept humans from communicating clearly and realizing their own formidable potentials. Mesopotamian stories *that predate similar Biblical ones* include: being cast from the garden of Eden, the tower of Babel, the great flood, and "God" or "angel" wrought holocausts.

Throughout history, Bramley contends, secret societies have spread false information and intentionally or unwittingly incited wars and strife. Power oriented businesses, religious groups, and governments have thus maintained control and kept humans in turmoil and darkness. This is one reason humanity hasn't realized the potential for peace on Earth *yet*.

In *The Twelfth Planet*, Zecharia Sitchin describes Sumeria as the first advanced culture, predating those in Mesopotamia, Egypt, Greece, and Rome. Astonishingly, however, "to this very day the scholars have no inkling who the Sumerians were, where they came from, and how and why their civilization appeared. For its appearance was sudden, unexpected, and out of nowhere."

Of this, noted social scientist Joseph Campbell states "With stunning abruptness... there appears in this little Sumerian mud garden... the whole cultural syndrome that has since constituted the germinal unit of all the high civilizations of the world." Mesopotamian clay tablets told of ET overlords who periodically visited and genetically engineered prehuman ancestors into Homo sapiens for use as slaves. Perhaps this explains the "missing link" in evolutionary evidence.

Sitchin makes a convincing case for ET involvement in the creation of Homo Sapiens and their culture, thus the evolutionary abruptness. Tens of thousands of ancient inscriptions have been uncovered that state "Whatever seems beautiful, we made by the grace of the gods." His book has many drawings and pictures of these "gods of Sumer" complete with their space gear, advanced technology, and "boats of heaven."

Sitchin describes pre-Biblical Sumerian writings about "EA", a *kindly* ET god who started the Brotherhood of the Snake to enlighten humanity and lighten their burdens under crueler ET custodians. After a battle between these powerful overlords, EA was banished and labeled "Prince of Darkness, Satan, the Devil, and Prince of Liars." He was portrayed by the victorious *malevolent* powers as the mortal enemy of a Supreme Being and the keeper of Hell.

Does this story line sound familiar? Have we been denied important information and told half truths or outright lies disguised as history and religion? One lesson from all this is that it's time for more persons to study, discuss, think, and feel for themselves. Since what constitutes the Truth is not widely agreed upon, trust your own heart, mind, and Soul.

These books describe a long history of negative influence by "bad" ETs, resulting in fear, calamity, and divisiveness. Have malevolent ETs indeed stirred up and fed on negative emotions while promoting hostility? Has this contributed to humanity's largely unhappy existence as confused slaves, a mockery of our original design and intended status? And do certain power structures have a vested interest in our continued ignorance of ETs?

Linda Moulton Howe, Emmy Award-winning filmmaker and UFO author, states "Unseen forces are leaving marks on animals, the earth and human psyches, while manipulating, traumatizing or inspiring. All these phenomena challenge us to confront other realities beyond the status quo. Yet, our human species, under the influence of rigid social, political and religious conditioning, rejects the accumulating physical evidence and human testimony."

I'm sure that—just like humans—there are many more good ETs than bad. Benevolent formed beings from other star systems and formless entities from other dimensions are assisting us now and their presence will be much more obvious in the future. Ze'ev Kolman's bioenergetic healing and other paranormal powers began after a UFO surrounded him with a cloud and ETs "changed his bioenergetic potential."

Says Dr. Hans Holzer "there are a number of well-known and properly documented cases of such encounters in the literature of UFO experiences, and many have been followed by extraordinary developments in the individual's psychic abilities or powers."

There is much potential good to be gained and nothing to be lost by knowing the truth. Ignorance is not bliss. If ETs exist, let's cooperate with the good ones and resolve problems with—or at least be aware of—the "bad" ones.

Howe concludes, "it's possible that another intelligence sees our environmental pollution, realizes that humans are on a path of self-destruction, and is taking steps on its own initiative to help us, even if we don't comprehend the actions or motives." Negative ET experiences were perhaps necessary given the time and setting, but it is now time for peace and harmony among all beings in the Creation.

Sexuality

Acknowledging and managing sexual energies is an important aspect of becoming a fully functioning person. When sexual needs are repressed or misused, imbalanced sexual drives can result. For example, in America, one in three girls and one in five boys are childhood victims of sexual abuse.

Sexual energies are centered at the second chakra; if these energies are over or under used, a fixation can occur, thereby blocking normal energy flows throughout the twelve chakras. That is, an imbalance in sexual energies can be due to or can create disharmony in other areas of life. The goal is to accept and acknowledge a healthy sexuality as a normal part of life.

This certainly is often not the case. Children are taught at an early age: "don't touch yourself there!" A very conservative friend was mortified when, after kissing his three year old daughter on the cheek several times, she replied "Daddy, kiss me *right here!*" while pointing to her clitoris. Awareness of sexual needs is a natural part of fully conscious living, even at a young age.

I remember playing "show and tell" with a female friend at around age 6. It was very innocent, no touching, just childish curiosity as we learned what girls and boys looked like. About two years later, I mentioned our little mutual exploration event and she got angry at me. She denied ever doing anything like that and said I made it up. (I guess that was my introduction to females and sex.) Repression of memories requires intrapsychic energy that can block or hamper higher emotional development.

A counseling client, "Fred", felt confused and guilty at a young age about sexual urges and masturbation. In his church, an "unforgivable sin" was mentioned in hushed and threatening tones. It was the perfect controlling device because everyone projected that their particular behavior was the one that would lead them *directly* (do not pass GO, do not collect $200) to hell forever.

No one ever mentioned masturbation—not his family, friends, books, or TV. So, he figured he was perhaps the only one who had discovered it and *certainly* the only one to do it. There he was, barely into puberty and doomed for hell, no doubt about it. Dating Lucy left and Ruthie right—that *had* to be the unforgivable sin!

He prayed in earnest, "Please God! I don't want to go to hell. Give me the will power to postpone this powerful urge till I'm married—that's *only* 13 years or so from now." That approach was usually effective for a few hours. No matter how much he tried to abstain, something invariably pushed him over the edge.

For example, one morning he tried intense praying at church in an effort to cool his adolescent sexual urges. But he made a serious strategic blunder when he picked up the Sunday paper and there they were: the women in the J.C. Penny bra ads. Men, back us up on this one; you know what we're talking about. Those voluptuous, curvaceous pictures were too much for any 12 year old. There he was again, locked in the bathroom only hours after church!

His parents thought he was constipated because Fred spent so much time in the bathroom and considered taking him to the doctor. Throw in a good measure of misinformation from the resident geniuses at school ("it causes acne, mental illness, hairy palms, and baldness") and the net effect was horrifying.

After what seemed like a lifetime later, Fred discovered that 99.9% of males and a high percentage of females have masturbated. His first reaction was profound relief ("I wasn't the only one!"), quickly followed by anger ("Why didn't someone tell me?").

How many other children have gone through such needless anxiety and shame? And, with a U.S. surgeon general recently fired for suggesting classroom education about the subject, how much progress have we made? These energies need to be dealt with and masturbation is a saner, safer alternative to teenage sex.

I share his adolescent angst to highlight a common source of needless worry and shame. Let's acknowledge these powerful urges and teach young people that masturbation is an acceptable way to handle sexual energies. Doing so will reduce teen pregnancies, psychological trauma, sexually transmitted diseases, and bathroom traffic jams.

Adolescents can also benefit from:

- honest and frank sexual counseling at home and school
- love and hugs from family and friends so they're not starved for physical affection
- yoga, energy, and body work to balance chakra energies
- sports and outdoor activities to expend energies in wholesome ways

Masturbation is also an appropriate outlet for sexual relief for persons of all ages including: adults who are without a partner, those whose partner is ill or otherwise sexually unavailable, and working parents with small kids.

The issue of sexuality surfaced at a recent holistic health retreat. I couldn't understand why, during spiritual growth ceremonies, I was checking out the babes and rating them for my fantasy harem. There I was, seminar speaker and holy man wanna-be, *thinking* like a 16 year old. As the week progressed, I discovered that other participants were feeling the same. The mayflies were mating, the setting was romantic, the moon was full, and second chakra energy levels were soaring.

The key is to acknowledge sexual feelings but not always *act* out on them. Enjoy the excitement of those energies while remembering that we each are really Eternal Souls, some in very attractive disguises. Then upgrade those energies to open higher chakra centers of love, planetary consciousness, higher wisdom, and cosmic consciousness. As always, balance is the key. For me, sex is one of the best 15 minutes — I mean 3 hours — in a relationship.

Severe repression of sexuality is one way to control humanity and keep them unhappy and confused. Pleiadians report that suppression of sexual urges is one way that controlling powers have historically kept humans in bondage and turmoil. Certain churches have scared the hell *into* guilt ridden parishioners about sex who are then afraid to trust their other natural instincts. Recall the unspeakable tortures and murders inflicted by churches/governments during inquisitions in an attempt to repress sexuality. Scars from these atrocities still exist within societal memory and unconsciously scare and control many.

Here's the scam: people are much more easily controlled if they can be convinced that their *feelings*, e.g., about sexuality, are wrong and dirty—even though such urges are instinctual and common. Those who desire power and fortune—whether extraterrestrial overlords, dictators, or corrupt officials—can then shame and harass people into giving away their money, time, and lives for "a more just cause."

Telling someone that their innermost urges are wrong creates distrust of self via a double message: "I feel this way. *They* tell me I shouldn't feel this way. I must be an ignorant or evil person. Thank goodness *they* know best and will tell me how I should live." Whether past control measures were malicious or intended "for our best interests", it's now time to trust our sexual feelings in particular and ourselves in general.

Sexual orgasm is a natural way to feel at one with the Universe and experience bliss. That's why some persons (who are sufficiently liberated to actually make noises during sex) spontaneously voice "Ahh" (the primordial sound of creation used during the meditation for manifesting), "Oh God," "Holy Cow," and other quasi-religious utterances.

Sexual behavior can be imbalanced to either extreme, too little or too much. Prolonged celibacy doesn't seem too natural or practical for most persons. Excess sexual activity can drain vital energies and result in disharmony. Yoga and various meditative practices help balance sexual energies and upgrade them for higher pursuits. Tantric sex techniques assist reaching higher levels of intimacy *and* spirituality. Nice combo!

Sexual activity is best enjoyed in a loving relationship. The negative consequences of promiscuity and unsafe sex are proving to be both short and long term in nature. During love making, partners experience and share unique energies and information. Safe sex between loving adults in a mutually desirable and committed relationship is a great way to enjoy life, to celebrate our Eternal Nature, and further awaken.

Spiritual Study Groups

In a spiritual study group, members explore and share various paths that remind us of our essential Oneness. The only rules are: confidentiality; speak from the heart, not the ego; and focus on hopeful, positive solutions (no bitching). People of all ages are welcome as we acknowledge that chronological age and Soul age are two different things. In our town, a few of us told friends with open hearts and minds and a study group was born. Our group of 25 meets once per month for about two hours.

Each month, different persons take responsibility for the opening and closing: inspirational readings, a group prayer or meditation, chanting or singing, or listening to the sound of a temple gong or bell. Some meetings feature a specific topic while others have an unstructured format. We sit in a circle and leave an empty chair to symbolize our openness to and respect for visitors from the Spirit World.

We cherish this time with others who are actively on the spiritual path. It's immensely healing and reassuring to have a community in which we can share our deepest joys, interests, and concerns. Prayer requests and upcoming "New Age" events are announced. Lots of hugging, networking, and fellowship follow. Establish a spiritual study group in your community; you'll be pleasantly surprised at the amount of interest in holistic and spiritual growth.

Years ago, our Unity center held a series of Native American spirituality classes. These were fascinating and offered a wealth of information and experiences. At the first one, I realized that, for some reason, I felt a profound guilt and shame about the genocide of the original inhabitants of North America.

I shared this with the group teacher, Rainbow Eagle of the Choctaw tribe. He gazed at me in silence then spoke gently: "Maybe you were a fierce Indian hunter in the past. Whatever the case, it is now time for *all people* to come together in harmony." Tears came to my eyes and a deep peace came over me; I felt about 80% better immediately.

Some residual guilt feelings remained though and I thought of that evening periodically. Several weeks later, my family attended a city festival that included many Native American dancers from all over the country. We were on the far opposite side of the park when suddenly I *just knew* I needed to be with the Native American group.

I quickly walked the distance and, just as I arrived, the announcer said it was time for the Peace Dance. This ceremony marked the time for forgiveness of all past wrongs and celebrated a new time of peace and understanding among all people of the world. I felt a thump in the center of my chest and the tears flowed again. The Peace dance was open to all people so there I was, circling and shuffling with the Native American dancers. And I never felt any shame or guilt after that.

Optimal Birthing

The Soul's entry into this life should be as gentle and conscious as possible. Even under the best conditions, the birth process can be a rough ride; spiritually sensitive persons will want to implement the following suggestions for welcoming a new Soul to Earth. Read *Birth Without Violence* by Frederick Leboyer, M.D., for a more thorough discussion.

In the *year before* you prepare to conceive, attain optimal neuro-musculoskeletal health with corrective chiropractic adjustments. Skeletal alignment and a proper nerve supply to the pelvic organs and muscles is especially important. Begin optimal nutrition with supplementation so mother and baby have the necessary nutrients for optimal growth and biochemical functioning. Pray for and visualize receiving a Soul according to God's will and plan.

At about *four months fetal age*, both parents should talk to the fetus so he or she knows their voices. During meditation, telepathically communicate with the unborn child, and remind him or her that a physically demanding process is ahead but everything will be OK. Play recordings of intrauterine sounds by Hajime Murooka, M.D., and music by Steven Halpern, Ph.D., that is specifically designed for optimal birthing.

Discuss your preferences for natural birthing with your doctor and/or midwife. Whenever possible, use *Lamaze* to avoid

drugs that may affect the baby or limit the mother's awareness during the process. Request that *Leboyer* techniques be
used, including:

- Dim lights as much as possible
- Play the music mentioned above that the baby has be-
  come accustomed to while in utero
- Talk to the little one in hushed and loving tones
- Place the baby's body in a basin of warm water as soon as
  possible after the birth
- After a gentle toweling dry, place the naked baby on the
  mother's bare chest (with a blanket over them) for warmth
  and bonding
- Attempt breast feeding as soon as possible
- Pictures should be taken without flashes; if desired, vid-
  eotape with a low lux camcorder and low light

The father or birthing attendant should stay with the baby
during any exams and the baby should stay with the mother
as much as possible. Continue to play tapes of the music and
intrauterine sounds to soothe and reassure the new arrival to
Earth.

Under hypnotic regression, some persons recall *birth trau-
mas* that must be released to allow normal psychological functioning. Consider how much easier it is to *prevent* such trau-
mas in the first place. Parents to be, take a little extra time,
energy, and money to give these precious first gifts to your new
born. In the future, enlightened holistic health care professionals will encourage and teach these techniques that are naturally right.

We used all these techniques with our daughters; the hospital nurses remarked they had never seen newborns look so
alert yet so peaceful and calm. Use of optimal birthing techniques is an excellent start for body, mind, and spirit wellness.
With a more peaceful journey to Earth, perhaps children will
better remember their birth-visions and fulfill their Soul's purpose.

Remember that there is more than one route for "parent"
and "child" Souls to meet again. Adoption is another route for
Souls to hook up when parents can't or don't want to give birth
to additional children. As discussed, adopting children of a dif-

ferent race is an excellent way to extinguish racism and preju-dice. Perhaps those Souls involved in the adoption volunteered in the Spirit World to suffer from an Earthly perspective (the children losing their biological parents, the adults not being able to bear children) in order to bring a higher blessing of harmony among all people.

Regarding children who die soon after birth, Newton says "These plans are all made in advance by the souls participat-ing in tragic family events. They involve a maze of karmic is-sues." Regarding a client who died from a birth defect in his last life, Newton asked "'What was the purpose of your life ending when you were only a few days old?' He replied, 'The lesson was for my parents, not me, and that's why I elected to come back for them as a filler.'"

Newton explains, "When souls return for a short life to help someone else rather than work on their own issues, because there isn't time, some call this 'a filler life.' In this case, the parents had abused and finally caused the death of another child when they were together in an earlier life... these par-ents evidently needed to experience the grief of having a child they desperately wanted taken away from them."

A patient, "Linda", came to my office for the first time in a year. She had been 4 months pregnant when I last saw her but I felt that I shouldn't ask how her new baby was. Linda ex-plained that she had suffered a miscarriage at 6 months fetal age for unknown reasons. I expressed my condolences and also my belief that there was a perfectly good reason for it.

After saying that, it immediately occurred to me that I should ask about her smoking. Although she had tried to quit several times over many years, Linda had not been able to suc-cessfully quit smoking. She quit immediately when she became pregnant, however, and had remained a nonsmoker.

We discussed that one of the *meanings* or blessings behind the miscarriage was that it helped her to quit smoking. Maybe it prevented needless suffering for her or others. In any event, this sad event will, no doubt, result in ultimately worthwhile and highly instructive lessons.

If a miscarriage, stillbirth, or early childhood death occurs, remember the wisdom inherent in all life. Perhaps a serious deformity or health problem was or would have been present. Metaphysically, the Soul may have decided to forgo the human experience and thus didn't join the body just before birth. Or the incoming Soul may have needed only to experience the birth process and a short life to reach its spiritual goals. In any event, trust there is a grand design greater than we can imagine. There is!

Optimal Passing Over

Preparedness for "death and dying" eases the transition as the Soul moves on to the next stage. Like birth, *passing over* can occur in an optimal setting that eases the Soul's journey. Both are vital parts of the exquisitely perfect Universal design. I used to wonder why death and change were necessary but now realize, as Alan Watts put it: "Without birth and death, and without the perpetual transmutation of all the forms of life, the world would be static, rhythmless, undancing, mummified."

I was present during hundreds of deaths while working in hospital emergency rooms and intensive care units. While attending theology school and studying pioneering work by Kubler-Ross and Ram Dass, I began attending to emotional-spiritual needs as well as cardiopulmonary resuscitation. I spoke softly into patients' ears, telling them not to be afraid, that every measure was being taken to revive them, and they were in capable hands.

After being present during many "deaths', I could almost sense when the patient's Life Force left the body. I perceived this through my peripheral vision as soft white rays of light or energy emanating upward from the chest region. If lifesaving efforts "failed", hospital personnel usually scattered quickly. "Death" was seen as a failure of medical technology rather than the timely departure of a happy Soul who had just graduated from Earth school.

After people "died", I continued to talk softly to them, encouraging them to follow the light, look for loved ones from the Other Side, and to trust God and Christ. Most of the other staff probably thought I was crazy but I didn't care. On several occasions a nurse lingered afterwards to say a word of prayer. Very rarely, a minister would be present to confer last rites. Spiritual counseling during the transition process is another obvious need to be addressed by sensitive health care professionals.

I frequently worked with two very old and severely ill patients for several months yet never saw flowers, cards, or visitors. These completely comatose individuals had multiple organ failure but held on for some reason. Tube feedings, suctioning, antibiotics and other measures kept them one step ahead of the pneumonia that would have mercifully allowed their crossing over.

After studying thanatology issues, I realized they might be *afraid* of letting go and passing on. So I spoke to them and reassured them that every measure was being taken to keep them alive; if they wanted to keep living in that body, we would continue to do everything possible.

But if their Spirit was ready to move on, I urged them to not be afraid. I suggested they look around and notice any loved ones from the Spirit Realms who had come to escort them Home. I reminded them that God loves and forgives them and that He would watch over them. Both of the patients I counseled this way passed on within 24 hours.

Having seen many persons suffer long and painful deaths shaped my views on euthanasia. We mercifully put animals to sleep yet make humans live out their final days inhumanely. Before advancements in medical technology, humans were put out of their misery by infection, dehydration, malnutrition, or other complications. Now each of those can be held in check, sometimes indefinitely. How natural and normal is it to keep a near-corpse barely functioning in a state that mocks true living?

On the other hand, I can't wholeheartedly recommend assisted death or timely suicide as a way out. I believe God understands and forgives those who take their life because of physical or emotional pain (for example, severe intractable pain or chronic depression) or confusion (drug abuse.) Although *usually* not the best option, I don't believe suicide is an unforgivable sin, nor do I think any such thing exists.

NDE lessons and most religious teachings agree that suicide is not a smart move for those desiring spiritual growth. We must face our problems eventually; suicide only compounds and postpones those lessons. Psychic Mary T. Browne says that suicide is not acceptable and is an act of rage against the Soul.

After suicide, "The spirit resides between the earth and the spirit worlds until the time of its normal passing... This state— not really dead or alive—is a terrible condition of existence... People reincarnate in a future life with the same problems that drove them to suicide. It's wiser to fight through the trouble during your lifetime than to be forced to repeat it in a future life... you *don't* escape any hardship by ending your life."

She notes that pain teaches and tests us and releases past negative karma. While noting that those who cannot live without life support should be allowed to die, she states "There's no mercy in mercy killing... it's the spirit that suffers beyond the grave if you take your own life or assist someone in doing this."

The Spirit of Arthur Ford, channeled through Ruth Montgomery, agrees and states: "No person has the right to take the life within himself, any more than that of another person, since all are a part of the Godhead."

In his past-life regression work, Dr. Newton has found there is no punishment *from an external source* for suicide. He describes Souls who commit suicide as feeling disappointed and sad at their poor judgment because they will just have to come back later and deal with the same things again in a different life.

Newton notes "This is the usual spiritual attitude toward suicide, but I want to add that those who escape from chronic physical pain or almost total incapacity on Earth by killing themselves feel no remorse as souls. Their guides and friends also have a more accepting view toward their motivation for suicide."

I see a significant difference between the terms "suicide" and "euthanasia." With suicide, the person has a potential quality life ahead of them and other, more preferable alternatives exist. In euthanasia (meaning good death), there is no appreciable quality of life ahead. There are no other options besides suffering in pain and waiting for the body to degenerate past even the current capabilities of medical technology's interference.

A person whose "death" was recently assisted by Dr. Kevorkian described her pain as if her entire body were burning and being stuck with a million ice picks at the same time. Who can judge that this 67 year old woman, who is of sound mind but suffering incredibly, cannot choose when she's had enough? Some would say only God can decide; what about when the *God-in-us* knows it's time?

Some Native cultures used to leave hopelessly infirm persons alone in nature to hasten their passing. I used to think this was cruel but now see the mercy and wisdom of it so this is what I plan to do with my parents. (Just kidding, mom and dad.) Seriously, is indefinitely postponing a timely and merciful death any less savage?

I remember a resuscitation attempt on a 93 year old man with terminal cancer of the brain and liver who had been in a nursing home for years. I asked one of the medical residents why we would attempt to revive someone in this condition. He answered that teaching hospitals took advantage of every opportunity to practice advanced procedures and were difficult places to die at all, let alone with dignity.

If we really *knew* about our Eternal Nature, would we go through all this? Understanding that life continues after the physical ends is the greatest antidote for ethical dilemmas. If we live countless incarnations throughout eternity, what's the big fuss about leaving this one when it's clearly time?

There are a number of factors involved. Fear of the unknown, of letting the body pass on, is a common underlying dynamic. Profits for health care providers and related industries are, sadly, another major factor. The gaps between religious teachings, philosophical ethics, and life support technology have not been satisfactorily solved.

Ancient admonitions against interfering with ones time of passing made sense when there were no methods to sustain life past reasonable limits. But medical technology can now keep a person "alive" who is certifiably brain dead and without functional kidney, digestive, heart, or lung activity. Where do

we draw the line? When does "life support" become an insult to
the quality of life we were meant to enjoy?

These are not easy questions and if we wait for a panel of
experts to agree, it will never happen. And who would choose
the members of this panel? The only obvious solution is to respect the wishes of adults who are capable of making sound
decisions. Discuss these matters beforehand with trusted family, clergy, and doctors; make your wishes known and legally
stated in a Living Will.

A very wealthy couple in their late 70's chose a joint suicide by carbon monoxide rather than face an inevitable decline.
He had to use a wheelchair because of arthritis and asthma;
she had Alzheimer's disease. They wrote: "We have the means
to afford the best doctors, hospitals and around-the-clock home
care to the end of our lives, but neither of us wants that kind of
life. It would also consume a substantial part of our money,
which through our will and through the mission work of our
church is destined to help many young people throughout the
world who may one day be able to help many more."

Their UCC pastor commented, "They were taking the high
road to death." To them, it would be a poor use of money to
spend it on their deteriorating bodies. I can understand their
decision. Which one of us can rightly judge them?

I asked an Incan Priest about ancient Peruvian understandings of death and dying. They recognize the importance of letting dying ones move on without emotional ties that hold them
back. When it's time to die, they don't have funerals. They have
a party and say good-bye.

Peruvian elders die while awake with their eyes open so
they know when they've left this world and entered the Other
Side. Or, they walk away toward the river or the mountains
and their bodies are never seen again. He explained that, after
passing on, "The soul just keeps on walking."

I asked if techniques existed for *consciously leaving the body*
when it was time to die. He answered that such techniques are
common knowledge among mountain dwelling people who have
maintained sacred ways of living. (Most Peruvian city dwell-
ers have lost contact with such wisdom.)

He said it would be a hundred years before humanity as a whole is ready for such information. When I stressed the great need for an answer to the "good death" dilemma, he said that current laws, potential legal tangles, and dangers of abuse prevent sharing this information now.

Learning to leave the body at will via enlightened practices is an obvious solution to the euthanasia dilemma. Techniques that allow spiritually advanced persons to pass on when they know it's time would bypass bioethical logjams. Such methods also have built-in safeguards; if it's not time or appropriate that the person passes over naturally, it won't happen.

Marlo Morgan described how Aborigines can leave their bodies when they discern the wisdom of such a move. Great spiritual masters, for example, Paramahansa Yogananda, have announced their intentions to leave the body, then entered meditative states from which their Souls exited peacefully. Years ago, an aged leader of the humanistic movement felt it was time to pass on and held a party, then went to sleep and naturally left his body.

Another suggestion for optimal passing over is the establishment of *centers for dying consciously*. The proper environment and staff would assist a good death and explore the excitement during life's biggest transition. Ram Dass established such a center but the "patients" were so happy and fulfilled that no one wanted to die.

That's understandable. In a loving, supportive, and enlightened milieu, who would be in a hurry to leave? This center obviously had valuable insights into establishing Heaven on Earth and was already much closer to being like life on the Other Side. Aging and disease will drastically diminish as we create an optimal environment on Earth—recreations of the Other Side with abundant opportunities for sharing, play, tolerance, wisdom, love, and exploration.

Think about all these issues and *feel your response* to the issue of euthanasia. Then trust yourself and your personal choice. Achieve body/mind/spirit wellness *now* so you enjoy a rewarding, healthy, and enlightened life for as long as possible. When your Soul is ready to pass on, perhaps you will be sufficiently advanced to give your own going away party, then pass over peacefully in your sleep or from a heightened state of consciousness.

When a loved one is "dying", remember the spiritual truths we've discussed. Let fear and worry go; remember you are privileged to participate in a process just as important and joyous as birth. Few loved ones can remain calm and clear in the face of death. Doing so is the last (in this lifetime) and greatest gift of love you can give a Soul in transition. Be with them, hold them, and remember passing over is not such a big deal.

Life transitions are excellent times to work on yourself and relationship issues with the departing Soul. Affirm and pray that you release any residual negative emotions linked with this person. Encourage the "dying" person to trust God, to follow the light, to look for departed loved ones and Heavenly Host. Remind them that no one passes from Earth to Spirit alone.

Tell them you love them, that you understand if it's time for them to leave, and that you'll see them again. Pray for their optimal transition and visualize them learning quickly and graduating upward through advanced spiritual levels. Remember that the most common reaction of Souls after "death" is: "Oh good, I'm back at my beautiful Home again!" Let this message of joy heal and inspire you.

The moment of "death" often occurs late at night or when loved ones momentarily leave the room. That's the departing Soul's way of saving loved ones from further grief. The Soul is then free from well-meaning but entrapping emotional efforts to keep them from "dying." They can also more easily pass over without inappropriate and expensive last ditch resuscitative efforts.

You can experience blessed teachings from the departing Soul if you remain centered and peaceful for even for a short time. During and after "death", Souls often send messages of higher wisdom and reassurance to love ones. These messages are best detected when you're calm and quiet.

Enlightened Souls know "death" and suffering are relatively trivial and temporary in the vast scheme of life. The more spiritually realized you are, the more life is clearly seen as a cosmic play, with actors and actresses coming and going, changing costumes, celebrating and suffering, being born and dying.

Dying then becomes like jumping into a cool pool of water. You may be hesitant at first and brace yourself for the momentary shock but soon the water feels great. An advanced Soul views every aspect of life—even "death"—as an adventure and willingly plunges in without fear to fulfill the mission. "Dying" is then more accurately understood to be not an end but an exciting new beginning with merely a change of scenery.

Anchor Part III

With God's ever-present grace and assistance *and* by consistently using this new information, you will become a totally successful Divine-human. *Resolve* to regularly use these methods and understandings to change yourself and the world for the better! After reviewing the topic headings in Part III:

A. List five "silver bullets"—powerful changes you *commit* to in the next *week*:

1. _____

_____

2. _____

_____

3. _____

_____

4. _____

_____

5. _____

_____

B. List five changes you *resolve* to make in the next *month*:

1. _____

_____

2. _____

_____

3. _____

_____

4. _____

_____

5. _____

_____

C. List five changes you *promise* to make in the next *year*:

1. _____

_____

2. _____

_____

3. _____

_____

4. _____

_____

5. _____

_____

Now call or write at least three Soulmates, your Master Mind Group members, and tell them *specifically* what you have committed to change and by when. Doing this greatly strengthens the probability you will carry through with your plan.

Now it's time to anchor in these positive changes you've resolved to make. Get in peak state: assume peak physiology and posture, call up empowering feelings, recall your power cues, play empowering music, and let your entire being celebrate. Now reread your 15 transformational resolutions from A, B, and C. Add this list to your poster and review in peak state for 14 days and then once per week. As you reach a goal, notice what you feel called to improve next. Review and amend your plans at least quarterly.

You'll lock these new goals in and exponentially increase your total success by consistently following through with these life-transformation exercises. Again, please don't leave this section without doing your homework. The successful outcome of the entire program depends on it. And the goal is nothing less than actually experiencing a personal and global Heaven on Earth!

Part IV:

REACHING A PERSONAL AND GLOBAL HEAVEN ON EARTH

It's time to put it all together! Enjoy a personal Heaven on Earth now while assisting a global transformation toward the same in our lifetime!

The Hundredth Monkey

"Almost everything you do will seem insignificant but it is very important that you do it... you must be the change you wish to see in the world."

—Mahatma Gandhi

Recently, I arrived at a hotel late at night. The room was hot and stuffy so I turned on the A/C and went to sleep with no covers on. Several hours later, I dreamt I was freezing but was too deeply asleep to act upon my body's signals. I eventually awakened and found myself curled up, shivering in the now cold room. Once fully conscious, it was an easy matter to turn down the A/C, pull up the covers, and resume sleeping comfortably.

Similarly, in the course of life, being asleep to our True Nature and great potential creates much suffering. We may, at first, think we have to suffer and can't prevent undesirable outcomes. *Awakening* alerts us to the need for adjustments in one or more areas of life. Making these adaptations restores harmony and balance again.

Abraham Maslow, Ph.D., stated that two important steps to becoming self-actualized are:

- be independent of what others think and stay on purpose
- avoid over-attachment to the fruits of your labor; freedom means losing ego's need for a particular outcome

A Course in Miracles says 'Infinite patience produces immediate results.' It's OK to set goals and have preferences about the results but don't get caught up with preconceived expectations. Trust in the Wisdom that created all and don't force the rhythm. Get ego out of the way and focus on serving others. Paradoxically, when you serve others, ego's desires are met without it getting in the way.

In 1972, my Russian language teacher told me about his visit to the Soviet Union in one of the first cultural exchange groups. He was surprised to find the Soviet people *were just like us*. Judging by news reports and fears in the U.S. during that time, I would have thought they were all bloodthirsty barbarians. In reality, they didn't want an active *or* cold war. They just wanted to live in peace and enjoy life—just like the great majority of all people around the world.

At a recent seminar, a professional soldier shared his decision to quit the military and contribute to world peace. He tearfully said, "I was trained to kill and we went all around the world looking for the enemy. But everywhere I went, I found only friends."

If lab rats are repeatedly electrically shocked for no reason, they eventually *turn on each other* and display aggressive behavior. They don't understand that researchers are studying their behavior and administering the shocks. Similarly, humans have historically turned on each other after being controlled by "the powers that be" and kept in ignorance.

War is a game that, if kings had to play, would not occur. It is time for all people to love, forgive, and cooperate. Humanity is awakening and realizing its vast potential for rapid and profound change. We have collectively slumbered in ignorance and darkness long enough. Break through your limitations and develop empowering strategies for a new way of life. We never know which one of us may be *the hundredth monkey*—the person who sufficiently tips the scales from darkness to Light so the whole world changes!

But don't burn yourself out thinking it's all up to you. Contribute what you feel called to share and know that your piece of the puzzle is important. Those who accept a life of service to humanity will always have more to do than is possible. Just be the best possible instrument or channel for God, then let go and let God. This attitude creates the optimal environment for doing all you can through a life of service.

A Golden Age

We are entering a New Age, a unique opportunity for a Golden Age of Heaven on Earth. The potential for it is already in place; we need only *realize* it in both meanings of the word: to accomplish *and* to be fully aware of its possibilities now.

Last week I called information for the phone number of the Sarasota Unity Center then dialed the number; a voice replied: "Ray here!" How unpretentious and enthusiastic, I thought.

Instead of "Sarasota Unity Center" or "Pastor Jones", just a friendly "Ray here!"

I introduced myself and explained my plan to give seminars about reaching Heaven on Earth at as many places as possible: "Would your organization like a promotional packet to evaluate for sponsoring my seminar in the winter of `98?" There was a pause and then Ray said "No, I don't think so."

I was crestfallen and shocked. "Ray, I'm surprised. May I ask why? Other centers in other cities have been enthusiastic about my seminars." Ray answered "Well, that's our busiest time of year and we'll be awfully busy." Now I was really surprised: "Isn't that good? The more people there the better. I'd think peak season would be a great time!"

Ray replied "I'm sorry, I just don't think it sounds like something for us." I was determined not to give up and responded "Ray, I don't want to be a nuisance but this is a great program. I'm sure your people will love it. I'm surprised your organization doesn't want to sponsor it."

Ray was caving in, "OK, I'll tell you what. Call tomorrow at about 11 AM and ask for Bob. If he is interested, I'll consider it." I answered "That's great, is Bob another minister there?" There was a long pause. "Minister?" Ray asked. Something felt definitely wrong about this conversation. I said "Is this the Sarasota Unity Center?" Ray answered "No, this is the Sarasota Taxi Service."

We laughed at how he must have thought I was crazy trying to give my seminars at a taxi business. Ray admitted that the seminars did sound interesting. After I got over feeling like a bonehead, I realized what a great lesson it had been:

- If you give up at the first rejection, you will miss out on possibilities and opportunities
- Communicate clearly; know and precisely state your intentions and goals
- Persist in your mission, even in the face of repeated rejection, to help usher in a new time of world peace
- It is definitely time to usher in a New Age of world peace; even a taxi service operator was considering sponsoring a *Toward Heaven on Earth* seminar!

The Australian Aborigines believe humankind is closer to experiencing Paradise then ever before. As her time with them came to an end, the Real People told Morgan "We have taught the Mutant much, and we have learned from her. It seems Mutants have something in their life called gravy. They know truth, but it is buried under thickening and spices of convenience, materialism, insecurity, and fear.

They also have something in their lives called frosting. It seems to represent how they spend almost all the seconds of their existence in doing superficial, artificial, temporary, pleasant-tasting, nice-appearing projects and spend very few actual seconds of their lives developing their eternal beingness... We pray they will look closely at their actions, at their values, and learn before it is too late that all life is one. We pray they will stop the destruction of the earth and of each other. We pray there are enough Mutants on the brink of becoming real to change things."

Bob and I were best friends all through junior high and high school. We became instant buddies and even at a young age had complete regard for and trust in each other. After graduating from high school, we followed separate paths. He married early and joined the military while I moved away to college. We kept in touch mainly through Christmas cards until a few years ago. Bob had become a lieutenant colonel in the military, earning a masters and Ph.D. along the way.

As we've spent more time together lately, we're amazed at the similarity of our life missions. His emphasis is on bringing Spirit, ethics, and higher consciousness into business and military settings. "How is it possible," he asked, "that we independently reached the same end result despite taking such different paths?" I believe that he and I are cluster-mates as suggested by our rapid, deep, and lasting friendship. Members of our "Soul pod" apparently chose bringing Spirit to the fore on Earth, thus our common lifework now.

He writes "there are many champions making contributions towards a more ethical way of conducting business. Further, it is apparent that the human race may be going through a metamorphosis that will lead to a new era of social consciousness... there are many thoughtful and action oriented people who share a common vision. The vision is one in which ethics, business, community, and nature all blend together to form a world where we can all achieve the highest level of joy."

Business executive and author John W. Horman says "I think we are in the darkest age of humankind we have ever been in. The reason is we have to become conscious. As soon as we become conscious, we are going to change our path because we will not consciously continue to do something bad. Large masses of people are still very unconscious, not really awake. And Mother Nature only has a few ways to push people into being more conscious."

Swedish CEO and business leader Rolf Osterberg states "If we go back to our contract with nature, which we left out in our previous way of thinking, we see that every human being is unique, but also a part of everything else. We can no longer consider ourselves the masters of nature, but a part of a whole system."

He describes the old business way of thinking as a competition with winners and losers. The old purpose of business was to exploit customers, natural resources, the environment, and the people of the Third World. The new purpose of organizations will be to serve as a catalyst for the personal development of those working and to serve the community. Businesses that serve and don't exploit will thrive in the future.

I've discussed this at length to help you realize that visions of world peace and Heaven on Earth are not just New Age or old hippie "pipe dreams." Many diverse groups of people expect major positive changes in this lifetime and are willing to stand up for what is right.

As discussed, many different religious, secular, and cultural viewpoints—e.g., Christian, Incan, Native American, Mayan, New Age, Aboriginal, and Western business interests—expect a Golden Age to come. Part of the anticipation is no doubt due to the anxiety associated with a new millennium. But there's much more to it than that. Many prophecies have long foretold of this coming age. People are awakening and *choosing* to make a difference now. Many believe humankind is now ready to make a quantum leap in consciousness.

We're Not Alone

Remember that we constantly and eternally have assistance and guidance from God and the Heavenly Host. They've always wanted the kingdom of Heaven for everyone and everywhere. Humanity is finally realizing the ever present potentiality of this plan. God and Her coworkers have always done their share; humans are now awakening that it's time to do their part in manifesting Heaven on Earth. Start by letting go of the fear that has blocked this process for far too long.

In *Running From Safety*, Richard Bach writes of facing these fears "Lean into your fears, I wished I could tell him, dare them to do their worst and cut them down when they try. If you don't, they'll clone themselves, Dickie, they'll mushroom till they surround you, choke the road to the life you want. Every turn you fear is empty air, dressed to look like jagged hell... before time and after, through every moment, Life Is and We Are. The one thing we fear most is the one thing that is not possible: We cannot die, we cannot be destroyed. Life Is. We Are."

Working with the *heart chakra* will help you realize the imminent opportunity for an inner and global Heaven on Earth and how we literally are assisted every moment. Imagine Jesus, an angel, or some spiritual master residing within your heart or 4th chakra. Realize that this High Being is with you, watching, and guiding you always. Then consider your every thought, word, and deed; are you proud to have your Heart Guardian know them?

Ask yourself: "Would my heart-centered Divine Being think, say, or do this?" You'll receive an automatic answer from your intuitive heart and grow closer to the spiritual level of the Heavenly Host you are emulating.

In *Angel Letters*, several messages from Spirit are summarized: "We are all one, and there is no such thing as death, merely a passing from one form to another. We are all sparks from the Creator, and our ultimate goal is to be perfected souls. The universe is far-reaching, beyond dimensions that we know here on earth, and we are never alone. There exists in every dimension "guides," whose purpose it is to help us advance spiritually toward a reunion with All That Is, the Universal

Intelligence that created all energy. We are all one group mind that exists throughout the universe, which is filled with light and love. We are all connected."

We've discussed several theories on why humanity has apparently been mired in darkness for so long. To recap:

- the *conspiracy* theory—powerful control institutions had a vested interested in keeping humanity dumb, barefoot, and pregnant
- the *malevolent ET* theory—powerful, mean-spirited beings from beyond Earth have fed on humanity's mass confusion and disharmony
- the *evolution of human consciousness* theory—humans are finally wising up after eons of learning the hard way
- the *cosmic hide-and-seek game* theory—everything is a dance of energy, all suffering and separateness is an illusion. God has just been experimenting and playing.

Whatever the case, clearly it's time for humanity to awaken and leave past discord behind. We have much more power and wisdom than we have heretofore imagined. In the tape series *The Science of Personal Achievement*, Napoleon Hill described the financial depression during FDR's presidency. The government, churches, business community, media, and many individuals worked together with a positive focus.

Partisan politics, denominational differences, profit considerations, and negatively oriented news reports were put aside for a higher cause. The tide turned with this immense emphasis on what was right with the economy—on positive solutions, not just rehashing the problem. Humans are now ready for a similar worldwide response from many people and institutions.

Responses needed include:

1. pray for world peace and harmony, for God's will to become manifest on our planet

2. use techniques that help *manifest* Heaven on Earth

3. educate yourself about Higher Thought through books, seminars, the Internet, tapes, and discussion groups

4. become all you can be and let your Light shine; every contribution is important and needed

5. actively participate in enlightened spiritual paths

6. visualize Utopia in our lifetime and spread the word about this realistic and obtainable goal

7. remember that we always have Divine assistance from God and all levels of Heavenly Helpers

When I first consulted a psychic several years ago, I was struggling with the decision to sell my practice and pursue full-time writing and teaching seminars. On the way there, I prayed that I would receive a *clear* sign that it was OK to follow my heart's calling. "Bill" lived 60 miles away and knew nothing about me except my first name. He held my keys and asked only my birth date and time of birth.

After pausing momentarily, he asked "Do you want to do what you're doing?" Tears came to my eyes and I gave thanks. He said it was time for me to listen to my Soul's longing and sell my practice. He knew that my dream and strength was writing and working with groups in life transformation seminars. Bill described seeing several spirit guides and angels around me who were assisting and guiding my progress.

When I returned to see Bill one year later, I had made important strides toward selling my practice and pursuing my new calling but he didn't know that. He immediately detected the change in energy, however. "By your decisions and actions, you have rejoined an original teaching Soul group", he explained. "Your auras reflect increased energy and harmony at every level. Even more spirit guides and angelic assistants are now participating in the outcome."

This is just one example of how we each are protected, directed, and assisted—as is our planet—during this exciting time, the unfoldment of a new golden age.

Enlightened persons realize their inseparability, their kinship with all life. This occurs, says Alan Watts, when you realize "the world outside your skin is just as much you as the world inside: they move together inseparably... What happens is neither automatic nor arbitrary: it just happens, and all happenings are mutually interdependent in a way that is unbelievably harmonious.

A Time For Peace

Aluna Joy Yaxk'in, author of *The Mayan Suns* and *Mayan Solar Destiny Readings*, shares Mayan prophecies that we are leaving the "age of belief" and entering the "age of knowledge." The spring equinox of 1996 marked the end of a 520 year cycle of darkness and signaled it's time for the reawakening of the "cosmic human."

Mayan wisdom says the veil between humanity and greater understandings of reality is becoming thinner, thus the deep spiritual calling that so many feel. She says "With the initiation of this new cycle of time we will no longer be veiled by illusion... This is a most auspicious time for humanity. We are on the threshold of a major shift for humanity moving into becoming cosmic human beings. We have been waiting for so long for this moment, 520 years to be exact, and we are almost home."

Aluna shares a message from Hunbatz Men, a Mayan shaman who said this sacred prophecy is "the call for the light workers of the earth garden to reunite and harmonize the earth; to bridge the gaps between continents, religions, cultures, and races for all ages, for all time. It is time to sing our heart songs and begin to live our true solar destiny." Be still for a moment and let these words resound within you. Feel this inner call and listen for your heart felt response.

Although we may not understand all the mysteries of life, we can trust there is a perfectly exquisite Divine Design. Many are awakening to the great spiritual Truth that everything in life has a purpose, a part to play, a good to impart. And when you can't see any hope, remember that it's always darkest just before the dawn.

For those who think "Heaven on Earth" is just wishful thinking consider the major social changes like the fall of the Berlin Wall, apartheid, and communism that culminated almost over night. Lasting world harmony and peace? Like the little boy in the movie *Angels in the Outfield* kept saying "It could happen!"

U.S. naval battle maneuvers were rescheduled several years ago when a helicopter gunship sighted sea turtles ensnared in fishing nets at sea. Navy destroyers veered 60 miles from their intended course to help free the turtles. This is just another example of how radically and positively things are changing. The military wouldn't have considered such an interruption in the past. Enlightened citizens are working in every sector of society to spread love and light.

Ex-Governor George Wallace recently apologized to Vivian Malone Jones, a black student he tried to block from entering an all white school in the 60's. He told her that Alabama is a better place because of racial integration and the desegregation of schools. The 77 year old Wallace has Parkinson's disease and has been partially paralyzed for 20 years, an abject karmic reminder of how suffering teaches and transforms.

Watch the Star Wars trilogy again and note Darth Vadar's eventual change of heart. He was the *last* person you would think could change for the better yet there was always that spark of good in him. No matter how ingrained the shadow or dark side, there is always a glimmer of light and hope. This is true for the most "evil entity", hardened killer, and even your boss or mother-in-law.

Have you ever traveled to a distant location and met a person from your own city or state? An immediate closeness and bond is felt: "you're from Ohio, too?" Extend that out and imagine you're visiting a distant galaxy where everyone is very different. Think how close you would feel to another Earthling you met there. Consider the vastness of the Universe and realize we on Earth are really one big family with much to appreciate and revere.

Our world will come together in peace as more and more persons acknowledge our essential Oneness and follow their Souls mission. Energy production and technological advancements that now seem impossible will be attainable as we apply time, energy, and money toward peacetime applications. Research into and development of paranormal powers will result in unforeseen benefits for humanity. Overpopulation, hunger, poverty, disease and war will be solved as more persons remember their birth-vision and contribute to a new world-vision.

Many persons have enjoyed major improvements in every aspect so their lives are much more like "Heaven" and less like "hell." Happiness, total success, peace, love and harmony are the benchmarks of this inner kingdom. I have a strong belief that peace on Earth in our lifetime is a realistic, imminently obtainable goal. I know from direct experience that a personal Heaven on Earth right now is possible.

I am much healthier, happier, more peaceful and prosperous that I ever have been. I do not fear death and know for a fact that I am One with all Creation. I enjoy excellent relationships with many friends and family members. I understand my Soul's mission and am fulfilling it to the best of my abilities. I am excited about a long life ahead with opportunities for learning, growing, loving, creating and serving.

It's not luck. I currently do or have done all the techniques in Part III. Reaching an inner Heaven on Earth is my passion, hobby, job, and calling; I make it a high priority in my life. I watch very little TV, am usually quite busy, don't drink or use drugs, and am disciplined to care for myself with regular body/mind/spirit wellness habits. If I can do it, anyone can. It's a decision, a choice to become all you can be—to thank God for all Her blessings and be a faithful servant.

A growing number of persons experiencing a relative inner Heaven are committed to assisting the realization of a global Heaven on Earth. Enlightened Souls come from every walk of life and contributions from diverse groups are now needed to put all the pieces of the puzzle together. Draw inspiration from the words of Margaret Mead: "Never doubt that a small, committed group of people can change the world. Indeed, it is the only thing that ever has."

One More Celebration

Knowledge is not power; knowledge paired with strategic and consistent action is power. Implement personal recommendations for body/mind/spirit wellness that *you know* are needed. Follow your plan for enjoying total success and Heaven on Earth on a regular basis and over time, you cannot fail. It's as simple and powerful as that. Unfortunately, most persons don't identify their goals and don't take the necessary steps to achieve them. You now possess powerful information and techniques for rapid and massive change. Will you use it? It's up to you. Only you can take the first step.

Just as individuals have suffered from unconscious negative incantations, humanity has been limited by erroneous mass incantations like "shit happens; life is a rate race; and it's a dog eat dog world." In the past, the idea of enjoying Heaven now was considered impossible and even sacrilegious. Most persons believed only God could decide where and when Heaven would happen—so it hasn't yet on Earth, at least on a wide scale.

God has always wanted Heaven for us but won't ram it down our throats. We have the freedom to choose; will you transform your life so you and others experience utopia? As more persons do so, humanity is ready for a new, more positive incantation: "Now is the time for all to enjoy a personal and global Heaven on Earth!"

Take heart in these words from God, says author Neale Donald Walsch in *Conversations with God*, "You are, have always been, and will always be, a *divine part of the divine whole, a member of the body.* That is why the act of rejoining the whole, of returning to God, is called *remembrance.* You actually choose to *re-member* Who You Really Are, or to join together with the various parts of you to experience the all of you—which is to say, the All of Me.

Your job on Earth, therefore, is not to *learn* (because you *already know*), but to *re-member* Who You Are. And to remember who everyone else is. That is why a big part of your job is to remind others (that is, to *re-mind* them), so that they can remember also. All the wonderful spiritual teachers have been doing just that. It is *your* sole purpose. That is to say, your *soul purpose.*"

Anchor this message deeply and strongly and share it wherever and however you can. Spin-off applications that spread the message of this practical, achievable goal are needed. You and other awakening humans are being called to share the good news about the potential for Heaven on Earth *now!* The goal is for this viewpoint to reach mass consciousness and occur in our lifetime. Do you share this dream? A team of many persons with varying expertise can make it a reality.

Imagine Heaven on Earth happening more and more every day. Imagination is not a weak or fruitless endeavor; it is the foundation, the vision for what is to come. In *Spirit Walker: Messages From The Future*, archeologist Hank Wesselman, Ph.D., states that in Hawaiian Kahuna mysticism, imagination implies "information, thoughts, and ideas that had their sole source in the spirit realm." *Imagine!*

Pray for inner and world peace. Make achievement of that ideal one of your life goals. Talk about attainment of Heaven on Earth with friends and family. Live as if it were a reality now; it will be when you believe it. And remember, we have help from the Creator and all manner of Heavenly Helpers. We have assistance and support from family, friends, and all people. Most of all, we have our unlimited inner resources that are just waiting to be tapped. With that in mind, answer these questions after you've reached *peak state*:

A. What are 3 positive beliefs about you and the world being ready for Heaven on Earth now?

1. _____
   _____

2. _____
   _____

3. _____
   _____

B. What are 3 ways you will contribute to Heaven on Earth?

1. _____
   _____

2. _____
   _____

3. _____
   _____

C. What is your new positive incantation about the imminent establishment of Heaven on Earth?

_____
_____
_____

Add these written Life-Transformative exercises to your poster where you'll see it often. Repeat them while in peak state daily for 14 days, then review at least once a week to keep your heart and mind on your birth and world vision. Part of every Soul's mission in this lifetime is to help establish Heaven on Earth. Are you doing your part? Anchoring this information greatly increases the probability that you will!

Don't wait until tomorrow to take action; tomorrow never comes. Many Lightworkers have been preparing over multiple life times for this crucial time on our planet. Today is the day to start implementing necessary changes and truly awaken to your Infinite Nature and awesome possibilities. Again, here's the game plan:

- *Remember your Soul* and realize your Real Self is Infinite, Timeless, Eternal Spirit.
- Feel the joy, freedom, clarity, energy, and power that flows from spiritual enlightenment. *Resolve* to make a real difference in the world!
- Identify your mission, vision, calling, dream, and purpose in life. Why is your Soul in this place at this time? What piece of the earthly puzzle do you feel called to fill? Then follow it without fear.
- To ensure the success of your mission, you'll need a strong and vibrant body/mind/spirit. You can serve the greatest number of people best by having maximum energy and well-being. Practice what you preach.
- The net effect is that you'll begin to experience a relative "Heaven on Earth" state. Life will increasingly be more happy, peaceful and successful in every way. This is your birthright, the high level of existence our Creator had in mind.
- As more and more persons enjoy an individual Heaven on Earth, a global transformation toward the same is just a matter of time.
- And after that? Who knows how far reaching the benefits of our return to Divine Harmony will be. There are always new adventures and challenges for Lightworkers who have eternity to enjoy, love, and serve one another and our Source.

Remember that I and many others are available for support and teaching. With God's help—which is a given—and a vast team of dedicated Souls working for Heaven on Earth, our eventual success is ensured.

Share Your Story

Don't hide your light under a basket; speak your truth and let your light shine. "Supernatural" events are much more common than most persons realize. You'll gain personal power and confidence by sharing your stories with others. In turn, those you reach will feel more open to the validity of the unseen world. As Willis Harmon, Ph.D., stated "Perhaps the only limits to the human mind are those we believe in."

I'm collecting stories about how others have remembered their Inner Self and their Soul's mission, then transformed their life and circle of influence for the better. What were the turning points for you, the events that "blew your mind" and helped you realize there is much more to life than meets the eye? Have you had any experiences discussed in part I that "prove" our Eternal Nature? Has a particular tragedy been a great teaching despite the pain? How has your life become more like Heaven on Earth?

If you are willing to have your story shared in my seminars and future books or articles, state that in writing with your signature and whether you want your real name used or not. Thanks for helping me help others! Namaste.

APPENDIX

Additional reading for the following sections include:

REINCARNATION: Death and Personal Survival by R. Almeder; Born Again and Again by John Van Auken; You Have Been Here Before by Edith Fiore; Reincarnation by Manley P. Hall; The Search for Yesterday by D. Scott Rogo; Edgar Cayce on Reincarnation by Noel Langley; Lifetimes by Frederick Lenz; and Reincarnation in Christianity by Geddes MacGregor.

NEAR DEATH EXPERIENCES: Saved by the Light and At Peace In The Light by Dannion Brinkley; At the Hour of Death by Karlis Osis; Embraced by the Light by Betty Eadie; The Case for Heaven by Mally Cox-Chapman; and the video Edgar Cayce's Life After Death with Rob Grant (RESOURCES #6)

ANGELS: The Physics of Angels by Matthew Fox and Rupert Sheldrake; Commune with the Angels by Jane M. Howard; Where Angels Walk by Joan Wester Anderson; Touched By Angels by Eileen Freeman; Messengers of Light by Terry Lynn Taylor; Angel Voices by Karen Goldman; and Celebration of Angels by Timothy Jones.

PAST-LIFE REGRESSIONS: Discovering the Soul by Robert G. Jarmon, M.D.; The Journey Within by Henry L. Bolduc; Eye of the Centaur by Barbara Clow; Your Past Lives and the Healing Process by Adrian Finkelstein, MD; Past Life Therapy in Action by Dick Sutphen and Lauren L. Taylor; Past Lives, Present Relationships by John Van Auken.

IDENTIFYING SOUL'S MISSION: Infinite Self by Stuart Wilde; Do What You Love, The Money Will Follow by Marsha Sinetar; Discovering Your Soul's Purpose by Mark Thurston, PhD; I Had It All The Time and The Dragon Doesn't Live Here Anymore by Alan Cohen; Repacking Your Bags by Shapiro and Leider.

TIME MANAGEMENT: Timeshifting by Stephan Rechtschaffen, M.D., a founder of the Omega Institute; Voluntary Simplicity by Duane Elgin; Down-shifting by

Amy Saltzman; and Inner Simplicity and Living the Simple Life by Elaine St. James

LOST YEARS OF JESUS: The Jesus Mystery by Janet Bock and the video The Lost Years by Richard Bock; Edgar Cayce's Story of Jesus by J. Furst; The Lost Years of Jesus Revealed by Rev. C.F. Potter; and The Aquarian Gospel of Jesus The Christ by Levi.

YOGA: Integral Hatha Yoga by Swami Satchidananda; Dr. Dean Ornish's Program by Dean Ornish, M.D.; Perfect Health and Boundless Energy by Deepak Chopra, M.D.; Yoga Over 50 and Yoga for Children by Mary Stewart; Yoga for the Young at Heart by Susan Winter Ward; Yoga by Richard Freeman; and magazines such as Yoga Journal.

VACCINATIONS: "But Doctor, About That Shot" and Immunizations: The Terrible Risks Your Children Face That Your Doctor Won't Reveal Robert Mendelsohn, M.D.; Immunization, The Reality Behind The Myth by Walene James; DPT: A Shot in the Dark and Vaccination, Social Violence and Criminality by Harris Coulter, Ph.D.; Vaccination: The Medical Assault on the Immune System by Viera Scheibner, Ph.D.; Lethal Injections and the Damage They Cause by W.C. Douglass, M.D.

CHELATION THERAPY: Nutrition, Health, & Disease by Gary P. Todd, M.D.; By-Passing ByPass—The New Techniques of Chelation Therapy by Elmer Cranton, M.D.; and Forty Something Forever by Harold and Arlene Brecher.

MERCURY AMALGAM REMOVAL: April 1994 issue of Extraordinary Science; It's All In Your Head: The Link Between Mercury Amalgams and Illnesses by H. A. Huggins, DDS, MS; DAMS (Dental Amalgam Mercury Syndrome) 505-332-3252

ALTERNATIVE AIDS THEORIES: "HIV is not the cause of AIDS" by Peter Duesberg in 1988 Science; AIDS and Syphilis, The Hidden Link by Harris Coulter, Ph.D.;

PARASITE REMOVAL: A Cure For All Diseases by Hulda Clark, Ph.D., N.D.; and Guess What Came to Dinner by Ann Louise Gittleman.

BALANCED PROSPERITY: The Seven Spiritual Laws of Success by Deepak Chopra, M.D.; The Amazing Laws of Cosmic Mind Power by Joseph Murphy, Ph.D., LL.D.; Think and Grow Rich by Napoleon Hill; The Richest Man in Babylon by George S. Clason; A Rich Man's Secret by Ken Roberts; and Walden by Henry David Thoreau.

UFOs and ETs: UFO's Explained by Philip Klaus; You Are Becoming A Galactic Human by Virginia Essene and Sheldon Nidle; Preparing For Contact by Lyssa Royal and Keith Priest; and books by John Lear, Dr. Fred Bell, Michael Lindemann, Colonel Wendelle Stevens, Len Stringfield, Trevor James Constable, Colin Andrews, Linda Moulton Howe, Norio Hayakawa, J. Allen Hyneck, Budd Hopkins, and William Hamilton.

OPTIMAL PASSING OVER: Life's Finishing School by Helen Green Ansley; To Die With Style by Marjorie McCoy; Last Rights: A Case for the Good Death by Maya Mannes; Letting Go by Richard Boerstler; Common Sense Suicide: The Final Right by Doris Portwood; A Practical Guide to Death and Dying by John White; Let Me Die Before I Wake by Derek Humphrey.

ENERGY WORK: books by Nikola Tesla and Wilhelm Reich;, A New Concept of the Universe by Walter Russell; Man's Supreme Inheritance and The Universal One by F. Matthias Alexander;, Blueprint for Immortality by Harold Burr, Ph.D.; A Model of the Universe by P. D. Ouspensky; Hands of Light and Light Emerging by Barbara Brennan; The Body Electric and Cross Currents by Robert O. Becker, M.D.; The Infinite Mind by Valerie Hunt, PhD; Biomagnetic Healing by Lloyd Graham, D.C.; The Nuclear Evolution by Christopher Hill; Life Energy by John Diamond, M.D.; Biological Effects of Magnetic Fields by Madeleine Barnathy, PhD.; and A Spiritual Philosophy For The New World by John and Jan Price.

RESOURCES

1. Integral Yoga Center (Yogaville): retreats, workshops, tapes, and books for realizing inner and world peace; founded by Sri Swami Satchidananda 1-800-858-YOGA

#2. "Lightworks Audio and Video"—tapes about angels, yoga, holistic healing, UFO's and ET's, metaphysics, spirituality, relationships, and body/mind awareness 1-800-795-TAPE

#3. EarthSave International; John Robbins' educational promotion of personal and world health 1-408-423-4069

#4. Inter-dimensional Music: music by Iasos 1-415-479-0700

#5. Celestial music for relaxation and peak efficiency by Steven Halpern 1-800-909-0707

#6. Association for Research & Enlightenment (A.R.E.) mail order bookstore 1-800-723-1112

#7. Unity School of Christianity: Unity Magazine, Silent Unity, Daily Word, books, tapes, and retreats 1-816-524-3550

#8. Seventh Generation: Products For A Healthy Planet; for environmentally conscious products 1-800-456-1177

#9. Lucis Trust for information about and copies of *The Great Invocation*: Box 722, Cooper Station, NY, NY 10276

#10. Institute of Noetic Sciences; research, books and workshops for exploring consciousness and guiding principles for a global society in the 21st century 1-800-383-1394

#11. Sounds True Catalog; audiotapes on spirituality, life skills, meditation, psychology, and more 1-800-333-9185

#12. Books For The Nineties; wide variety of enlightened books on anthropology to world religion 1-800-331-3761

#13. Pacific Spirit Whole Life Products; products, books, tapes to assist body/mind/spirit wellness 800-634-9057

#14. Explorations; resources of healing wisdom and spiritual treasures from around the world 1-800-720-2116

#15. The Spirit Collection; books, tapes, music, seminars for higher consciousness by Stuart Wilde 1-800-962-4457

Index

About the Author

Mark Pitstick, B.S., M.A., D.C., has over 25 years clinical experience in hospitals, mental health centers, pastoral counseling settings, and private practice. His training includes premedical degree, graduate theology school, a master's in clinical psychology, and a doctorate in chiropractic.

His first book, *Balanced Living: Realizing Your Fullest Potential*, was endorsed by Drs. Wayne Dyer, Elisabeth Kubler-Ross, Deepak Chopra, Bernie Siegel and others. He has practiced and studied holistic health, meditation, yoga and "Higher Consciousness" topics for over 20 years. Dr. Pitstick teaches his *Toward Heaven on Earth* seminars across the country as his full-time life's work. He and his wife, Michelle, have two daughters, Faith and Rae Lynn.

Are you ready to experience Heaven on Earth

Dr. Mark Pitstick's experiential
***Toward Heaven On Earth Seminars* will help you:**

✦ Know the REAL YOU is an Eternal Spirit, a timeless Soul who does not die and cannot fail.

✦ *Identify* and follow your Soul's special mission.

✦ Become an enlightened and courageous Lightworker with vibrant vitality of body, mind and spirit.

✦ Enjoy total success and Heaven on Earth living.

✦ Assist global transformation toward peace and harmony, one person at a time.

Seminar format includes lecture, music, group sharing, visualizations, life-transformative techniques, demonstrations, Angel Walk, and Sufi dancing (weekend intensive only).

Call or write for information on seminars in your area:

Dr. Mark Pitstick
PO Box 387
Chillicothe, OH 45601
800-976-9310
Fax 614-774-4478

Share Dr. Pitstick's books with others...

Balanced Living: Realizing Your Fullest Potential
discover your vast potential in every area of life:

✦ Physical wellness: the cleansing crisis; alcohol, tobacco, and illegal drug abuse; aging gracefully, environmental issues.

✦ Rest and sleep: when to sleep; sleep positions; naps; insomnia.

✦ Wellness and exercise: why and how to exercise and stretch.

✦ Chiropractic care: the vertebral subluxation complex; how to choose a great chiropractor; and recommendations for neuro-musculoskeletal health.

✦ Balanced nutrition: optimal diet, reaching proper weight; breast-feeding; supplementation; vegetarianism; living foods; food-combining principles; juicing and sprouting; fasting.

✦ Self-actualization: Stress management; meditation; relaxation; the love, acceptance and forgiveness technique; goal setting and affirmations; loving relationships.

✦ Spiritual enlightenment: the nature of God; Jesus and the Christ consciousness; prayer; Heaven within; service to others; remembering who we are.

Balanced Living $12.00

Toward Heaven on Earth: Remembering Your Soul
shows how **you** *can:*

✦ remember you are an Eternal Soul, a timeless Spirit Being, and One with God

✦ know *your Soul's mission and how to best achieve your* birth-vision

✦ reach *vibrant levels of body / mind / spirit wellness to fulfill all life's roles* and *follow your bliss*

✦ *enjoy relative utopia living now*

✦ *follow your* world-vision *and help assist the* transformation *toward a global Heaven on Earth!*

Toward Heaven on Earth (248 pages) $12.00

Send check, money order, or credit card (Discover, VISA, MasterCard) info to:

Dr. Mark Pitstick
PO Box 387
Chillicothe, OH 45601

Phone or fax orders:
800-976-9310
Fax 614-774-4478

Qty	Title	Price	Amount
	Balanced Living	$12.00	
	Toward Heaven on Earth	$12.00	
	Subtotal		
	Shipping		
	Ohio res. add 6.5% sales tax		
	Total		